The funniest and most real book written by a suburban dad who dared to let God transform his perspective and his life as he fulfills God's mission for him in Africa. You will love this book.

—TED BARNETT, US Director, Africa Inland Mission

As you read this compelling story of a real man trying to make a real difference where it really counts—the story of an ordinary man who dared to pursue a big dream—you may find your purpose and your dream. Steve's story will touch your heart as it touches the Father's.

—LAMAR BOSCHMAN, author, teacher, and worship mentor

Every so often, you read the story of a life that inspires you. Why would a technology manager in Texas pick up his family and move to Kenya? How does he feed thousands of children each day and create school computer hubs wherever he travels? Steve explains it all, amid great stories of hilarious chaos and absurd Kenyan politics. Read the book and be amazed.

—COLLEEN CARMEAN, PhD, Assistant Chancellor,
University of Washington Tacoma

During his time in Kenya, Steve has done two things: First, he has maintained a loving, caring heart toward the needy. Second, he has resisted being overwhelmed by the impossible, believing that God can use him to make a difference. May this book open your heart not only to the desperately needy children of Kenya but also to the needy whom God brings into your life right where you live.

—TIM COOK, former Superintendent, Rift Valley Academy

Steve's lesson for all of us is that all you need is a big heart, energy, and faith, and you can accomplish anything. Thank God for Steve, Nancy, and their family, and the work they have done, and their never-say-never approach to all of the world's problems. *A Dream So Big* will inspire you.

—BRIAN DEEVY, Chairman and CEO, RBCDaniels;
Director, The Daniels Fund

Steve Peifer has a rare and precious gift—he can make you laugh while you are crying. In his memoir, he skillfully transports you into the heart of Kenya, where he and his family have spent more than ten years feeding and educating thousands of poor and hungry children. A must read.

—ARIELLE FORD, author, *Wabi Sabi Love*

How does a white guy from the suburbs of Chicago receive global acclaim for changing the lives of thousands of children in Africa? Unintentionally. And by encountering his own pain and grief, allowing God to redeem them for the sake of others. With his gift for self-deprecating humor and poignant insights, Steve Peifer weaves a humble story of genuine adventure, profound transformation, and authentic heroism.

— CRAIG GLASS, President, Peregrine Ministries International

Heroes: ordinary people faced with desperate need taking courageous action. Through humorous musings and anecdotal reflections, Steve, a white, suburban technology executive, shares the journey that took him halfway around the globe as he grieved the loss of his son. His story reminds us that one man courageous enough to take action can make a difference.

— TIM HALL, Superintendent, Rift Valley Academy

Steve Peifer's journey from suburban America to the countryside of Kenya is one of moving from despair to hope, from pain to promise. Along the way, the Peifer family discovered God's greater family in the most surprising places and in the most inspiring ways. Turn the page and journey with them.

— RAY HOLLENBACH, writer, *studentsofjesus.com*

The Peifers' unselfish commitment to helping others is inspirational, and their tale of getting there will make you laugh, cry, and see hope in humanity.

— KELLEY, AMANDA, AND SUMMER, founders of Linda's Voice

Come along with Steve Peifer on a journey that will fill your heart with joy and tears. *A Dream So Big* is an unvarnished look at missionary life. *Thumbs up mbili!* (Kiswahili for "Two thumbs up!")

— DR. HARRY KRAUS, author, *A Heartbeat Away*

Steve and Nancy Peifer tell their journey in a candid way that draws you into their passion and moves you to step out of the routine of life and into God's purpose and plan. This is a great inspirational read for those with a global perspective, and for those who need one.

— TOM LANE, Executive Senior Pastor, Gateway Church

A Dream So Big chronicles the story of one family that just said yes and made a difference to countless children in Africa. Through humor and raw emotion, Steve unwraps the journey of his family and the longing of God's heart for the children in Kenya.

— JULIE MEYER, International House of Prayer–KC

I don't know anyone like Steve who has done more in the care of poverty-stricken kids by making the ultimate sacrifice of self. Steve's story is one of inspiration born of giving of oneself. After reading the first paragraph, you won't want to put the book down.

—MIKE MUHNEY, CEO, VIPorbit Software

This is the story of a man who successfully climbed the corporate ladder only to realize that real happiness came when God asked him to leap into the depths of African poverty. This insightful and humorous story allows you to walk into an African village and feed hungry children, build a computer lab, and guide young high school students to a future which is as foreign to them as Africa is to you.

—DR. MARK W. NEWTON, Associate Professor of Clinical Anesthesiology, Vanderbilt University

It has been a special privilege to watch God use Steve Peifer's extraordinary gifts to impact the lives of so many kids in Kenya. Steve was a hero long before CNN recognized him. His story is an inspiration and a testament to God's sovereignty and grace.

—DR. WARREN RICH, former Chairman, Rift Valley Academy School Board

A Dream So Big is the story of reckless surrender, a heart unfolding to the will of God for a desperate, precious people. Peifer's belief has hands and feet. It's messy but real, and lives have been transformed because of it, including my own.

—NATHAN SMITH, speaker and author; President, Love Africa

Heroes are people who attempt to do what others consider impossible. Steve is a hero who has learned to cry about the things that make God cry. His heart for children, and especially the children of Africa, is transparent and beautiful.

—STEPHEN M. SMITH, President, Naviance

A great and funny story of how my friend and his family adventured to Africa and made a big impact on people's lives. And Africa made a bigger impact on them. You will wish you had done the same. I laughed and cried reading the book. I am awed that there are people like the Piefers who answer God's call.

—PAT SULLIVAN, CEO, Contatta, Inc.

This is a riveting read about Steve Peifer's process of making dramatic change. In the world of education, his story is even more remarkable: from the students he cares for at Rift Valley Academy to the twenty thousand Kenyan children his lunch program feeds every school day. This book will inspire you to accomplish something as wonderful and important as Mr. Peifer has accomplished.

—REBEKAH WESTPHAL, Director of International Admissions, Yale College

How does a normal couple living in Texas win the CNN Heroes Award? It begins with heartbreak, followed by compassion, and then overwhelming need. The stories Steve shares with his unique style and humor will remind you of your own humanity and daily opportunities to make a ripple in the lives of others.

—KYLE WILSON, founder, Jim Rohn International

I cannot think of another book that captures in such an accessible manner the astounding contradictions that define current-day Africa. While we intend to praise someone by saying that he has written "with a clear eye," this book's effectiveness comes from Peifer's courage in sharing what he has seen through eyes often filled with tears. I hope many people will find this book a call to action.

—ROBIN M. WORTH, Director of International Admissions, Harvard

A DREAM
SO BIG

A DREAM SO BIG

*Our Unlikely Journey to End
the Tears of Hunger*

Steve Peifer with Gregg Lewis

ZONDERVAN.com/
AUTHORTRACKER
follow your favorite authors

ZONDERVAN

A Dream So Big
Copyright © 2013 by Steve Peifer

This title is also available as a Zondervan ebook. Visit www.zondervan.com/ebooks.

This title is also available in a Zondervan audio edition. Visit www.zondervan.fm.

Requests for information should be addressed to:

Zondervan, *Grand Rapids, Michigan 49530*

Library of Congress Cataloging-in-Publication Data

Peifer, Steve.
    A dream so big : our unlikely journey to end the tears of hunger / Steve Peifer and
Gregg Lewis.
       p. cm.
    ISBN 978-0-310-32609-0 (hardcover)
     1. Peifer, Steve. 2. Missionaries — Kenya — Biography. 3. Missions — Kenya — Biography.
4. Church work with children — Kenya. I. Lewis, Gregg, 1951- II. Title.
    BV3625.K42 P45   2013
    266'.0237306762 — dc23   2012034384

Published in association with Yates & Yates, www.yates2.com.

Cover design: Kirk DouPonce / DogEared Design
Cover images: Steve Peifer, Shutterstock®
Interior design: Beth Shagene

Printed in the United States of America

13 14 15 16 17 18 19 20 /DCI/ 24 23 22 21 20 19 18 17 16 15 14 13 12 11 10 9 8 7 6 5 4 3 2

To Stephen Wrigley Peifer
Born March 4, 1998

—

Having fulfilled the purpose the Father had for him,
he returned to the Father March 12, 1998

Contents

Acknowledgments

To Nancy, whom everyone else sees as the cute, smart, nice one in our marriage: I see all of that, but I also see the deepest well I know, someone who has never stopped seeking. However, mostly I see the most fun person I know. I love you so.

To JT, Matthew, Ben, and Katie: you are the greatest gifts Mom and I have ever received. Thank you so much for your love and your courage.

To Janelle: we are so grateful that you are a part of us and we are a part of you. JT has very good taste.

To Margaret, who is in charge of our food program, and Lucy, our head computer teacher: no one has more yako than the two of you.

To Walter, the genius who designed the computer center, and Bruce, the force of nature who built so many of them.

To Metroplex Covenant Church, Woodland Heights Baptist Church, and Gateway Church.

To Jeff and Amy, Chris and Lucy, Bob and Marianne, and James and Karen: thank you for your guidance and kindness to us.

To Tim and Becky, who gave us not only our invitation to Africa but our examples.

To CNN, for an undeserved but very appreciated honor, and to Nelson and Cory for nominating us.

To NACAC, for helping a clueless corporate guy become a Kenyan high school's college guidance counselor, and then honoring him in such an unexpected and amazing way.

To Dan Crabtree and Jan Miranda, for their mentorship in college counseling, and to NACCAP, for their kindness to me.

To Rift Valley Academy, for taking in someone who was as wounded and as unqualified as me to work at a school for missionary kids, and for somehow becoming a place of healing and restoration.

To Tim Hall, who saw something in me that no one else saw and opened the door for college counseling.

To Mark Buhler, the person I most admire in the world, for being an example in all things.

To all the students at Rift Valley Academy, with special thanks to Sam, Andy, Brad, Wan, Emily, Jessica, Joel, Chris, Ji-Hee, and Peter, the first brave students who broke out the ceiling.

Very special thanks to Sarah, whose excellence inspired the Prestigious Scheenstra Award. If you go on YouTube, you will be astonished at my skill in crafting the Prestigious Scheenstra Award Theme Song. I wrote all the lyrics myself, with no help and no training.

To Covenant Christian Academy, for their care of our children when we are back in America, with special thanks to Keith and Tami.

To Rex and Lisa, Ray and Kim, Don and Laura, Rich and Kathy, and Don and Vicky.

To Robin Worth, who, in her own way, has done more for Africa than anyone I know.

To the Coleman Mob.

To Old Jeff, because he is a pretty great guy.

To my brother and sisters, for putting up with too much.

To Mark, Tim, Jim, Alan, and Jon, who had the rare joy of managing me.

To Bruce Boeck, Tom Roberts, and Nancy Chaps: thank you for high school friendships that somehow survive the decades.

To Nathan Blick and the PB and J Project at A&M: you guys are SUCH an inspiration.

To Africa Inland Mission, especially for those who serve in Peachtree City, Georgia, for service beyond the call of duty.

To the missionary community, who put themselves at risk because they love others more than themselves. We will never know why I get this attention and you don't, but I understand where I stand in God's economy, and I'm not worthy to wash your feet.

To all the great teachers at RVA, and special thanks to Brian Wagner, whom I call to thank whenever an RVA student is accepted into a competitive college, and who always yells at me for it. Even though I get credit, I know the real reason. Thanks for being the world's greatest math teacher.

To Tim Cook and Tim Reber, for being extraordinary leaders.

To Tom Lavery, the smartest guy I know (and this is the most painful sentence I have ever written).

To Dr. Glenn from NIU, the greatest teacher I ever had. Transformational.

To Jon Levin, the world's greatest boss.

To Ivy, whose invitation started so many things.

To Jenny, for making the Harvard Summer Institute come true.

To Clint and Edie, for being the best neighbors ever.

To Gregg Lewis: this book never would have happened without him, so all blame should accrue to him. We will always be grateful.

To Sealy, for being the greatest agent I've ever had. (He is also the only agent I've ever had, but that is beside the point.)

To Zondervan: thanks to all for midwifing this LONG pregnancy.

To John Stouffer and Alicia H., and everyone at CSA who got the computer idea before anyone else ever did. If it weren't for you, nothing would have happened.

To Len and the entire Bergstrom family: I'm so grateful for decades of friendship.

To Bill Bludworth: the tough years in that salt mine were worth it to work with such an example of a righteous walk.

My first album was *Tap Root Manuscript*, which included Neil Diamond singing in Swahili. I ran outside and shook my fist and KNEW that someday I would be in Africa. That is not a true story, but it would be so cool if it were. Thanks to Neil Diamond for his inspiration by being the greatest singer/songwriter of all time. Special thanks to Micah Blalock for the Doug Rhone introduction, who allowed me to actually go backstage at a ND concert, surely the high point of human existence. You were right.

Whenever you read this, the Cubs will win the World Series in four games this year. Bet everything you have on the Cubs; I have, and see where it has gotten me.

So many people supported us when there was absolutely no reason to do it, except that you were kind. We are so grateful to you.

Most of all, thank you to Jesus, who saved a wretch like me.

Prologue

THE LIGHTS GO DOWN IN THE PACKED-OUT NEW YORK CITY CONCERT hall. From my front-row seat next to my wife, Nancy, I look up to see myself suddenly projected onto a huge screen above the stage. The video instantly transports a glamorous, star-studded celebrity audience—dressed to the nines in diamonds, designer dresses, and tuxedos—around the world to a rural Kenyan hillside where a video-me stands looking out over the Great Rift Valley. And my amplified voice fills the auditorium, saying, "Africa will change you. Africa gets under your skin and won't let go." The screen shot shifts from a rural setting to an African street scene as my voice-over continues. "We were a typical American family . . ." I cringe to see my own much larger than life image, speaking and moving across the screen. I listen to my voice drone on and make what sounds in this moment to be a public confession: "My wife has always wanted to be in Africa; I never wanted to be in Africa."

A part of me can't help marveling at what is happening to me here tonight, at a live television event being broadcast around the world. Yet a bigger part of me almost has to laugh out loud at what feels like just another very strange chapter in a strange life that is no longer my own and hasn't been for almost a decade.

Then a young makeup artist crouches down beside me and hurriedly tries to make me "presentable" for my acceptance speech. I want to tell her she has a hopeless job. Instead, I bite my tongue. And as she goes about her business, I determine to refocus on the screen and review in my mind the words I've written out to say.

When the attentive young lady whispers, "We can't have you looking all shiny up there," and begins powdering my entire countenance, three nearly simultaneous thoughts arise in my mind: *I've never before in my life worried about being "all shiny," whatever that means. It's hard, if not impossible, to focus your thoughts on anything else while a makeup artist is powdering your face.* And, *I have found myself in more than my share of weirdly unsettling situations before, but this feels weird on a much bigger, harder-to-believe scale!*

As the video rolls on, my mind wanders. How does the college guidance counselor at a hundred-year-old, rural Kenyan boarding school for missionary kids ever get nominated for, let alone win, the annual CNN's Hero for Championing Children Award? For that matter, how in the world did a guy living a "normal" American life — complete with a wonderful, loving wife, two terrific kids, a nice big house, and a solid career as a corporate manager with one of the world's leading technology giants — find himself residing on the far side of the earth feeding lunch and teaching computer skills to hungry African schoolchildren, some of whose families still hunt with spears and live in mud-hut villages without electricity or running water?

The answers to all those questions require a story that does not begin at a glitzy gala in New York City. Neither does the story end as the screen goes dark, the house lights come back up, and Tyra Banks, one of the world's most famous fashion models and now also a television show host, stands at the microphone saying, "It is my honor to present the CNN Hero for Championing Children, Steve Peifer."

That night, as unreal as it felt at the time, as nice an honor as CNN made it on such a big stage, is a small, albeit memorable, scene in a much larger real story — a personal and family pilgrimage that began more than ten years before and far beyond the bright lights and big city. A story that has taken me to many places and situations where I have had to do what I did that special night in New York: stop, look around, pinch myself to see if I was dreaming, and wonder, *How in the world did I get here?*

1

"What in the World Am I Doing Here?"

TWO CONTRASTING YET INTERRELATED FEELINGS HIT ME THE MOMENT I walked through the exit doors of the terminal at Nairobi International Airport at 6:00 a.m. and stepped into Africa for the first time. Number one was the worst, most exhausting case of jet lag I'd ever experienced. The second was a sudden, heightened awareness of my own alienness.

After a twenty-eight-hour journey from the United States, including a fifteen-hour layover and whirlwind tour of London, with my wife, Nancy, and our seven- and ten-year-old sons (who'd had all of six hours of sleep over the previous two days) in tow, I understood the exhaustion. I was simply glad to have survived my very first international travel experience and have all eight pieces of our luggage arrive in Kenya with us.

What caught me by surprise was how suddenly and totally out of place I felt. We definitely weren't in Kansas anymore. I'd lived in Kansas for a few years before I moved to Texas. And Nairobi wasn't anything like anywhere I'd ever been before.

Most of the hour-and-a-half drive to our final destination remains a blur on my memory screen. Any travel-guide spiel offered by the man who met us at the airport and drove us out to Kijabe went right over, or in and out of, my head, although I clearly remember that I found driving on the left side of the road so disconcerting that I couldn't count the number of times I flinched in anticipation of a horrendous crash.

But a few of the sights and sounds and smells of Africa penetrated the fatigue enough to leave some lasting impressions. All of which fed my out-of-place feeling. Every direction I turned, everything I saw looked so ... so *foreign*.

15

More than three million people live in Nairobi, Kenya's capital and largest city. Most of them seemed to be out walking shortly after dawn on this weekday morning. The rest rode in matatus (privately owned vans and minivans) that serve as the country's primary "mass" transportation. As many as thirty Kenyans will pack into a van built to hold nine people comfortably; I saw some matatus with riders on top and others with "outside passengers" standing on running boards or hanging from luggage racks or clinging to open and swinging back doors.

Neither drivers nor pedestrians hesitated to cross multiple lanes of moving traffic wherever and whenever they wanted. Then there were the donkey carts using the same lanes as motorized vehicles. And the chickens, goats, and sheep that wandered all over the place.

The city was so crowded and dirty, even the new buildings looked tired. Vendors peddled anything and everything you can imagine (and some you can't) in what looks like an endless roadside flea-market. The farther you get from the downtown business district, the more frequently you see and smell trash burning right along the streets. Somewhere between one and two million people make their homes in Nairobi's slums, living in sheet-metal shacks with dirt floors.

Even if you aren't a big city fan, you can enjoy the energy of New York, the vitality of Chicago, the diversity of San Francisco. It was hard to find anything in Nairobi to appreciate, except for the more than three million individuals who live there in some of the most deplorable conditions you can imagine.

When I managed to look past the constantly moving mass of people walking along, and back and forth across, the roadways to focus on one person at a time, what I saw was even more unsettling—young kids the age of our JT and Matthew carrying around large jars of glue, sniffing all the time. And as I looked more carefully, I was amazed by how many people I noticed in the background—sitting, staring, and going nowhere. There seemed to be no hope in their eyes.

Even after we got out of Nairobi, a steady stream of trudging pedestrians paralleled the road, as many people walking away from the city as walking toward it.

There wasn't quite as much to see in the countryside, but what was there in that vast rural landscape felt just as foreign to me as anything I'd seen in Nairobi. Which made me wonder yet again (and not for the last time), *What's an ordinary, unadventurous (some might say "humdrum"; I prefer "typical"), suburban*

American guy like me doing in a place like Kenya—for a year, no less? What was I thinking when I agreed to this?

The short answer is that it seemed like a good idea at the time. Our family had recently gone through such a painful and difficult time that Nancy and I decided a change of scenery and the chance to leave the past and get away for a while would be good for all of us.

Friends had convinced us that spending a year in Kenya as short-term volunteer dorm parents at a boarding school for the children of missionaries would be just the way to provide the time and opportunity for even the deepest of our emotional wounds to heal. But that was before I realized just how far away we were getting. After two days of travel that landed us half a world and eight thousand miles from home in a place that felt like a different planet, a year suddenly didn't seem very short-term at all.

It wasn't as if I didn't expect to have to make some major adjustments, coming from American middle-class suburbia to life in rural Kenya. Almost every instructor at the intensive three-week orientation and training session we'd gone through just before leaving the States had emphasized a variety of challenges we should expect. I'd been particularly interested in and focused on the cross-cultural differences we were told we might encounter.

Three examples had stuck in my mind.

One instructor illustrated a difference in cultural mindset by saying that in our Western culture, if a kid hits a ball through a window during a game, it is considered his fault and he's responsible for the repair bill. In Kijabe, Kenya, if a kid hits a ball through a window, the whole team bears the responsibility for it because "the game did it." I thought there was much to be said for that sort of shared community and family spirit.

A veteran missionary at our orientation training told about being invited for a meal at a national family's home where a tribal tradition is to give the oldest male present the honor of eating the head of the chicken being served for supper. When the missionary asked his host how to eat it, the national laughed until he fell down, and then summoned all his neighbors because he could not believe that an adult male did not know how to eat a chicken head. (FYI: You eat it all, including eyes and beak. It is considered rude not to try, but if you truly cannot eat something, you apologetically say, "It defeats me!" which I suspected would quickly become a Peifer family tradition with Matthew whenever we had spinach.)

A professor of anthropology had talked to us about how different cultural views of the world can lead to very different conclusions. He told of visiting one tribe (there are fifty tribes in Kenya, and tribal loyalty is still the strongest and primary source of affiliation among Kenyans) that still practices multiple marriages. The custom in that tribe is for each wife to live in a different hut, and a husband stays overnight in a hut with a wife only if he is planning to be intimate with her, which means the entire village knows when he is going to be with each wife. The professor looked at a man with four wives and concluded that the national was oversexed. But then the national came to the professor's home and looked at the bedroom and asked if the professor slept there. The professor said, yes, he did. "Where does your wife sleep?" the national asked. "She also sleeps here," replied the professor. "Every night?" asked the incredulous national. His conclusion: Americans are oversexed.

It had been one thing to contemplate rather fascinating cultural differences from thousands of miles away. Somehow the differences seemed a lot bigger, or at least a lot more real, now that I'd actually landed in Kenya. The differences, the reminders that we were indeed in Africa—for a year, no less —were suddenly all around me. And they were all I could really absorb that first morning.

I was reassured somewhat, if only temporarily, when we turned off the main, trans-Kenyan highway and drove down a steep, rutted gravel road into Kijabe, where we pulled into a long drive and then through a gate into what felt like an oasis of familiarity right there in the African bush. Rift Valley Academy had the look and feel of many small college campuses I'd visited back in the States, a haven that instantly felt more like home than anything I'd seen since we'd walked off the plane at dawn that morning.

In our family's three-bedroom upstairs apartment in the dorm that would be our home, it took all of twenty minutes to unpack and put away everything we'd brought to wear for twelve months. Then as Nancy further explored and inventoried our new residence, I took JT and Matthew down to the playground just across the road to release some of their pent-up energy after two grueling days of confinement and travel.

As I watched my sons run and play, an American man about my age walked up and introduced himself. I told him who I was, that my wife, Nancy, and I were going to be the fifth grade boys' dorm parents, that we were from Grapevine, Texas, and that we'd just landed in Nairobi earlier that morning.

No sooner had I articulated those few particulars than he asked, "Hey, do you want to preach down in the valley this Sunday?"

"Well, uh ..." I was a bit taken aback by his question. "I've never preached before, but if you really need someone to speak ..."

"You've never preached before?" he exclaimed. "What Bible college did you go to?"

"I didn't go to Bible college. I graduated from Northern Illinois University with a degree in political science." Why did I suddenly feel like I needed to apologize for that?

My new colleague just looked at me, as if he simply didn't know what to say to that. Finally he asked, "Well, how long you here for?"

I'd learned that some people come to teach or work at RVA for only a term. So I proudly replied, "A whole year."

"You came all this way for just one year?" he asked. And before I figured out how to answer such a judgmental question, which sounded more like an accusation, he abruptly left. Which I took to mean I wouldn't be expected to preach in the valley that Sunday after all.

I figured that was probably just as well, since I felt rather more prepared to eat a chicken head than to preach a sermon.

Truth be known, until we'd landed in Nairobi and I felt so suddenly out of place, I hadn't been worried so much about adjusting to African culture as I was that being a missionary might be what would "defeat me."

I wasn't a preacher, a teacher, a doctor, or anything else I'd ever thought a missionary needed to be. And much of our experience at orientation school had underscored my sense of inadequacy. Other people there preparing to come to Africa not only seemed so much better equipped professionally; they all seemed to be so much better people, so much more sincere Christians than I was. Many of them had an obvious passion for Africa I'd never felt, or a lifelong sense of calling that I'd never experienced. I felt privileged to be among such committed, faith-full people. But I also found it humbling because I realized I wasn't at their level.

Now my playground encounter with a real-life, experienced, veteran missionary only amplified the question I'd asked myself during our training and again on the long drive from the airport to Kijabe: "What in the world is someone like me doing here?"

———

Before we left the States, we promised family, friends, and other people who gave financial support so our family could go and work in Kenya that we'd stay in touch by sending regular emails to keep them updated on our experiences. I wrote my first email report after we'd had a chance to recuperate from the trip and had a week or so to settle in. After recounting some of our orientation school experience and a few details from our journey, I offered this brief description of where we were:

The Rift Valley Academy (RVA) is located at an elevation of seventy-five hundred feet, to be above the malaria level. It is almost one hundred years old, and it is like a small college campus. There are dorms and classrooms throughout the campus. Teddy Roosevelt laid the cornerstone for one of the oldest buildings during one of his African hunting trips. Although we are at the equator, our elevation means that it is cool during the winter season, which is now. There is no heat except our fireplace, and the house is cement block (which all houses are here because of termites), so it can get pretty cold for us Texans. It was fifty-three yesterday. We also have a fireplace outside to warm our water for bathing.

The official languages here are English and Swahili, so Nan and I will be attending language school next week for several weeks. My bride received her college degree in linguistics, so she is thrilled. Since her slow husband can make her break out in a rash with his French accent, I am sure Swahili will be more of a challenge to me, but we are excited about it.

It is beautiful here, and the nationals are wonderful people. The poverty is almost beyond understanding; the average African makes two hundred and eighty dollars a year. Kenya has the highest amount of AIDS in the world, and the large mission hospital just down the hill from the campus says one out of four patients are there because of HIV. There is currently a drought too. We are in the rainy season, but are not getting any rain, just fog and damp. The crops are already damaged, but if no rain comes soon, they will be totally lost. Please be praying for rain.

RVA was between terms when we arrived in late July. Which meant the campus felt almost deserted with many of the faculty and staff away during the break and no boarding student scheduled to return until the first of September for the new school year. But that gave us time to get acclimated and prepare for all of our responsibilities, which would begin with a bang when the kids got back and the term started.

As part of our introduction to Africa, a group of us from RVA, including a number of new staff members, took a day trip to Lake Nakuru National Park a couple of hours away. It is a large park, almost two hundred square kilometers in size, where you can drive around grasslands and forests on unpaved roads and see, in their wild and natural habitat, fifty-six species of mammals and four hundred fifty species of birds, including a flock of hundreds of thousands of flamingos.

After touring the park for several hours, our group stopped to eat lunch. As we sat around enjoying our picnic, a baboon leaped into our circle, grabbed a sandwich, and plopped down to eat it.

There are several things I didn't know about baboons before I arrived in Africa. To be honest, I don't recall ever giving baboons a thought until I got to RVA and realized we shared the campus with a number of them. But they have two-inch canines, and four of them can take on a lion, so you don't mess with them. A common defense is to throw stones near them; you don't want to throw at them, because that can make them mad and they will charge. Or they'll pick up the stones and hurl them back!

So after a stern warning from a veteran missionary not to show our teeth, because that is a sign of aggression, we drove them off with stones and moved our picnic. Five minutes later, they invaded again, and grabbed potato chips and calmly ate them, until we got more stones and drove them off. Then we stood guard so they wouldn't swipe our food for the rest of the meal. It seemed even African picnics required some cross-cultural adjustments I'd never considered before.

—

In one of my next emails home, I reported on yet another cross-cultural dining adventure our family experienced when the electrical power on campus was off all day and we went "out to eat" for the first time since we'd arrived in Kenya.

We walked down and out the main gate of the campus to the dukas (or shops) serving the neighborhood that line the road that runs past the school. Dukas like these are a common sight everywhere we've been in Kenya, but if they were in the States, we would think they were abandoned and would never imagine they were places of business. They look like shacks made of wood or tin with tin roofs. They are painted bright colors, if they are painted. And they usually have any available surface covered with large signs advertising everything from Coke to Blue Band (the margarine of choice here) to cell-phone providers.

We walked into a duka that said Nehemiah's Hotel. (Hotels here are restaurants.) There was a dirt floor, open windows and doors (no screens), and no electricity, so it was semi-dark. There were five non-matching tables and about fifteen chairs, each different from the others.

On the wall was a chalkboard with the menu. It was primarily for decoration; we'd been told it is better to ask, "What do you have?" than to request different items that they don't have. Chickens regularly walked in and out of the restaurant. Coke, which is ubiquitous in Africa, is served from the bottle and is warm. A friend from here swears that he was in one duka and ordered chicken, and the cook grabbed a chicken that walked in the door and prepared it as they watched.

So we didn't order chicken. We all ordered kitaweo and chapatis. Kitaweo is a vegetable stew relying heavily on potatoes and cabbage. The meat is like a garnish on top, but it is excellent! Chapatis are flat, fried breads. They are made of wheat flour, but are much heartier than a tortilla — also excellent. A large plate of stew and a chapati (enough to fill non-teenage male appetites) cost forty-five shillings, or about sixty cents. If you splurge and get a soda, add seventeen more shillings and you still have a great meal for less than a dollar. This gives you an idea of the local economy, where the average income is probably between two hundred fifty and three hundred dollars per year. And this is a more prosperous area than much of Kenya. I am quickly becoming aware that in the eyes of many of our national neighbors, we are millionaires. It's an odd feeling and somewhat uncomfortable.

And yet another cross-cultural adjustment I never anticipated having to make.

—

The boys adjusted much faster than Nancy and I did. They quickly made friends with the few kids whose families were on campus during the break and could hardly wait for the rest of the students to arrive so they could meet all the new brothers that would live with us in the dorm for the year.

We hired a national to help us with our lawn and firewood. Fred was a wonderful young man, with a real heart for kids. I asked him to teach the boys to cut firewood with him. You should see our seven-year-old Matthew operate a panga (a large machete) or our ten-year-old JT swing an ax. You don't get to, or need to, do much of that in Grapevine, Texas. So right from the start, I realized Africa would provide an even bigger educational experience for our boys than I'd ever expected. And I knew that was a good thing.

—

Speaking of educational experiences ...

Most married men probably know, at least deep down, that their wives are better people than they are. Guys like to scratch and spit; women tend to be deeper and more refined. Anyway, I have always known this about my bride, who is smart, kind, gracious, tactful, encouraging, beautiful — the list could go on forever. And I am usually silently grateful for that.

But on rare occasions, our differences seem to shout, and our first week of language classes in Kijabe was one of those occasions. Nancy graduated from college in three years with a linguistics degree; I still struggle with my mother tongue. The first day (okay, more like the first minute) of Swahili class, it became so, so, *sooo* obvious how gifted she is. And how amazingly unproficient I am.

Our instructor, Richard, was a tremendous teacher; I am sure that given enough time, he could help me master his language. I'm just not sure there will ever be that much time. But, speaking of eternity, one hour into our language course, I remembered an old silent chant from seventh grade math: *Go, time, go. Go, time, go. Go, go, go, go. Go, time, go.* Alas, the mantra worked no better for me in 1998 in Africa than it had in northern Illinois in the late '60s.

This is what I wrote in my first email report on my language progress:

One day in class, our instructor gave us an assignment: "Go out and introduce yourself to someone, ask where he or she is from, what he or she does, and how his or her day has been." After being rebuked for asking, "Can I do it in English?" I ventured outside and met a very nice man named Peter. I am sure that was his name because it was on his badge.

I'm a bit fuzzy on how the conversation went from there. After I introduced myself to him, I was pretty certain he asked me to repeat what I said to two other Kenyan workers standing nearby, who, when I did so, broke out in gales of laughter. I was never certain whether Peter told me he worked in the fields, or if maybe he had acknowledged having an open sore. But after further cordial and enlightening conversation, my new friend Peter placed his hand on my shoulder and kindly said, "I will pray much for your Swahili teacher."

We're scheduled for another language practice outing to the market on Tuesday — to bargain. If you discover that we have sold our house in Texas, this may be a possible explanation. Nancy, on the other hand, is beginning to have real conversations with folks. Beauty and the Beast indeed.

It was time. My seven days of Swahili had prepared me to go to the Masai Market. To get there from the spot where our instructor dropped us off, we followed a steady stream of Kenyans up a rather precarious path along the edge of a steep hill, high above the noisy traffic of a major highway, until we reached a large, level hilltop where hundreds and hundreds of Africans had spread out their goods for sale on the bare dirt ground. As I stood there trying to absorb the colorful scene, I felt as if I had a large target on my forehead, and inside the bull's-eye was a sign, flashing, "Here lies a dumb, rich white person; charge as much as you can!"

My impossible mission? (Whether or not I chose to accept it.) Bargain. It's an art form in Kenya, and anyone who pays full price for anything is considered as naive and foolish as someone who pays the full list price for a new car in the States. And the car analogy is an apt one, because I quickly learned

Kenya is a land of used-car salespeople—without the cars—who will say anything to make a connection. And a sale.

JT was wearing a Dallas Cowboys shirt, and at least a dozen men loudly proclaimed, "I love the Cowboys Dallas!" I saw one gentleman wearing a U of Chicago sweatshirt and told him I once attended a class there. He told me he had also, and pointed to the date on the shirt: 1892. Another guy told me it was a bad omen if I didn't buy; I told him I didn't believe in omens. He then loudly proclaimed, "I am again borned." Whatever they thought you wanted to hear, they said.

I saw a batik I thought Nancy would really like; it is dye on cloth, and it is quite the art form in Kenya. "Steve" (there were about twenty "My name is also Steve" guys that day) responded to my question, "Ni shillingi ngapi?" (How much?) with, "Ten thousand shillings." I grabbed my heart and moaned, "Ni ghali sana." (It is very expensive.) He protested about the integrity of his artistic vision, or that he was going to eat bratwurst for lunch —I'm not sure which. But it didn't really matter. Because I told him that his price was so shockingly high that I was about to suffer a heart attack, fall down the hill, and be hit by a car. Our conversation, consisting of at least as much body language as Swahili, went on and on until we finally got down to seven hundred shillings. What a day!

—

I'm sure my cross-cultural business acumen could be at least partially explained by the fact that I had read the *Wall Street Journal* from the time I was nineteen, starting my sophomore year in college and continuing the habit as I climbed the corporate ladder. But when I inquired about the possibility of scoring a WSJ fix in Kenya, I was informed that a one-year subscription costs twenty-seven hundred dollars and it arrives five to seven days late. So I realized I had no choice but to give up my habit, go cold turkey, and remain sadly uninformed.

Instead I had to find different ways to become informed about a whole new world. This was one reason Fred and I were having a memorable discussion one day. It was a chance for me to work on my Swahili and to get to know a national better; for Fred, it was mostly an opportunity to laugh at my accent and pronunciation. At one point in our conversation, Fred told me he was hoping to save up to buy concrete (his home had a dirt floor) and windows (because the cardboard he used at the time was an invitation for thieves). My new friend Fred was considered well-to-do by African standards. But as he excitedly shared his remodeling dreams, I simply did not know what to say—in any language.

—

I also struggled to adequately communicate my thoughts and feelings about this new African experience with my old friends back home. But I knew I needed to try. So one of those early Sundays in Kenya I sent an email saying:

We went down in the valley to a Masai church today. It had a tin roof, dirt floors, and wooden benches with no backs. The service was in Swahili, so much of it flew by me. But the worship was joyous, the singing beautiful. When they took the offering, I watched people with nothing give their tithes. And at the end of the service, they presented our whole family with wristbands and necklaces.

I don't know how to adequately articulate this. But when I saw these people, most of them barefoot or in shoes with huge holes in them, offering their tithes, I felt as if my entire life passed before my eyes, and I saw myself for the first time. I didn't feel worthy to be in that place. And the truth is, I'm not worthy. For months I've been telling people I wanted to come to Africa to learn, not just to teach. The school kids are arriving here tomorrow, and I will begin teaching. But I'm already learning more than I could ever teach.

2

Questions without Answers

THE IDEA OF SPENDING A YEAR IN AFRICA AS BOARDING-SCHOOL DORM parents and surrogate mom and dad to a bunch of missionary kids had seemed like a timely, worthwhile, perhaps even noble way to seek relief from the long months of excruciating pain and grief Nancy and I had endured after our family's loss. But what had in theory appeared to be a rather simple and appealing prospect was put to the test of reality the day our ten-year-old male dorm residents—nine of them: four Koreans, one Indian, one Kenyan national, and three Americans (although two of the Americans had spent most of their lives in Africa)—arrived on campus for the first term of the new school year.

Rift Valley Academy is like boy heaven for ten-year-olds; our dorm was right across the street from the school, a huge playground, *and* the soccer field. They have lots of trees to climb, some of those trees contain live monkeys, and all their pals live no more than five minutes away. But boarding school also means being separated from parents, and that can be tough. So that first night proved rather traumatic, with more than a few tears. And a whole lot of trying to hold back those tears because ten-year-old boys are not supposed to cry, no matter what their nationality or cultural background. One poor guy wailed away in the privacy of our bedroom for nearly two hours as Nancy and I took turns trying to console him. I'm convinced he wasn't so much homesick as he was mortified to be crying.

We tried to reassure him, as we did all the fellows, that it was okay—perfectly normal, in fact—for them to be sad and miss their families. Though I don't think they were convinced; after all, how many ways can you prove you are indeed a big, tough ten-year-old other than by not crying?

From the outset, our dorm-parent gig promised to be an interesting learning experience. Every one of the boys listed pizza as their favorite food, though the Koreans like pizza and noodles. Beyond a few such cultural variations, I quickly discovered a great universality among ten-year-olds, much of which centered on gas. Fifth grade boys, especially those living among a group of their peers, seem to have a fascination with flatulence that distinguishes them from any other segment of the human race. They take the subject seriously; within the very first week, I walked into one very animated late-night discussion on whether, if they hooked tubes to their bottoms and connected them to the stove, you could actually cook with it.

Thankfully, there are a few other serious subjects for discussion among ten-year-old males, whatever their cultural backgrounds. Females, for example. In passing, I overheard this question posed: "Is it true that the first time you kiss a girl, you go home and throw up?" I paused long enough to hear several responses. But the response that has stuck forever in my mind is, "I don't know if you *have* to, but I know that I'm *gonna*." This was not said to be funny. And nobody laughed. (Except me — and of course Nancy, when I filled her in on the results of my eavesdropping.)

I quickly determined the vilest insult a ten-year-old boy can hurl at another ten-year-old boy. It is *not*, "Hey, you stink!" That particular accusation merely results in good-natured agreement and a welcome opportunity to talk more about gas. No, I discovered the ultimate hot button for ten-year-olds when the first of our guys had a birthday early in the term. We have a tradition in the Peifer family: we all take a turn telling the birthday boy at least one thing we like or appreciate about him. When we tried that during our dorm celebration, one of the guys said of the honoree, "I like that he is handsome to girls!"

With great fury the celebrant replied, "I am not. *You* are." The first boy's loud and sharp retort was, "Only to my mother, and she's not a real girl." Fortunately, all anger dissipated as a deep theological discussion ensued regarding whether mothers are girls, or exactly what they are.

—

Prior to my dorm-parent experience, I would have thought it difficult to find *any* bright side to having no water. But I soon learned never to underestimate the indomitably optimistic nature of the male child. When we awakened one Tuesday and turned on the faucets in our bathroom to discover we had no running water, my immediate thought was, *This drought is making it tough on everyone.* Everyone, it turned out, but ten-year-old boys. The moment this *cruel* reality sank in, euphoria swept through the dorm like a brushfire in a windstorm: "We can't take a bath!"

Surely, I must have witnessed such rapturous joy before, but for the life of me, I have never been able to remember when or where. It was as if the principal had proclaimed, "School is canceled for the rest of your lives. Play soccer!" Great excitement lasted until the following day, when, unfortunately in some eyes (and gratefully to our noses), both water pressure and the horror of bathing were restored.

—

We had other daily reminders of the infrastructure problems of Africa. I wrote about one of them in this weekly email home:

Email was down for the entire nation of Kenya this last seven days. Kenya has only one satellite that handles all its email, and when it goes down, there is no plan B. When email goes down for an extended period, I start to imagine all sorts of wonderful news items I will receive when it comes back up:

> *"Cubs Win World Series"*
> *"Dow Hits 30,000"*
> *"Cure for Cancer Found"*

Instead, what I received was a message from my good friend who is renting our house (in Texas), informing us that water is leaking from the downstairs bathroom and it will cost thirteen hundred dollars to repair and would I reply ASAP? Unfortunately, I received this message on Saturday and he had sent it the previous Sunday. We are grateful for email, but in Kenya, it has its limitations.

—

One more bit of news: We also inherited a dog this week. She is a black lab named Jessie, who is supposed to be watched by another family while her owners are in the States on a furlough. But from the first day, she developed a deep dark crush on JT. She would chew through her leash to sleep outside our dorm so she could greet him in the morning and go with him to class. So we finally made it official on Tuesday, and she moved over to our dorm. Five hours later, we got the call: "Your dog stole our dog's dish." Some of my old friends know of my tendency to attract stupid dogs and bring out the dumbest in them. The streak continues.

—

Another morning partway through the fall term, we had a chapel speaker who made a presentation about the drought and the impact the ongoing local famine was causing. A number of his stories really touched our RVA students, and their response touched *me*.

Most of our dorm kids received just seventy cents a week spending money. So I found it unexpectedly moving when the boys in our dorm decided to forego spending their treat money on Cokes or candy bars to make a donation to famine relief instead. But the kids wanted to do more, so we talked about what kind of fundraiser might be feasible. The obvious, traditional stuff like washing cars won't work in a part of the world with few cars during the middle of a drought. We brainstormed fruitlessly until the boys finally went to bed.

Later that night it hit me. As background, and at the risk of sounding immodest, I have to acknowledge that I had twice in my life come up with marketing ideas that captured the attention of a nation. But that success had been in a different occupational world, in a galaxy far, far away and long ago. So I have to admit that it came as a bit of a surprise when I realized that there in Africa, I may just have thought up the greatest fundraising idea ever.

But first, a little more background: At the start of the semester, all of our dorm kids were issued band instruments—five trumpets, two saxophones, one trombone, and a flute. As enthusiastic beginners, the boys loved to practice, often simultaneously, inside our dorm, which was built with cement-block walls. Believe me, these kids gave a whole new meaning to the phrase "the sound of music."

For weeks I'd had dreams about how many different ways "Hot Cross Buns" can sound flat. The phrase "Listen to this!" made me break out in a rash. But the boys had been so excited to be taking beginning band that it was hard not to have fun with it. And while I don't consider myself personally qualified to evaluate the progress made during the first weeks of the term, I could certainly attest to the fact that their enthusiasm had not waned, which brings me back to the brilliant fundraising idea.

We named our little dorm-boy band The Joyful Noises and began visiting other dorms, offices, and assorted campus residences to give free concerts. Yes, the genius of this plan is that we played for free. The secret to our fundraising success was that we charged a fee if our audiences wanted us to *stop* playing.

And the longer we played, the more reasonable that fee sounded.

Response was overwhelming. Reviews included, "I've never heard anything like that before." Our first number was technically our warm-up. The second song was the classic and aforementioned "Hot Cross Buns." I can assure you that with the talent we had, no lesser expert than John Philip

Sousa himself would have found it difficult to distinguish between the two. When we decided during one concert that our third number should be the RVA fight song, two of our guys yelled, "We don't know that one!" before boldly entering into playing it anyway.

Gift certificates for our concerts soon became popular. Some people even paid us to perform concerts for friends with whom they'd recently had a small tiff, no doubt as a way to make up. That resulted in doubling our earnings by collecting both for starting and stopping our concerts. In just a matter of days, The Joyful Noises raised enough cash to buy three large bags of maize and set out delivering it around the community. Our hope was not merely to help hungry people but also to impact some ten-year-old boys about the reality of life for many of the Kenyan people who lived near our school.

Our outing not only accomplished that; it also gave opportunity for another lesson in empathy: I've never seen a Kenyan man do it, but the Kikuyu women around Kijabe routinely haul as much as a hundred and fifty pounds on their backs, even as they hike up and down incredibly steep hills. So after we'd delivered maize to a number of grateful families in the nearby community, we spotted a lady we knew walking ahead of us and balancing on her back a bundle of firewood sticks almost as big as she was, and probably heavier. So I asked if our guys could carry the load for her. It took four of them. And they didn't get very far.

That night, as JT headed to bed, he said, "Dad, I'll never look at those women the same again."

—

We were all looking at many things differently since we'd arrived in Africa. And I continued trying to convey some of those lessons to our family and friends in the emails I sent out almost every week. Like the one in which I wrote:

We saw a different side of Beauty and the Beast this week when our family all went out (with some other missionaries) to deliver maize in the valley for the famine relief effort. We filled a large flatbed truck to transport the food to seven different churches. While we were driving across terrible roads (or no roads), we spotted zebras, gazelles, and other kinds of magnificent wildlife. That is one part of Africa—the Beauty.

But there is also the Beast. It's called "drought." Its impact is everywhere; the visual evidence is horrible to look at and impossible to fully describe. We stopped at one orphanage where kids get barely enough for one meal a day. The churches where we delivered food had floors of dirt and mud walls that didn't reach the ceiling. Many of you know—a few of you went with us—that Nancy and I sometimes volunteered

*feeding the homeless in Dallas. But I have to tell you, this is like no poverty you've
seen before.*

Back in Texas, I would look at rain and think, Now I won't get to see the
Rangers game tonight. *Less than three months here and I have begun to realize,*
If it doesn't rain soon, lots of people are going to die. *What must it be like to
look up at the sky and think,* If it doesn't rain, I'm going to die. *Or worse,* If it
doesn't rain, my children are going to die. *I can't imagine. I can't even begin to
get my mind around a question like that.*

*I don't want to end this email on a down note, but I need to be honest. I wish I
had answers. I just have questions.*

———

During a hike our family took to explore the area back before school started,
we'd been surprised to see a tree on fire in the forest above our school. But
we found out that's not unusual. Cutting down and burning trees is how
many Kenyans (and Africans in other countries) make the charcoal millions
of people across the continent use for cooking and heating their homes. The
problem is that every tree that comes down means the water supply suffers.

Much drought occurs because Africa is destroying its forests. Deforestation affects water tables and climates in devastating ways. Forests surround
RVA, and every day we hear trees being chopped down by men who can
earn two hundred dollars a year making, bagging, transporting, and selling
charcoal. It is against the law to cut down the forest, but when the police
were first told what was happening, they claimed they didn't have enough
petrol to run their police cars. Without the resources to transport the miscre-
ants to jail, they saw no point in making any arrests. But our school finally
protested loudly and long enough that the local government officials agreed
to enforce the law.

So the police went through the forest in force — destroying all the charcoal pits, confiscating tools, and gathering all the stockpiled charcoal. The
next day, several men marched up to the gates of our school grounds. We
learned later that when they first saw what had happened to their livelihood,
their plan was to storm RVA and kill several of our leaders. But they had
thought better of that idea and came instead asking for help.

I talked to one of those men for some time. He was pretty rough around
the edges, but he told me he had six kids and wanted to know how he was
going to feed them without charcoal. I asked him what would happen to his
children and grandchildren if the forest was cut down. And that is the issue
in Africa today: how can people look to the future when getting through the

day is so hard? If you are making only two hundred dollars a year from selling charcoal, you don't think about the long term. You think about right now.

In the States, when you are newly married, you cut out some things to save money so you can buy your first house. Short-term sacrifice equals long-term gain. But when you start with nothing, how do you cut back?

One more question for which I had no answer.

—

I tried to articulate this dilemma in my next email report.

The problem becomes this: Every day I encounter good people with legitimate needs for money and resources. Robert's granddaughter needs chemo; Grace has school fees due; Fred wants to cement his home's floor; Margaret has no food and relatives are coming; the list goes on and on. We try to do what we can do, but there is no way we can support all the people with needs around here.

They had career day here at RVA a few days ago. Each participating adult introduced themselves and their profession. I introduced myself by saying, "I'm a filthy capitalist pig." So much of what this country needs is just companies relocating here and providing jobs. I can't blame a hungry guy for cutting down trees to put food in his kids' stomachs. Kenya needs alternatives. Africa just makes it so hard for companies to provide that alternative; the government is corrupt, the roads are atrocities, and the power is off more than it is on.

Despite that, we need to hope that rich nations invest in Africa. If we lose the battle for the forest, it will be devastating for more than just Africa. If we lose that battle, we all lose. I'd hate to lose the forest for a billion dollars; to lose it for two hundred dollars a year makes me sick.

—

We asked Fred to come for dinner one night with our family. By midway through our meal, I was astonished to realize that most of the usual things I like to ask someone I'm just getting to know don't work in Africa. How do I ask, "What is your favorite restaurant?" of someone who has eaten at a restaurant only three times in his life? "What is your favorite movie?" doesn't work for someone who doesn't have electricity. And, "What are you currently reading?" seems like the wrong question to be asking of someone who views books as one of life's sweetest luxuries.

In Africa, I clearly needed to relearn how to make a new friend.

—

As I told all of my old friends in my next email home:

Africa never lets you forget you are in Africa.

Like the time just this past week when Nancy got a call to come down to the local mission hospital to donate blood for a baby. The Kenyan nurse who drew Nancy's blood casually remarked to her that most local nationals can't give blood; it isn't rich enough because of their diets.

We had another reminder this week. In the States, we would plant a garden for fun, or because we wanted real tomatoes. In Africa, if your garden doesn't come in, it is that much less food you and your family eat. So many people here are hungry because their gardens haven't come in because of the drought.

The poverty here puts such tremendous pressure on folks. There is no free education for children in Kenya; if you can't pay the school fees, your children are pulled out of school until you can pay. Do you spend what little money you have on food or education? What a horrible, grievous choice, and the reality for so many parents here.

—

We had a class from a national school visit the Rift Valley Academy campus one day partway through that first semester. I was to show our visitors the computer lab, where I had intended to demonstrate how we had set up the network, share our plans, and talk about our immediate intentions to replace our routers.

But none of these Kenyan students had ever seen a computer before. Or an aquarium. Or a piano. They had seen pictures, so they knew what they were, but they had never seen real ones before. One of the teachers gasped when she saw our eight-year-old Macs and wanted to know, "Are these all for the children?" She was attending a university and taking a computer class. She told me she was eight weeks into the course and had not been on a computer yet. Her class had only practiced "typing" on a printed cardboard keyboard.

These young Kenyan visitors were nice, bright kids, and better off than most; I saw only a couple of toes sticking out of shoes. Yet none of them had ever seen a computer. When I showed them how I could save work to a disc and bring it home to work on, one of the kids looked at me incredulously and asked, "You have a computer at home?" I put on a good face for them, but when those schoolchildren left, I had myself a real long cry. I just wanted those Kenyan kids to have a shot. But I couldn't help wondering, *How does a nation compete globally when its kids have never seen a computer, let alone know how to use one?*

I didn't know how to answer that question either.

—

But nowhere did Africa remind me where I was more frequently or more poignantly than whenever I visited a hospital pediatric ward to distribute toys and other gifts our friends and supporters sent to share with the children of Kenya. I reported on these experiences in an email I sent home, thanking those who'd made the donations:

There were three special moments in the hospital this morning. One was visiting a boy with no fingers, playing with a Matchbox car someone sent us. He played with such joy and animation that you forgot he was having to pick it up and push the little vehicle around with his elbows. He was having so much fun it was fun to watch him.

The second special moment involved a mother. In Kenya, mothers stay with their hospitalized kids and usually sleep in the same bed. There are no private rooms in this hospital, just one very large children's ward for young patients.

One little girl was asleep, so I gave a coloring book and crayons to her mother. The woman actually embraced them, and then told me with a broad smile, "All my life I wanted a coloring book, and I never had one. But now my daughter will have one." In the hospital this morning, another little girl just sat on the floor and patted it. I didn't understand what she was doing, so I asked her mother, who explained, "We have a dirt floor at home; she has never been in a room with a floor." One of the doctors told me later that many of their young patients have never before been in a building with a floor. What's more, for many of them the hospital is the first place they've ever slept in a bed or eaten three meals a day.

There are so many things here in Africa I hope I never forget, but I actually prayed that this memory from today would be seared onto my heart. I've never thought about floors before I came to Africa. So I consider this one of the greatest miracles of being here—seeing the world in such a different way.

Even the floor.

—

And that new perspective on the world was giving me a new perspective on life. Not just on the new life our family was making in Africa but on the one we'd left behind that had led us to Kenya.

3

Our Story Started with Stephen

TWO YEARS EARLIER, WE HAD BEEN LIVING THE AMERICAN DREAM. Nancy and I had just celebrated twelve years of a happy marriage. We had two wonderful and well-loved sons, ages five and eight. At the age of forty-two, I had a management position with Oracle Corporation, the giant, multinational computer systems and software company; my job was to oversee the recruitment and work of Oracle's nine thousand outside contractors and consultants across North America. We'd recently moved into a bigger house. We had many terrific friends—even a faithful dog. Life was on track, and everything was under control. The future looked bright. It was all good.

Then, surprise, we got pregnant again. At first we didn't know whether to laugh or cry as we considered all of the implications of this news. We'd really thought the baby phase of our lives was over. But it didn't take long for both Nancy and me to get excited about having another child.

Nancy's first trip to the obstetrician included a sonogram because he liked to do an early one to confirm due dates. We knew his routine, since he delivered Matthew. What wasn't routine was the call Nancy took from the doctor himself that night during supper. She didn't say anything when she came back to the table, since we hadn't yet made the announcement to our boys. So it wasn't until after we got them to bed that Nancy told me what the call was about.

The doctor had phoned to inform us the sonogram showed more amniotic fluid than usual at this point in a pregnancy. He wanted to refer Nancy to a specialist because this sometimes indicates early problems with a baby's kidneys. I could tell Nancy was upset by the call, but she acknowledged,

"He's probably just being overly cautious because I just hit the red-flag age of forty."

We prayed together for our unborn child, and Nancy called to make the appointment with the high-risk specialist. Back before JT's birth, she had shopped around for an OB because we didn't want to deal with a doctor who performed abortions. But this time we just went to the specialist recommended to us by our doctor, without asking any questions—primarily because we didn't expect to deal with him beyond this initial exam, which would show everything was fine.

When we walked into the specialist's office, the receptionist told us the first person we needed to see was their genetics counselor. What was *this* all about? We just wanted the super-duper sonogram that would show our baby was fine. But we met with a nice young woman, who had an unpleasant job to do. She was supposed to (1) convince us to immediately do an amniocentesis test to find out exactly what was going on with our baby, and (2) offer us the choice of an early abortion should a genetic disorder be found.

We preempted her talk right there to inform her that we would carry him or her full term no matter what was found out about our baby. And we would love him or her as the God-given child he or she was. The genetics counselor listened graciously, but after we'd explained our position, she continued on her course. I could tell my wife was now quite upset. And later Nancy told me she was thinking, *I don't believe I am sitting here having someone offer me an abortion. And I don't believe anything is wrong with my baby!*

After that ordeal, we saw the doctor. I suspect he'd already read over the genetics counselor's notes, because the first thing he said to us after greeting us was that he felt we should go ahead and have the amnio done, "right now." Nancy told him we would not undergo a test that had a 25 percent chance of miscarriage without reasons that outweighed that risk.

The doctor was not happy, but said he would perform the super-duper sonogram. He did, and they found two notable concerns: enlarged kidneys and, more significant, a two-vessel umbilical cord. The doctor told us, "While it is possible to have a healthy baby when there is a two-vessel umbilical cord, 100 percent of all genetic disorders have two-vessel umbilicals."

So did we want to have amnio? No, we did not. He asked us to return in two weeks. When we returned for that next appointment, we did not have to see the genetics counselor again, but we were greeted with the same recommendation of amniocentesis. After we again declined, the doctor asked what we would do if the baby had Down syndrome. We replied that we would love him as long as God allowed the child to live. He did not appear happy with our response as he proceeded to do another sonogram.

The kidneys still looked enlarged, and there also appeared to be a cleft lip/palate. (It is truly amazing how much detail sonograms show at four months.) The doctor informed us that cleft lips/palates are common in trisomy 13 and trisomy 18 babies. I had no idea what he was talking about there, but I did catch his meaning when he added, "Those conditions are not compatible with life." Then he again asked us to do an amnio. Once more we declined.

Much prayer and many tears followed that appointment. But what happened at our next appointment will be clearer if you hear about it in Nancy's words from a personal account she wrote sometime later:

I had been continually praying about the situation and felt the Lord said to my heart that an amnio would provide clarity. This time the sonogram showed that the kidneys were still enlarged, and a hole was found in our boy's heart. (This third sonogram suggested strongly that we had another son on the way.) The doctor again asked us to undergo amnio. Steve and I asked for some time alone. I shared with Steve what the Lord had spoken to me, and we decided at this point we needed to take the risk to get clarity on how best to help our boy.

The doctor returned, and we gave him our consent. The procedure took just a matter of minutes and wasn't as bad as I'd expected. But then the wait for the results began. I clung to the words the Lord had spoken to me about clarity and prayed fervently that the clarity was that our baby was perfectly fine.

The doctor called the day after Thanksgiving 1997. Nancy and I were both on the phone to hear him say, "It's trisomy 13." At that point, the only thing we knew about trisomy 13 was what the doctor had casually said at our first appointment, that it was "incompatible with life." I put my arms around Nancy. I think we both went numb. We just weren't ready to believe that the "clarity" could be our worst fears realized. The doctor said little else during that phone call, at least that either Nancy or I remember, other than to ask us what our "inclination" was now that we'd gotten the test results. He still wanted us to have an abortion. Without hesitation we told him we would continue with the pregnancy, to have and love our boy—the amnio confirmed his gender—for as long as God gave him to us. And we set another appointment.

What happened next also has to be told in Nancy's words from her written account of this experience:

Monday morning, following that long holiday weekend, after Steve went to his office and the boys were in school, I grabbed my Bible and sat down on the living room couch knowing I would be uninterrupted for several hours. Then I proceeded to tell God

I didn't think I could walk the path he was leading us down. I told him so in fairly strong terms—which is not my usual modus operandi. I told God that his Word, the Bible, said that all his ways were perfect and I did NOT see how this could be a part of any perfect will.

Then I began to enumerate a long list of reasons why I didn't believe I could do this: "I'm not a strong person. I faint easily, even at routine medical procedures. This child will require many nonroutine medical procedures, if he lives. If he doesn't live, then ..."

My list went on. But after every argument, God softly spoke to my heart, "I know you can't, but I can, and I will."

Finally I threw my last card up in God's face. I said, "I don't know how you think I can continue the last four months of this pregnancy, carrying a baby I am loving more each day, but knowing he is going to die." And ever so gently, with the grace of his very nature, God said to me, "I too watched my son every day of his life on earth, knowing what his end would be." Nothing changed, but everything in me changed. My only response was to fall to my knees and worship. This God who had sent his own son for me, who understood a parent's love for their child, who had also lost a son, was leading me down this path, and when I couldn't, he could.

We named our boy Stephen Wrigley Peifer. (Wrigley Field was my special place with my father, and we wanted Stephen to know that even though he probably would never make it to Wrigley with me to watch the Chicago Cubs play baseball, he was special too.) And we all, Nancy and I and our boys, called him by name when talking about him or to him.

We also started doing research online about trisomy 13. What we learned was not encouraging. It is a genetic disorder with an extra chromosome on the thirteenth pair. Down syndrome results from an extra chromosome on the twenty-first chromosome pair and is also known as trisomy 21. The smaller the number of the chromosome pair, the more important the genetic material stored on that pair. Trisomy 13 is the most serious genetic disorder for a recorded live birth.

But those statistics were not encouraging either. Fifty percent of trisomy 13 babies either do not go full term or are stillborn. The longest a trisomy 13 child has ever lived is two years. Common symptoms of trisomy 13 babies are kidney problems, heart problems, cleft lip/palate, and sometimes extra fingers and/or toes.

We tried to process what this meant for us and our family. We explained to our young sons that Stephen probably would not live long, he might not look good, and he would have many health issues, unless God worked a miracle. And we prayed for that miracle, even as we prepared for the realities of a baby with many special needs. It was a hard season. One day we planned Stephen's funeral as we painted his nursery.

We also met with the neonatal specialists at the hospital to discuss options. They didn't expect any surgery to be feasible. We needed to decide if we would go "no code" or request medical "intervention" when our son was born. Because of the nature and extent of his problems, Stephen probably would not be in good shape at birth. If we opted for intervention, the medical team probably would whisk him away to the neonatal ICU before we could even hold him; there he would be hooked to machines for monitoring, and we probably never would get to take him home or hold and cuddle him. If we went with the no-code option, the medical staff would not try to resuscitate him no matter what his condition at birth. They simply would give him to us to hold and love on.

What a decision to have to make. We prayed and decided for the no-code option. If his life was short, we wanted to be a part of it. We didn't want his brief experience on earth to be tied up to tubes and machines.

Our friends and church family were amazingly supportive. Nancy's best friend, Leslie, hosted a frozen-meal shower for us, rather than a typical baby shower. We didn't want to have to get rid of baby things if Stephen didn't live long. So friends filled our freezer with home-cooked meals for the days after his birth.

Again, only Nancy can effectively tell this next part of the story:

As Stephen's due date approached, I became more and more anxious, and sad. I needed to hear from God again. One Sunday in church as I prayed, the Lord graciously did speak to my heart to say, "Stephen has more purpose than just fulfilling your motherhood."

That hit me and turned my whole mindset around. What a selfish posture I had taken. I was worried about my son, of course, but I was more worried about me—how sad I was, how sad I would be to have a son with disabilities, how sad I was my son would probably die early, just how sad I was.

With that simple word from the Lord, everything came into focus. I realized Stephen was a precious, God-created child with a purpose to fulfill on this earth. Stephen's problems were not the result of an oversight on God's part. But the Lord had allowed Stephen to be formed as he was because God had a special purpose for him. I needed to look beyond my grief to allow this son of mine to fulfill that purpose.

I still shed buckets of tears, I still prayed for a miracle, I still wanted my boy to be fine, but I now believed not only that God was in control but that he wanted to use Stephen to work out some mysterious part of his perfect way.

At the last doctor's appointment prior to our due date, the doctor told us

Stephen was in footling breech position, not a good position for a baby with heart issues. Nancy told the doctor she wanted a C-section, for Stephen's sake. Our OB was reluctant, saying he didn't want to add risk for Nancy when the baby was going to die anyway. I knew my wife's feeling on this, so I added my voice, insisting we did want a C-section. The doctor relented.

Nancy had just dropped JT and Matthew off at soccer practice and was climbing back into the van when her water broke. She went home to call the doctor. She tried to call me, but I was already on my drive home and, in that era before cell phones, she couldn't reach me. Her OB instructed her to get right to the hospital. But Nancy was not about to head to the hospital without me, so she packed her bag slowly and arranged for JT and Matthew to stay with friends after informing the boys that Stephen would be born soon. By that time, I had arrived home, and we took off for the hospital in Fort Worth.

Our doctor was the OB on duty for the night, so as planned, they prepped Nancy for a C-section. They rolled her into the operating room, gave her an epidural, and the doctor proceeded with the operation. Nancy's previous two deliveries had been all natural, fairly quick, accompanied by a wonderful sense of excitement, anticipation, and joy. The atmosphere in this delivery room was unmistakably different, almost silent. Again, in Nancy's words:

As the doctor pulled Stephen out, the nurse anesthetist bent down to my ear and said, "Honey, there is something you need to know ..." She was so gentle, so caring. I turned to her and said, "Oh, I know, and I'm ready for him." They cleaned him up just a bit, took his first Apgar scores, swaddled him, and handed him to Steve.

Stephen wasn't making any noise. Steve bent down with him so I could see our son. He wasn't a pretty sight. His skin was blue, a huge bilateral cleft lip/palate formed a gaping hole in his face, and his eyes were shut. But he was my precious boy. And he was alive!

As Steve held our son, he started talking to Stephen, telling him of our love, praying over him. And as he did, Stephen started to fuss and make those sweet baby sounds. I am convinced that Stephen's daddy had the privilege of blessing our son and giving him the affirmation and love he needed to find the will and the strength to fight through the coming days.

The nurse, unbelievably, told us that our baby's second set of Apgars were almost that of a perfectly healthy newborn.

Stephen arrived around 10:30 that night. So we let the hospital nursery take our boy after a couple of hours so Nancy could get some sleep. Early the next morning, a neonatal intensive care nurse came in to tell us that they had tried to feed Stephen during the night, but even using a specially designed bottle, his huge cleft lip and palate made it impossible for him to create any suction. She said we needed to discuss a feeding tube.

I was holding Stephen at the time, so I asked if I could try. The nurse looked at me, as only nurses can do, and assured me the most experienced neonatal intensive care nurses had tried everything without success. I told her, "I'd like to try anyway." It was easy to tell from the way she walked out of the room that she thought my request was pointless. But when she returned a few minutes later and handed me a bottle, and I placed the strangely shaped nipple in his mouth, Stephen began to suckle. Nancy grinned as she and the nurse watched Stephen empty the entire bottle. That may have been the first time our boy asserted his will, but it wasn't the last. As Nancy observed later, "It was as if he knew his time was short, and he wanted every moment to be with us, not with strangers."

That night, Nancy and I both were exhausted. Many friends had come by to meet Stephen; we'd called and suggested that any relatives who could come should do so soon, as his days were probably short. But we hadn't caught on to Stephen's determination yet, so we again asked the nursery to please give him his middle of the night feeding so we could sleep. Around one in the morning, the neonatal ICU nurse apologetically wakened Nancy to say none of the staff could get Stephen to eat. Would she please try? Stephen took every drop in the bottle from his mother.

The next evening, Stephen was very fussy. Nancy couldn't soothe him and was exhausted. To give her a chance to rest, I took him and walked up and down the hall for a time. He continued to cry. One of the nurses finally stopped me to say, "Let me take him for a little bit; you need some rest too." I teared up as I admitted, "I'm afraid if I put him down I may never get to pick him up again." The kind nurse eventually coaxed me to let her take Stephen. She headed back to the nursery, and I rejoined Nancy in her room. Within five minutes, the nurse walked into the room carrying Stephen and laughing. "Here," she said as she handed back our son. "He's fine now. He just had a stinky diaper." We had been filtering everything through a life-or-death scenario and had not even considered that he might just need changing.

Earlier that day, we'd talked with two neonatal specialists. One doctor was gracious and kind; the other one clearly thought we had made a mistake in choosing not to have an abortion. We asked about Stephen's prognosis. They said they would need to do an ecocardiogram to determine the extent of his heart problems. We'd consented and they had performed the test. Thankfully, the gracious doctor came back to share the results. The test showed two holes in Stephen's heart. But they'd spotted an even more critical concern: the valve on the pulmonary artery was backward. No blood was being oxygenated by flowing through that artery as it should. A tiny fetal blood vessel called the PDA directly connects the pulmonary artery and the aorta. In utero, it also sends blood to the lungs to be oxygenated. The PDA usually shuts down within twenty-four hours of birth once a baby is breathing on its own.

In Stephen's case, because of the backward pulmonary valve, this tiny blood vessel was the only thing keeping him alive. It couldn't handle that stress for long; the doctor estimated he had, at most, three weeks. When we asked about the possibility of operating, he shook his head. With Stephen's other complications and his low blood-oxygen levels, he would not survive anesthesia.

We began setting our minds and hearts to enjoying our son while we had him. When you know your time is short, you are so much more aware of things. We realized early on that Stephen responded to Nancy's and my voices more than he did to anyone else's. While we had certainly enjoyed our interaction with our older two boys from the moment of their births, I don't think we recognized their personalities in those early weeks.

With Stephen, we really got to know him right away. He was an opinionated, spunky little guy who loved us and clearly wanted to spend time with us. He developed a routine of eating, sleeping just a little, and then awakening to be held. If Stephen was awake and *not* being held, he let us know he should be. To borrow an apt description from *Mrs. Katz and Tush* by Patricia Polacco, one of our family's favorite children's authors, "He was such a person."

On his fourth day, March 8, it snowed in Texas, an uncommon occurrence that time of year, making it a unique day for the homecoming of our wonderfully unique boy. We hadn't known if we would ever be able to bring him home, but we did! It was such a big celebration for a little guy who was "such a person."

Knowing that unless God performed a miracle, Stephen faced a short life, we had contacted a hospice service. They had already supplied an oxygen tank and morphine drops for when we might need them. But for now those provisions were hidden in a corner as we rejoiced at having our son home. JT and Matthew loved their little brother despite his deformities. They held him, talked to him, and also held stuffed animals out to him to play with him. Early on, they learned beauty is in the heart, not the outer appearance.

Fortunately, Stephen was not suffering. He stayed on the bluish side because of his low blood-oxygen levels. But he was very content, unless he was hungry. Family and friends came to meet Stephen and were an amazing support to us. One of the blessings of the clarity that amnio provided was that we had cleared the decks of our lives. We could simply enjoy our boy for however long he was with us. Friends took care of meals, picked up relatives at the airport, ran errands for us, and did anything we needed so we could just be a family with our new boy. We were blessed to have such a group of friends.

We made an appointment to have a family portrait made that Saturday. But on Thursday night Stephen started to struggle. Because he looked bluer, we began giving him oxygen. That helped, but he still struggled to breathe. We called hospice. They gave us some advice, but also told us we needed to realize this might be the beginning of the end. Late that evening, we administered his first morphine drops to ease his discomfort. Nancy and I alternately held him, giving him oxygen continuously now. Around midnight, he had a seizure, and we called hospice again. They suggested we use more morphine as needed and prepare ourselves for the end.

Throughout the night, we took turns holding him and dozing. Early in the morning, I told Nancy to go to the other bedroom and get some real sleep, and I would take Stephen for a couple of hours. Nancy recounted what followed:

The next thing I knew, my sister-in-law was waking me, telling me to go be with Steve and Stephen. When I walked into the room, Steve told me that Stephen had just returned to his heavenly Father.

We knew it was coming. Actually, we had known for months it was coming, but that doesn't lessen the pain when death comes. We held our boy and cried. We brought JT and Matthew in, and we all cried together. What an impact a tiny life can have in eight short days.

My sister arrived a little later that morning, before we contacted anyone else. She got to hold Stephen's little body. Then we changed his clothes, contacted our pastor, called the funeral home, and started "making arrangements."

I helped plan my mother's funeral when I was eighteen; now I planned my son's. Neither was easy. Steve and I had already decided on what we wanted to happen with the service itself. But there are so many other decisions to make: choosing the casket, open or closed; what time; how many times to receive guests; what about flowers, or not; who attends the graveside; and on and on.

When asked if we had any idea what we wanted on a gravestone (the one item that didn't have to be decided immediately), we didn't hesitate. Steve and I agreed it needed to say:

Stephen Wrigley Peifer
Born March 4, 1998
Having fulfilled the purpose the Father had for him, he returned to the Father
March 12, 1998

And that, as Nancy wrote, was our "testimony." He came, brought love, and changed our lives. We were deeply grieving our loss, yet were confident that Stephen had fulfilled his mission and that his short life was not a mistake. Everything that has happened since—for me, for Nancy, and with our family —has proven that testimony true.

4

An Emotional Toll

WHILE BELIEVING THAT STEPHEN'S LIFE PURPOSE HAD BEEN FULFILLED made it a little easier to accept his death, I don't think it significantly shortened the seemingly endless road of pain, sadness, and loss Nancy and I found ourselves traveling for months afterward.

Grief is such a weird, uncontrollable beast. You never know when or where or how it's going to pop up and demand its due. The triggers for Nancy were different from what they were for me. Some you realize you might have seen coming, like the family going to church on Mother's Day. Nancy seemed fine and glad to be there among friends—until they began recognizing mothers and she just lost it and had to get up and rush out of the service. The boys and I followed, and we all went home.

It was hard seeing my wife hurting so, never knowing when the grief would hit her or having any idea how to help when it did. Sometimes, with no noticeable trigger at all, Nancy would just be overcome by a wave of grief and yearning to have Stephen back in her arms. One day while shopping at Target, Nancy ended up in a checkout line behind a group of teenage special-needs kids with their teachers on a field trip. They were learning about shopping. As she thought how Stephen would have been like them, she began to cry and couldn't run out of the store fast enough to the car, where she could sob safely. Then she drove straight to the office of a good friend whose special-needs daughter had died a few years earlier. They held each other and cried a long time.

—

Another family at church had a baby right about the time Stephen was born. Every time I saw that baby, I thought, *That's how old Stephen would be*, and then I'd be hit right in the gut by the thought, *I'm never going to see my son grow up*. Sometimes grief ambushed me. I remember taking a walk around the neighborhood, just enjoying the evening. As I passed this one house, I noticed some little kid's toy lying in the front yard, and a sudden sorrow descended on me so hard and fast I almost fell down under the weight of it. I felt that overwhelmed.

Grief exacted its emotional toll in every area of our lives; no doubt in some ways we never even realized. I know it impacted me at work. I'd been with Oracle through much of the wild and crazy tech and dot-com boom of the 1990s. Like everyone in the information technology industry, I'd had to scramble to keep up, but when the demands threatened to swallow me, I prided myself in always being able to find another gear. Not only had I kept pace; I'd managed to outrace and survive the explosion to advance within the company. But in the months following Stephen's death, everything at work seemed to slow down. And it wasn't just the beginning of the end of the tech boom. *I* was slowing down too.

Work felt almost like a slow-motion battle scene in some epic movie; I observed the action going on all around me, yet I was not really a part of it anymore, at least not in the same way. I knew I had a wife and two sons who counted on me. I needed to keep moving forward, to keep fighting. But everything in me just wanted to lie down and give up. No matter how hard I tried, I couldn't maintain the level I'd been on. I couldn't understand it. It was like I suddenly didn't know how to do what I'd always done before. I didn't even know how to help Nancy with her grief; she couldn't even *hold* a baby anymore.

—

For months I prayed and asked God to ease our grief and to help me know what I could do to help relieve Nancy's pain. I prayed to know what I needed to do differently at work, and to try to start putting back together the pieces of our shattered lives.

After a time, as I wrestled with all this and with God in my daily devotions, I felt the Lord saying to me, *Make your wife's dreams come true*. Day after day as I prayed for answers and help, I sensed that same response. *Make your wife's dreams come true*. I thought I knew what he meant. But I didn't see how I could ever do it. And I tried my best to explain this to the Lord. But before

I try to explain it to you, I need to share a little background about this relationship I had with God, with my wife, and with her dreams.

—

I grew up in a nominally Catholic family in the northwest suburbs of Chicago and attended a parish school there until fifth grade. That's when my parents enrolled me in public school and we pretty much stopped attending church altogether, which bothered me not at all. Church bored me to death, and I didn't really believe in much of anything anyway.

In high school I kept getting invited to this Christian club called Campus Life. They tried to reach out to school leaders and, since I was president of the student council and active in lots of stuff, I was the kind of kid they targeted. They invited me week after week. But I wasn't at all interested, *until* this girl I had a mad crush on invited me to go to a prayer meeting. I said, "Yeah, right. What do you do at a prayer meeting?" When she said, "You just hold hands and you pray," that sounded good to me. The holding hands part anyway.

It turned out that Campus Life did more than pray. They had lots of fun activities and interesting discussions about real-life issues. It was there I eventually understood enough of Jesus' gospel message to pray for salvation and accept Christ into my life. But it was more of a head thing than a heart understanding. I talked a good game, but I wasn't following Christ closely enough for it to make a lot of difference in the way I lived my life. I'm not sure you'd find a greater hypocrite than me back in those days.

I met Nancy during high school. She came with a friend of hers to a Bible study some buddies and I led. She was so taken with me that it took me only ten years to get her to go out on our first date. You could say we were opposites who didn't attract from the start. She was quiet and shy. I wasn't. As one of the "leaders," I took it as my responsibility to draw her out and get her more involved in our group. It took a while, but in the process I got to know enough about her to realize just how different we were.

Nancy had grown up in what I considered a strict conservative Christian family. She thought I was pretty wild to be leading a Bible study. And she was right, because she was a lot more mature in her faith than I was. An active churchgoer all her life, Nancy had prayed to accept Christ when she was eight years old. She'd been a committed follower of Jesus ever since. As a fifteen-year-old at a church youth conference, she went down to the altar because she felt God was calling her into full-time Christian service. And she spent the next couple of years trying to figure out what that might mean.

By the time I met Nancy in her junior year of high school, she'd decided she would be a missionary, and she already had a five-year plan. One more year of high school, three years to graduate from college with a degree in linguistics, then a year at a Bible college to study God's Word in depth, and off to the mission field in Africa. (One of her earliest vivid memories from five years of age was of a black-and-white photograph of a missionary woman reading to a group of African children; she'd been enamored with Africa ever since.) She had her life all plotted out.

I went off to college two years before Nancy did, mostly planning to have fun. While I got involved with Inter-Varsity Christian Fellowship at Northern Illinois University, I'm ashamed to say I still wasn't the best or most consistent witness for Christ. Since I could lead a pretty good Bible study, you might think I had the talk down better than the walk. But I had some issues with the talk as well. When I was with non-Christians friends, I could swear with the best of them. I did get involved in a church during those college years; that and my exposure to discipleship training through Inter-Varsity gradually nurtured my spiritual growth.

After I graduated from college with a degree in political science, I landed an entry-level job with a maintenance services company in Louisville, Kentucky. The only good thing about my short stint there was that I made contact with Nancy again through mutual friends. Her mom had died during Nancy's first year of college, which dealt her quite an emotional blow.

Then about halfway through college, she began to have doubts about her five-year plan. She had set aside a weekend to pray and fast, and she felt the Lord say, "That's a great plan, but it's not my plan for you." Nancy told me she had reluctantly laid down that plan and prayed for God to show her his plan. Meantime she continued her major, graduated on schedule in three years, moved to Louisville with a bunch of college friends, and found a job as a technical writer for the data-processing division of a manufacturing company.

Soon after our friendship was rekindled, I left Louisville to run a college bookstore in Manhattan, Kansas. And while I was there, Nancy moved to Dallas to help start a computer/IT department for a large church. I worked in banking for a time, and then transitioned into the computer technology industry, which took me to Dallas as well.

Some people might have considered it fate or God's leading or at least a significant coincidence that we found ourselves yet again living in the same town. We didn't see it that way; we were just old friends. Romance was so far off our radar screens that when our pastor suggested we date each other, we both laughed at the idea. With a little more coaxing from the pastor, however, I did ask her out, and we started dating. But that was going so poorly within a couple of months that we were on the verge of parting ways and even ditching our friendship.

The pastor told us he thought we should go out one last time to patch things up enough to at least preserve our friendship. When we did, we both just "knew" we were supposed to marry one another, although it took a few months for our hearts and emotions to line up. Before I finally asked Nancy to marry me, knowing her longtime ambition to be a missionary, I wanted to make one thing clear. I told her my one caveat was this: "We will help *send* missionaries, but I'm never *going* to the mission field." She accepted my proposal and told me she'd prayed about it and was absolutely convinced I was God's man for her. She admitted to being puzzled as to why her heart still burned to be involved in missions if I was never going, but trusted that it was so we could be supporters of missionaries, or perhaps because one of our children would go.

—

All that explains why when I felt God telling me during my quiet time thirteen years later to *make your wife's dreams come true*, I could think of only one thing that might mean. And as I pointed out to God, we had indeed regularly supported missionaries all of our married life, but my going to Africa was simply out of the question. I didn't have any of the skills necessary to live and work in the African bush. I wasn't a preacher, a teacher, or a doctor. I'd never even had a Bible course. Even if my wife's dream was to go to Africa as a missionary, there was no way I could do that. End of story.

That was right about the time a couple of those missionaries we supported called to say they were going to be in town and would like to get together with us. We told them we'd be thrilled and invited them for dinner. They were home from Kenya for a while and were traveling around, speaking at churches and meeting with individuals in an attempt to raise enough funds to cover their next term overseas. Tim and Becky McDonald were longtime friends; Tim had been a lay pastor and teacher in a church I attended, and we were financially supporting them and their work as teachers at Rift Valley Academy, a boarding school for the children of missionaries working in countries throughout Africa.

Tim and Becky were great people, but their fundraising skills left something to be desired. After we had a great time sharing a meal together, talking, and catching up on each others' lives, they said, "You don't want to watch this video about the school where we work in Kenya, do you?"

We told them, "Yeah. That would be great." They assured us, "That's okay. Nobody else has wanted to watch it." "No, we really do want to watch it."

So we watched it, and I was impressed. Rift Valley Academy reminded me of a small college campus. The students I saw were an interesting mix of nationalities and races. The facilities looked well-kept and reasonably modern. The scenery in the video was beautiful. I could see why our friends loved it there, and I told them so. Becky made an offhanded comment, something to the effect that "you guys ought to consider coming over for a year. You'd love it. RVA is going to need another set of dorm parents next fall." My immediate response was, "I could do that."

I'd just blurted it out before filtering the thought through my brain. Becky and Tim, who'd known about and probably picked up on our heartache as we'd told them about Stephen, suggested that it might be good for us to get away, have a change of scenery, and allow some distance to aid our emotional healing. As they told us more about RVA and answered some of our initial questions, I kept thinking, *I really could do that*. I also began to think they might well be right about a change of scenery. We needed something different to help get us far away from the pain of our grief that was consuming our lives in Texas.

After we bid our friends goodbye, Nancy turned to me and said, "Don't you play with me about this!" I assured my wife I'd been serious. I could see us going for a year to a place like this school where our friends taught. The next morning, Nancy questioned me again. I guess she was almost afraid to get too excited, and then be disappointed. *Make your wife's dreams come true.*

"I think I could do that," I told her.

"You're serious; you'd really go?" I could see the excitement growing in Nancy's eyes.

"Yes. I would. Really." Almost immediately I had buyer's remorse, thinking, *If everything works out that needs to work out, I am willing. There will be a few hurdles to clear. But JT and Matthew aren't going to want to do this, to leave their home and school and friends.*

Nancy wanted to raise the possibility with the boys immediately to give them time to consider the idea. We did, and they didn't need any time to think. They were as excited and ready to go as their mother. The McDonalds had planted the seed when they came to dinner that November evening. Nancy didn't waste any time; the next day after we talked with the boys, she started researching what all would need to happen. (She said later she knew once I'd said I would go that if she let that dream die, it would die. And she wasn't about to let that happen.)

As soon as the holidays were over in January, we applied to Africa Inland Mission (AIM), the parent agency of Rift Valley Academy, for a one-year, short-term assignment as dorm parents at RVA. We received word we'd been accepted by February. We started sharing our plans with family and friends in March. And we were more than a little surprised by the reactions we received. Since I was the most unlikely, ill-equipped, and unqualified person in the history of the world to become a missionary, I was prepared for uncontrollable laughter and exclamations of disbelief when friends heard the news. But people were amazingly affirming; I think most of our closest friends knew how much we'd been grieving, and immediately recognized this as an emotional balm for our healing.

One night we went to dinner at the home of some old friends. We told them what we planned to do and even showed them the same RVA video the McDonalds had shown us. Then we thanked them for dinner and a nice evening and said goodnight. We hadn't even left their driveway when they came running out to catch us and say, "We want to help support you!" I remember the surprise I felt as the thought hit me, *Something special, something bigger is going on here. This really is going to happen.* Every week, Nancy and the boys seemed to get more excited. But once the Africa Express started moving, everything happened so fast it seemed all I could do to hold on for the ride.

I remained a little concerned about the fundraising hurdle. While we would have a monthly stipend and our living expenses at RVA would be low, it wasn't cheap to move a family of four around the world and back again after just a year. The costs would add up. But we sent a letter of financial appeal to relatives and friends in April, and so many responses came back, from friends old and new, postmarked all over the country, representing every segment of our past and present lives—community, work, church—that by May we had enough in one-time gifts and monthly pledges to cover our support for the entire year. Yet another surprising, not to mention humbling, confirmation that indeed something special was going on here.

We signed a rental agreement with an old friend who would live in our house for the year we were gone. And in June, soon after the boys' school ended, we packed and headed for AIM's US headquarters in Pearl River, New York, for three weeks of training and orientation. In July our family boarded a plane in New York City, and a day and a half later, we landed at the international airport in Nairobi, Kenya, East Africa, a place I'd always said I'd never go to do something I'd always insisted I'd never do.

5

No Sweat, Real Heroes,
and the Joy of Rain

A FTER A FEW SHORT WEEKS, WHAT I WAS *DOING* IN AFRICA INVOLVED much more than our roles as dorm parents. Nancy and I had other responsibilities on the RVA campus. She served as librarian for the elementary school, or "Titchie School." My role was more like the proverbial "jack of all trades, master of none." My primary task was to help implement new accounting software in the business office. This part of my job proved challenging for a number of reasons.

First, because of frequent power outages, including a planned one every morning until noon Monday through Friday because of the drought.

Second, because we had email but no other internet access and phoning was so expensive, which meant we had no technical support we could easily access.

But third, and mostly, because of my limitations. At Oracle, my job had been to help recruit, hire, and oversee the work of some nine thousand outside contractors who did the work. Thinking that somehow qualified me to be a point person on this software project made as much sense as expecting me to begin repairing television sets because I once watched one. But I had a ball learning the capabilities and idiosyncrasies of Blackbaud software and vowed to be more sympathetic to all consultants when I returned to the States. Incidentally, RVA's old software was not Y2K compatible, so there was some time pressure to finish well before the last day of 1999. No sweat!

My second task was running the elementary school computer lab and instructing first through sixth grade students how to use it. The lab was equipped with Macintosh computers, and my personal history with Macs was limited. Back in the '80s, I sold computer hardware for a time. My company marketed both IBM and Macs, but I had never sold a Mac until my boss announced a sales contest with extra commissions and prizes for every Mac we sold.

That month I sold more Macs than anyone else in the company, which earned me the chance to participate on a conference call with Apple founder Steve Jobs. Once the sales contest ended, I never sold another Mac. Who would have guessed that experience would qualify me to be an elementary school computer lab instructor—in Africa, no less? But again, no sweat.

My third staff assignment, however, resulted in considerable sweat; I was drafted to teach driver's education. This proved particularly challenging because:

1. I myself could not legally drive in Kenya for the first three months I lived in country.
2. Kenyans, like the British who colonized their country, drive on the left side of the road, which I had never done, at least not intentionally.
3. I had no training in secondary education, and in fact I had not been in a high school classroom since I graduated from Arlington Heights (IL) High School twenty-six years before.
4. For reasons I will never understand, I was required to teach driving to a class of multinational, multicultural teenagers in rural Africa using old driver's education textbooks (written and published by the good folks at the University of Nebraska), which were so bad that I instituted a contest in which a regular (and favorite) assignment for my students was to identify and nominate what they considered to be the most stupid or inane instruction in each chapter. I still recall this gem: "When leaving the car, lock all doors but the door you will exit the car from. Lock that door *after* you exit the car."

I am not making this up.

As my class approached that highly anticipated day when they would finally get behind the wheel, I was absolutely determined not to be that stereotypical, emotionally hyper driving instructor who frequently and involuntarily screams in panic or bursts into tears for no apparent reason. "Stay *calm*" was my mantra. (Though I have never been completely sure what a *mantra* is.)

I vowed to affirm and gently reassure my students as I guided them through their first happy driving experiences, the warm memories and important lessons that would prepare them well for wherever their lives' roads might take them. After all, we'd already spent the first weeks of the term thoroughly covering the curriculum by augmenting the admittedly inadequate textbook with wisdom gleaned from my many years of personal driving experience. I enjoyed the diversity of the students in my class. I felt we'd truly bonded during the course of our classroom instruction.

So I figured the first day of actual driving would go just as smoothly. I actually slept the night before.

Sure enough, I remained the picture of *calm* when my first behind-the-wheel student proved herself a competent driver. No doubt the exceptional classroom instruction she'd received was every bit as responsible for her good showing as was her prior experience driving in Nairobi with her father.

Then my problems began. Driver number two stalled out twenty-two times (I counted) trying to get started in first gear. (Automatic transmissions aren't practical for Kenyan roads.) For a while there, I worried I might have to sit on her lap and operate the clutch for her if she was ever to pass a driver's exam. But she came up with a different solution. She hunched down enough to see beneath the dashboard and gave her full and undivided concentration to the pedals on the floor.

The moment she managed to get the car started and into first gear without stalling, we rolled forward. And I realized my second student remained slumped down in her seat, staring with pride, and no little surprise, at her own feet.

Calm remained my mantra. So in the gentlest and most affirming voice I could muster, I said, "It is good that you got the car in gear, but once we start moving, you must also *steer* the car."

Her reply will live with me the rest of my days (which at the time I feared might not be many). "Oh!" said she, clearly more bemused than enlightened by my instruction, because she continued to study the position of her feet on the pedals until the left wheels of the training car rolled up a steep embankment, tilting us so sharply that my startled student instinctively lifted both feet, which wasn't at all what I (or the University of Nebraska) ever would have recommended. But thankfully her sudden surrender of all control stalled us out for the twenty-third time and allowed the grace of gravity to gradually bring us to a stop.

All passengers were present and accounted for, grateful for the seat belts holding us tightly in place, but at such an angle that, looking out the windshield toward the distant and now diagonal horizon, I felt like a tipsy astronaut preparing to launch into space from one very cockeyed planet. After taking a few moments to appreciate my new perspective on life and to begin to breathe again, I calmly asked my would-be driver to "please, carefully get out of the car" so I could slide over and maneuver the vehicle safely back down to level ground. At which point I became aware that I was, in fact, perspiring.

The next student, before starting the car, conscientiously confessed that she could not drive and had always fancied buses anyway. She too stalled the car several times in her attempt to get started. So in my most soothing voice, I told her, "Just ease off the clutch and gently touch the gas pedal at the same time."

Several things happened next, and pretty much simultaneously. She managed to put the car into gear, which was a good thing. But as she released the clutch, she pressed the accelerator all the way to the floor, which was a bad thing. As she screamed rather loudly, I patiently encouraged her: "Ease off the gas. But you got it into gear; great job!" However, she then steered the car toward another steep embankment with the gas pedal still pressed flat against the floor. "Ease off the gas and STEER THE CAR!" I yelled in a somewhat panicked voice.

"WHERE IS THE GAS?" she screamed in a *very* panicked voice. By this point, I was practically standing in my seat, yanking the emergency brake up as far as it would go, while screaming as loudly (but as calmly) as I could, "GET OFF THE GAS! GET OFF THE GAS!"

When we finally ground to a stop, one of the students in the back seat asked, in a shaky voice, "What is that smell?" "That," I said sadly, "used to be the brake." And since there was no other damage to the car or any of the passengers, I decided that would be a great time to end class for the day. Fortunately, I had the weekend to recover. Unfortunately, we had to start all over again the next week.

—

You've never heard of him. When he returned to the States, no crowds were waiting for him at the airport with "Welcome Home" posters. No band played. He never wanted anybody to do that anyway. But in my short time in Africa, I had come to consider him a true hero. And I wanted someone to know that besides me, so this is what I wrote about him in one of my weekly emails that semester:

Jim is from Iowa, and looks it. You would never know that he is a PhD in applied sciences and a college professor back home. Not because he doesn't appear bright; he just doesn't call attention to himself. But he has been the primary person responsible for making the technical part of Rift Valley Academy run. And he has managed it with unskilled labor, limited money, and all-too-often inferior materials.

Yet I have never heard Jim complain. Not once. And this place runs great because of his work. In his "spare" time, Jim built a church in his back yard. Then he transported it down into the valley and assembled it in a Masai village. He also built benches for the congregation to sit on.

If you knew how little money he and his wife live on here, you would be shocked. And yet Jim regularly delivers food he has purchased with his own funds to feed hungry families. He has that rare gift of being able to help someone without wounding their dignity or injuring their spirit.

Jim's family has been here in Kenya for several years, but it's time for them to go back to the States. One of his daughters is approaching high school age, and he needs to prepare for her future. People coming and going is a regular occurrence in life here at RVA. But the parting still hurts, and I am going to really miss my friend Jim.

Back home in Texas, I once skipped work to watch a Dallas Cowboys' victory parade, where I screamed myself hoarse. So I hope you will indulge me this shout out to someone who has given and given, at great personal and financial sacrifice, without any fanfare, to make this part of the world a better place. I know next week's issue of People *magazine will feature the latest media or sports "hero" on its cover. I feel so lucky that I got to know a real one.*

—

One day that semester, a Kenyan preacher who had just returned from studies in Chicago spoke in chapel. He shared the old familiar story about the young boy walking along the seashore, picking up and throwing back starfish the storm waves had washed up onto the sandy beach. A cynical old man out for a stroll came upon the boy, watched what he was doing, and said, "Son, there are thousands of starfish stranded on this beach this morning. You can't possibly throw enough of them back in the ocean to make any difference."

The boy stopped and looked up at the old man for a few seconds. Then he bent over, picked up another starfish, pivoted, and tossed it out into the surf. When he turned around to the old man again, the boy said, "It made a difference to that one."

I'd heard that story more than once. But it really put things in perspective for me this time. Like the old man in the story, from the time I arrived in Africa, the overwhelming need I saw all around me made me painfully aware of my limitations. I knew I couldn't come close to even really understanding what caused so many of Kenya's problems, let alone helping solve them. I admitted this and referenced the starfish story in another of my weekly email reports to friends and supporters:

I've also begun to identify with an old senator from Illinois who once explained his fight against the destruction of sand dunes in my home state by saying, "When I was a young man, I wanted to save the world. When I became middle aged, I wanted to save the country. Now, as an old man, I just want to save the dunes."

Since I'm no senator, I figure I better start out thinking small. So there are three things I would like you to know about:

1. *The famine continues. We would love to distribute more maize and beans in the valley. A seventy-pound bag of maize costs about thirty dollars.*
2. *We work with an orphanage nearby. There can't be too many rougher blows in life than to be an orphan in Africa. I can't change that, but I wish we could give them something for Christmas. A perfect gift would be a Magna Doodle—one of those magnetic drawing tablets you can get almost anywhere in the States. They're sturdy toys that don't require batteries or much explanation. I would love to see every kid in the orphanage get a Magna Doodle.*
3. *We also work with a Crippled Children's Hospital. In Africa, one of the saddest facts of life is that children with problems are often hidden away because they are an embarrassment to their families. Often, their parents don't seek treatment until something that might have been a relatively simple problem to correct after birth becomes a major health crisis as the child grows older. The kids here play with anything they can find—sticks, rolled-up rags, whatever. They create their own soccer balls out of large wads of cheap plastic grocery bags tightly wrapped and tied in a kickable size. So I think it'd be great to have lots of crayons and coloring books, Matchbox cars, and children's books to hand out. Nothing big.*

I know lots of you folks have asked what you could do for us. We really don't need anything more ourselves; we're just really grateful for all the support you've already given us. Which is why I hesitate to ask this, and so early. But we expect more power outages and email problems, not less, over the next couple of months. And I wanted to let you know now so you might have enough time before Christmas if you wanted to help us give something to Kenyan kids who have nothing.

—

It rained in October—finally. Not enough, but still welcome. In Dallas, when it showered in the afternoon, I would think, *All the morons are going to take their stupid pills and try to outrun the raindrops and cause a million accidents, and I'll probably get home late for dinner.* In Kijabe, Kenya, the first rain in months brought everyone outside. Many of them had tears in their eyes, tears of joy. Adults were walking around getting wet and looking up just to enjoy the feel of raindrops hitting their faces. The drought wasn't over yet—far from it—but what an amazing feeling it was to be so genuinely grateful for rain.

We had our three-and-a-half-day midterm break a little later in October, when school ended one Friday morning and resumed the following Tuesday. We used the long weekend off to take our first-ever Peifer family African road trip. We went with friends and set off halfway across the country to visit another American missionary family. We'd never met them, but our church in Dallas had supported them for years. When they'd made the invitation, they sent us much more interesting directions than I've ever gotten from Google or MapQuest:

> Come on the main road from Kijabe all the way to Eldoret. Don't take Eldama Ravine road, because it will be too late in the day when you come through there, and it can be dangerous because of bandits! If you have a map, just follow the main road through Eldoret, and about five miles outside of Eldoret you will go under an overpass ... after that, you will come to a big main road (paved) that turns to the right. Take that road ... it may or may not be marked. But there are some dukas on the left side of the road as you turn and there is often a family of about twelve giraffes that wander around on the right side of the road late in the afternoon.
>
> Follow this road all the way to Kitale—until you come to the Total station on the right ... turn right on the road that goes beside the station ... follow that to a dead end ... it is a very rough road, so drive slowly ... turn left at the dead end and take an immediate right ... follow this road until you come to St. Martin's Cottage Hospital on the left ... the first gate past the hospital on the right is ours. Just honk and the guard will open the gate for you. If you should get lost ... our phone number is 30949 in Kitale ... outside of Kitale it is 0325-30949.

We missed the bandits, saw the giraffes, made the Total turn, survived the rough roads, and safely arrived at our destination after an adventurous, five-hour-long, hundred-and-fifty-some-mile drive that Friday afternoon. We also made some new friends and for the first time in two months relaxed for three nights without any responsibility for nine extra "sons."

The rest of that term raced by, crammed full of classes, special programs, and many more memorable experiences and people.

Like the time we delivered food to folks whose homes were smaller than some office cubicles I'd worked in back home in the States. I particularly recall one old, blind woman we met. She was crippled (her feet were curled up), and her tiny home gave off the most horrible odor I can remember ever smelling, anywhere. When we handed her a big bag of food, she thanked us profusely and then wanted to pray with us. At the end of her prayer, one of us commented that she obviously really loved God. She smiled broadly, nodded, and said, "Completely."

Earlier that day, I had whined about a bug in the accounts-receivables system, complained that we were out of strawberries, snapped at one of the kids, and spoken poorly about a friend I hadn't heard from since we'd left America. As we left this sweet woman's house, all I had done that day came flooding back to me.

As we trudged back up the hill toward the RVA campus, I thought to myself, *One reason I came here was to see Africa. But Africa makes me see myself — as I really am. It's not a pretty picture.*

—

I've always enjoyed Thanksgiving, but for much of my life, I must confess its primary purpose for me was twofold: (1) eat until it hurts, and then (2) eat more.

It's not a holiday recognized or celebrated in Kenya. But since Thanksgiving 1999 for us fell the last week of our first term, Nancy and I decided to invite all of the single staff of RVA over to celebrate with a big traditional holiday meal.

I came to Africa with my bride and my sons, so if I'd never made a friend in Kijabe, I still would have had a good time. But I found myself marveling at people who had come to Kenya to work and teach and serve at RVA without any family, with no one to come home to at the end of every day. I'd watched them. They worked so hard, always giving of themselves.

So we determined to make sure they weren't forgotten on this special day. We had expected a few to show up. But sometimes, plans take on a life of their own. By the time the last Thursday of November rolled around, twenty-seven guests had shown up. But Nancy had prepared a big turkey, and everyone who came brought something to contribute to the feast.

We had African, American, Canadian, and English folks all crowded around our table. So I drew on all my newly acquired cross-cultural sensitivities and communication skills in answering when my closest Kenyan friend, Fred, asked me what I thought Americans were most thankful for. The crowd hung on my every word as I explained to Fred that all Americans were most grateful for two things: "Number one, we are very, very thankful we got out of England. And number two, we are almost as thankful that we didn't end up in Canada."

But I quickly made up for that crack on all the Brits and Canadians in attendance with a more serious tradition Nancy and I have practiced every Thanksgiving of our marriage. We go around the table telling each person why we are grateful for them. Thankfully (no pun intended), this tradition transferred easily to Africa, and we had a wonderful time celebrating our holiday with our new international friends.

At the end of the feast, Fred happily remarked that he felt like he had been to America for the first time. "Not yet!" I responded.

At Thanksgiving, for the first time since we'd left Texas for Africa, I found myself missing *things*. I'd missed family and friends and church, but Thanksgiving evoked a longing for a number of other, "lesser" things that surprised me: being able to just call people on the phone, the luxury of friends and family close by, newspaper ads for cool toys that I really wanted for me but could give to the boys, and NFL football.

"You haven't experienced a truly American Thanksgiving," I told Fred, "until you've watched a football game after your holiday meal. But you're in luck."

I had wanted to watch a football game on Thanksgiving, and I'd voiced that desire loudly around campus for weeks. A dear friend on the RVA staff had offered his tapes of the Buffalo Bills to watch. But to a Cowboys fan, the idea of watching the Bills play on Thanksgiving was about as enticing an idea as kissing my sister. With all due respect to my lovely sisters, that would just never feel right.

But then an even dearer RVA friend, learning of my desire, offered to loan me a Dallas Cowboys tape that her dearest-of-all brother-in-law had sent her. So I can testify that dreams do come true, because after we finished a memorable meal with a houseful of new friends, we all gathered around our television set and introduced them to all-American football by watching a Dallas Cowboys game on Thanksgiving afternoon in Kijabe, Kenya, East Africa. I'm certain it was a highlight of their lives.

I amazed myself at how engrossed I got in the game even though I knew the outcome from the beginning. I cheered and yelled with a ferocity that alarmed Grace, amused Fred, and undoubtedly made all the Canadian and English folks grateful that my people had long ago made their way to settle in the great US of A.

On a more serious note, I have to admit that I had never been a particu-larly grateful man. But being in Kenya for just a few months made me realize, in a new way, how much I had been given and how much I had simply accepted without ever stopping to think about being thankful for it.

I'd waited more than twenty minutes the last time I tried to get a dial tone in Kijabe. But I vowed that the next Thanksgiving I would burn up the phone lines back home, calling my family and friends, thanking them for all they mean to me, and apologizing for how I've too often taken them for granted.

Africa had already helped me become grateful.

6

The Sound of Hunger

JUST BEFORE THE END OF THAT FIRST TERM, I HIRED A LOCAL KENYAN craftsman who made his living carving wood into ornaments and spoons to give a carving demonstration for our dorm boys. Charles is an amazing guy; as a young man, he had his thumb bitten off by a hyena that attacked his family's cow. He fought off the hungry predator but lost his thumb and the use of one finger in the battle. Yet somehow he still had managed to develop an incredible skill in carving.

He brought ten pieces of wood in various stages to show the boys the steps in the process. Then he took a raw chunk of olive wood and began the work of making that into a serving spoon. Charles's only tools were a machete, a file, one piece of sandpaper, and a log. He made all the cuts with the machete, and then he used the file and sandpaper to smooth out the rough cuts and the edges. The log served as his workbench, vise, and measuring tool.

In two hours, he turned the piece of wood into something beautiful, a real work of art, without a thumb and using the crudest tools imaginable. The boys, who'd been spellbound the entire time, were amazed. I hoped the demonstration they'd witnessed had been etched in their memories and that the lesson Charles exemplified would sink into their hearts.

Africa can break your heart, but it is full of people who have made something beautiful out of so little.

—

There may be times, however, when understanding is overrated. Like the time I walked into the kitchen to discover Nancy and Grace discussing the cross-cultural differences on the subject of circumcision. The discussion went like this:

Grace: My children were all circumcised when they turned ten.

Nancy: I can't believe it! *(shocked face)*

Grace: When did your boys get circumcised?

Nancy: When they were born.

Grace: I can't believe it! *(shocked face)*

Me: Can we talk about something else?

⁓

The first term of the school year at Rift Valley Academy concluded at the end of November. The boarding students headed home to spend the holidays with their families, and the RVA staff got a much-needed, month-long break to reconnect with our nuclear families, make plans for Christmas, gear up for the second term, and maybe even squeeze in a little R & R. But the first thing on the campus calendar at the beginning of December was the big annual five-day conference for all the AIM missionaries from a number of African countries.

This conference was not something I'd looked forward to. You see, for much of my life, I'd thought missionaries were dweebs, well-meaning but out-of-touch folks with bad haircuts and dated clothing who droned on and on about dull stuff. If one came to speak at my church, I usually managed to volunteer in the nursery.

But the AIM staff I met at this gathering were committed, hardworking, kind individuals, couples, and families who had felt called to Africa and were trying their best to demonstrate God's love for African people any way they could. Many of them had gladly invested decades of their lives doing just that.

One night, the conference organizers recognized several retiring missionaries. I will never forget one particular retiree, in large part because the moment she stood to speak, I realized how perfectly she fit my stereotype: dated dress, out-of-fashion hairstyle, and all. But she told a story about how one young African friend of hers had become offended when a national pastor referred to her as white. The friend had protested, saying, "She is African in her heart!"

This woman, a nurse, had worked tirelessly for years to eliminate polio in the Congo, and she routinely traveled on treacherous roads, alone and at dangerous times of the night, to reach patients, just because she cared.

The rest of that conference, whenever I saw that woman and thought about how I had judged and thought about people like her all my life, I felt a shame I had never known before. Everything in me had looked down on people like her for stupid, superficial reasons, while she had dedicated her whole life to helping others. So I determined during that conference to spend the rest of my life looking beyond the surface to better appreciate people, and to place a higher value on service to others.

My resolve lasted two days.

Until I received a late night call from the hospital asking me to come down and donate blood for a newborn. The caller reminded me that most Kenyan blood was unsuitable for transfusions; it wasn't rich enough because the local population's diet lacked so many important nutrients.

However, it was storming outside that night. The hour was late, and we had invited people over to our place for the evening. Plus a trip to the hospital meant a long trek down and then back up the hill, in the dark, through mud and rain. So even though I quickly agreed to come, I headed down the hill in a less than gracious mood.

But as I walked, I recognized my horrible attitude. *Here I am with a chance to help save a baby's life, and I'm whining about it.*

Suddenly, the sense of shame I'd felt during the conference two nights before flooded over me again, and as the rain ran down my face, I wept over my selfishness and superficiality, even as I prayed to the Great Physician that this tiny, struggling little baby would be okay.

When I reached the hospital, the doctor informed me, "The baby's taken a turn these last few minutes. She's doing better now; we won't need your blood tonight, after all. Sorry you came down in this weather." You've never seen a happier person walking back home, uphill, in the rain, thinking, *Two wake-up calls in one week. Suppose Someone is trying to tell me something?*

———

I told about another meaningful experience in one of those weekly electronic missives I continued to send to a steadily growing email list of our friends, families, and supporters back in the States:

We have begun to receive toys from a number of you, and I went to the Crippled Children's Hospital Sunday morning to distribute some of them. (We needed to wait until we had enough to give something to every child, or there would have been more tears than I could bear.) It turned out to be an experience that was sobering and exhilarating at the same time.

In much of African culture, deformed children are thought to be a curse and an embarrassment. So they are hidden away from the community. One of the doctors told me, "If only we could get to them earlier, we could correct many common problems very easily. But so many families wait out of shame, and then it is often too late to help."

I saw a little guy named Martin who had a concave head; it's the only way I can describe it. And there were many, many burn victims. In Africa, so much cooking is done over an open fire on the floor of a hut, where it is all too easy for little ones to wander where they shouldn't and fall into the flames. My experience with those kids reminded me again what a blessing our son Stephen was in my life. He was born so deformed that it forced you to look at the beauty within, because he did not have any on the outside. Because of my time with him, I could look at these children and not react negatively to the horrible damage that had been done to them.

One little girl named Ketisha had much of the left side of her face burned off. Her left eye looked horrific; deep, ugly burns covered her body, and she walked with a painful limp. But I have never seen a more mischievous smile on a child in my life. Every time she walked by me, I reached out and tickled her. And she squealed and ran away. If I missed her, she would run back to get her tickle. Ketisha is four, with more strikes against her than I could count, yet she had more life in her than most people I know.

I played with those children for an hour. But after I pulled out a Magna Doodle for a little boy named Emanuel, I never saw his face again. He drew and wrote on that thing for an hour. The entire Kenyan staff gathered around to watch, because none had ever seen anything like that inexpensive little toy. When it came time for me to leave, I told Emanuel, "This is a gift from people in the United States who love you." And he cried. The nurse who walked me to the door dropped her voice to tell me, "Emanuel has had three painful surgeries on his feet [he had a club foot] and never cried once. Now he cries for this!"

But love is a good thing to cry for, isn't it?

⁓

Everything is different in Africa, even vacations.

In mid-December, the Peifers spent a fun and relaxing week at the beach when one of the other RVA families graciously invited us to ride nine hours with them to Mombasa, Kenya's largest coastal city on the Indian Ocean. Several African distinctives made the journey a memorable part of the experience:

1. *Kenyan roads.* The highway to Mombasa was so bad that our driver frequently had to veer into the opposite lane to avoid potholes that threatened to swallow a van. What made things really interesting was watching for the potholes in the other lane so you could anticipate

when the vehicles heading in the opposite direction might need to veer into your path. On some stretches, we crisscrossed lanes a time or two every mile.

2. *Public restrooms.* You might find fifteen people working at a gas station —operating the petrol pumps, washing your windshields, checking your oil, repairing vehicles, patching tires, and manning the cash register of the "convenience store" inside. None of them ever seemed to have been assigned the job of cleaning the bathroom. You're in for an even ruder shock if you haven't been warned that many African toilets are not stocked with toilet paper. So either you carry your own, or you wing it.

3. *Convenient cuisine.* You might drive three hours on a cross-country trip in Kenya without even seeing a gas station. And fast-food establishments are even rarer outside of a handful of major cities. If you are fortunate, you might happen upon some enterprising vendor selling fire-roasted ears of maize (which can be quite tasty) along the side of the road. But when you travel, you plan to bring your own food, or do without.

4. *Daily drive-time redefined.* Never drive after dark in Kenya if you can help it. When a mzungu (that's a Swahili word for "white person," "foreigner," or "outsider") friend reported being held up at gunpoint one night, the police yelled at him for being so stupid as to be out driving after dark. Bandits, who operate with impunity on unlit, deserted stretches of highway, will place large rocks on the roadway and lie in wait. Whether motorists slam on their brakes and stop in time to avoid the hazard or stop to survey the damage because they didn't, the armed robbers leap out of the shadows and take whatever they want from the helpless travelers. Which is why we left Kijabe at 4:00 a.m. to allow plenty of time to reach Mombasa before nightfall.

5. *African warning signs and roadblocks.* In the States, when you see a flare, flashing lights, or an illuminated sign, you recognize it as a warning that there's an accident, construction work, or some other sort of road hazard ahead. In Kenya, people simply lay branches out in the road, which certainly works to slow you down. But I always wondered how you could be certain it was not the handiwork of a gang of creative bandits who had slyly altered the usual banditry MO in hopes of waylaying unsuspecting motorists.

Despite all the distinctly Kenyan challenges of our cross-country road trip, we reached Mombasa safely with daylight to spare, though we did drive through the worst slums I'd ever seen in search of our hotel, right on the ocean, with a nice clean room. We checked in and decided to take a walk along the waterfront with our sons.

Over the years, Nancy and I had been to Hawaii, Barbados, and Acapulco. But I had never seen a more beautiful beach. It had white sand. Warm, clear water. And no crowds at all. Tourism was still way down in Africa just a year after the deadly bombing by Muslim jihadists of the US embassy in Nairobi. Our hotel was only about 20 percent occupied—a plus for us, if not for the hotel.

JT and Matthew had always been water bugs, so they had a wonderful time in the ocean. And what is there *not* to like for two preadolescent boys when your hotel is just a stone's throw from the water on a tropical beach, there are monkeys on your balcony, and three-foot-long lizards are sunning themselves on the stairs? The only downside was that the coastal region of Kenya is a malaria area, so we had to take preventative medication for it. But the medicine worked.

We went snorkeling several of our days in Mombasa, including one time when we paid to ride a dhow (a traditional Arab sailing vessel still used for transporting fruit and other commercial cargo along the coasts of the Arabian Peninsula, India, Pakistan, and East Africa) down the coast to a nature and wildlife conservatory.

Matthew and I were snorkeling over a gorgeous coral garden when he excitedly waved to get my attention and pointed to a fish bigger than he was that swam right under us. Noting the thrilled look in the eyes of my eight-year-old son, I thought, *This is not your father's childhood.*

My biggest thrill as an eight-year-old was riding my bike down to the 7-11 to buy a Slurpee.

—

Back home from the coast with only a short time to finish up Christmas preparations, I managed a quick email to the folks back in the States:

This week the Peifers are going out with some of the other RVA staff to help deliver maize and gifts to Kenyans around the area, which just may be the most wonderful and meaningful way ever to celebrate the holiday.

I say that in part because last night a friend and colleague here at the school told me a story that put a whole lot of things in perspective. There is this Kenyan guy who works here at RVA and has eight kids. His family was getting along fine until his brother and sister-in-law died of AIDS. So this guy took in his six orphaned nieces and nephews, and now he and his wife are suddenly struggling to raise fourteen children.

When my friend asked him how they would celebrate Christmas, he said they couldn't afford to do much. So my friend asked him what he would like to make the holiday special for his family. This hardworking father of fourteen said, "We eat ugali [a cheap dish of coarsely ground cornmeal mixed in water and boiled to the consistency of very thick and stiff cream-of-wheat cereal] for dinner every night. It would be nice to eat something else for a day."

My friend bought him a goat. So his family's Christmas meal will be different this year. I hope I look at all my meals differently this Christmas and from now on.

As we delivered food and gifts in those days before Christmas, again the amazing contradiction that is Kenya came into play. Our school is perched near the top of a high, steep escarpment marking the eastern rim of the Great Rift Valley at a breathtaking (literally) elevation of almost eight thousand feet. But one day, we made deliveries to homes and tiny communities scattered at even higher elevations in the hills above Kijabe. That required a lot of wild and woolly off-road driving, and when our four-wheel-drive vehicles could go no farther, some rigorous uphill hiking was necessary. But the effort rewarded us with unbelievably spectacular views.

In North America, you might have to pay a million dollars an acre for the panoramic vistas we enjoyed that day. Of course, that assumes you have a car. For those who don't, like virtually everyone who lives back up in those hills beyond the end of any road, the view may be great. But it also means hours of walking to work every day, while it enforces an even greater sense of isolation than you find in most of rural Africa. We were delivering food to some of the poorest of Kenya's poor, who had some of the most amazing views in the world.

How humbling it was to bring food to people with so many strikes against them, who had such wonderful attitudes. One old crippled woman with just two remaining teeth and an obvious problem in her left eye lived all alone in a tiny one-room hut with a thatched roof and a dirt floor. After we gave her a sack of food, she insisted on singing us a song and told us how much she loved life. She had so little but was so obviously grateful for what she had and for what we brought her.

The boys and I went out with a bunch of other RVA folks to deliver maize in the valley right before the holidays. We'd done drought relief before, but what impressed me this time was how much effort was required of everyone involved. First we hauled out two-hundred-pound bags of grain and hoisted them onto the trucks. Then we bounced for hours over nonexistent roads.

When the herds of grazing zebras, galloping gazelles, and surprisingly graceful giraffes could no longer distract me from the discomfort of my bruised and battered backside, I began to daydream of the time when I would return to the States and laugh in disdain at all those American drivers whose four-wheel-drive pickups and SUVs never leave the pavement.

Finally arriving at our destination, we found dozens of people waiting. A lot of them had walked many dusty miles to get there. Now they stood patiently in ragged lines as we opened the bags and began the long and tediously precise process of measuring out a ration of grain for each family.

We did so knowing that in this culture, during a drought, if someone perceives that another person is getting extra grain, a riot can start faster than a dust devil can spring up and sweep across the dry Rift Valley landscape. So we poured carefully measured grain into people's empty bags, prompting a relieved smile, a fresh spark of hope in their eyes, and an occasional *asante* (Swahili for "thank you") as our only reward. That and the satisfaction of seeing people turning and beginning their return journey with a little more determination, a little more spring in their steps, despite the heavier bags of hope they now carried on their backs or balanced on their heads for many miles before they reached home.

On this particular relief outing, I realized that after almost half a year in Africa, I had grown accustomed to the *look* of hunger. Up close and personal, poverty felt a lot more real than what we North Americans have seen long-distance and once-removed in our media's coverage of famine around the world.

Yet I experienced something new this time. At our second or third stop, one of the people waiting in line for a ration of maize was a gaunt, young mother with a tiny baby swaddled in a cloth sling. So the baby hung within easy reach, at her side, on her back, or just beneath her mother's breasts.

The infant swaddled in that sling had a cry unlike any I had ever heard before. But since I usually gravitate toward babies, I asked her mother if I could hold the little one. She handed over her tiny daughter, who weighed next to nothing as I nestled her in my arms and attempted to soothe her with my best cross-cultural daddy repertoire. But after several minutes of my gentlest arm-rocking and my best back-patting failed to calm or quiet that little girl's pathetic protests, I asked the mama what she thought was wrong with her daughter.

That young mother shrugged and told me, "She is just hungry."

On the long, rough ride out of the valley and back up to Kijabe, I don't remember once noticing my body's aches and pains. If we passed any wildlife, I didn't see them. Nor did I daydream about someday being back in the States watching pristine four-wheel-drive vehicles travel over smooth, eight-lane expressways. I couldn't seem to erase that baby's cry off the soundtrack in my mind.

Back on campus, when Nancy asked how our day had been, I told her about the baby and how its cries had moved me so. I'd seen the look of hunger many times since we'd arrived in Kenya. Now I knew the sound of hunger. It's a combination of desperation and fatigue. And it is the saddest thing I had ever heard. I never wanted to hear it again.

But at the same time, I hoped I never would forget what it sounds like.

7

Dreaming of a Baboon Christmas

I ROSE EARLY THE MORNING OF CHRISTMAS EVE TO EXERCISE AND ENJOY THE cool, crisp mountain-morning air. And as usual, Jessie, the codependent dog we'd inherited with the dorm, wanted to go with me.

But when I stepped out the door onto our dorm's front porch, I found myself face-to-face with a large and rather imposing male baboon standing maybe five feet away. I think he may have been as startled as I was by our encounter, because we both froze, staring at each other for what may have been the longest two seconds of my life. At which point this man's loyal, brave (though not terribly bright) best friend growled and lunged at the baboon, which leaped off the porch and went racing across the yard with Jessie hot on his heels, and I started breathing again and silently cheered, "You go, girl! Get him!"

But after all of three to four seconds of dog chasing baboon, the big ape must have had an epiphany, something like, *Why am running when I am obviously bigger and stronger, not to mention smarter, than this foolish creature chasing me?* Because that's when the pursued primate suddenly stopped, pivoted, and became the pursuer of said dog, who then sprinted for her life—right back toward me.

As I watched a terrified dog and an angry baboon get closer and closer, I was struck by an epiphany of my own: *I've never had a Christmas Eve like this before.*

Fortunately, the baboon abandoned the chase short of the porch, gave me one last superior look, and ambled away. I pondered that thought in my heart throughout the remainder of the season.

—

Baboons may not have been part of our holiday plans, but Nancy and I had determined we would celebrate a memorable, different, and low-key African Christmas with our sons. So we had decided our family would give each other only local Kenyan products as gifts this year.

We gave Matthew some wooden and soapstone carvings, a locally made slingshot, and a thumb piano. A thumb piano is a small, rough wooden box with a hole, and over the hole are some varying lengths and widths of flat metal, attached to the box at one end and free at the other, which create a musical note when the loose end is thumbed.

And JT received a genuine Masai spear, a Masai knife, a traditional red Masai blanket, and a Masai rundu (a beautifully carved and smoothly polished wooden club carried for defense).

The Masai people are dark and very tall cattle herders. So seeing my fair-haired, fair-skinned, ten-year-old son all decked out and imagining himself as a Masai warrior seemed amusing, yet fitting at the same time. However, answering honestly the question, "Dad, do I look like a Masai man?" was a challenge I'd never anticipated as a parent.

And yet one more wonderful reminder that this was not just another Christmas.

—

An additional Peifer holiday highlight that year came the day we invited our Kenyan house-helper, Grace, and her family to lunch with us in our home. Although Macharia, fifteen, Charles, thirteen, and Martin, ten, were older than our kids, they interacted well with JT and Matthew. Boys will be boys, at any age, in any culture.

But again it struck me how difficult it can be as an adult to converse politely with someone when you have little or no common context. I don't know much about chicken farming; Grace's husband, Peter, has never heard of E★Trade, which might have made for awkward, stilted mealtime conversation if not for our second grade son. When the occasion called for it, Matthew was able to make surprisingly appropriate and often humorous comments on anything and everything from chickens to E★Trade and many more subjects between. So a good time was had by all.

After dessert, we walked our guests over to the school's computer lab. Learning that none of Grace's family had ever worked on a computer before was initially depressing for me. I couldn't help but think, *Three kids who have no experience with computer technology will find it hard to compete in today's world.*

But something wonderful happened when we sat both parents and the three boys down at five different computers. The adults obviously felt intimidated and uncertain. But the kids soon began to catch on. Grace and Peter's sons all started on MathBlaster, and Macharia worked through two levels in record time, having figured it out on his own. His two brothers hunched over their own screens, working away.

Witnessing those boys' intensity and excitement as they sat in front of a real computer for the first time in their lives made an indelible impression on my mind. But it was when I noted the expressions of sheer pleasure and pride on Peter and Grace's faces as they watched their sons that a more encouraging thought struck me: *If these kids just get an opportunity, they can make up for lost time.*

Of course, I wasn't sure how in the world they would ever get that chance when most Kenyan families live in homes without power, and 60 percent of Kenyan kids drop out of school after junior high because their parents can't afford the tuition to continue their public school education.

Still, I was convinced that if sharp kids like this were given a shot, they would run with it.

But will they get their shot?

—

I wrestled with that question throughout the remaining days of our Christmas break, and I reported my conclusions in this email:

Grace's oldest son has finally received his assignment for secondary level training. He was accepted at a boarding school where the annual tuition is about what the average African makes in a year. There is so much graft, corruption, and unfairness in the educational system here that it put me in such a foul mood I wanted to scream: How can the government justify this cost when so few Kenyan families can afford it?

And, Why do they require uniforms that cost so much? Why do they require kids to buy books instead of lending out texts like we do in the States? *Why would a country cripple its children this way? I didn't know the answer to that one. So I was mad, as mad as I have ever been since we arrived in Africa.*

With the generous help of some of you—our friends, family, and faithful supporters—we were able to help Grace and Peter cover the first year's tuition. However, the Kenyan educational system is so broken that even after the national government announced a recent 50 percent reduction in school fees across the country, local school officials simply ignored the decree and maintained tuition at the previous level.

Yet another blow came after we helped get the necessary money together (now twice what the average African makes in a year). That's when school officials informed Grace she couldn't pay in cash; all tuition payments needed to be by money order. And the money order cost the equivalent of another three weeks' wages.

I have never really understood the motivation behind revolutions before I came to Africa. And I worry that if there was widespread unrest in this country, the poor would be the most hurt. Yet I wonder, at what point do citizens of any country throw up their hands, shout "Enough is enough!" and trash a system that robs and steals from its own people? I don't know the answer to that question either, but I understand the question now.

—

We received word over the holidays that a big shipment addressed to us had arrived in Nairobi. We'd been expecting several more boxes of toys to distribute at the local hospital and orphanages. But when we checked to see when and where we could pick them up, we were told they had not yet cleared customs. And we would be notified when they did, maybe sometime in January.

We were already frustrated they hadn't arrived in time for Christmas. But our Kenyan friend, Fred, assured us that few if any Kenyan children would be disappointed to get those toys later. They never expected gifts on Christmas anyway. He reminded us that he was twenty-six and had never received a Christmas present before that year.

Earlier in December when I'd asked what he would like for a Christmas present, Fred said he had never slept on a mattress. So that's what our family had given him. And he'd come back after the first night to tell me it had been the best night of sleep in his life, which meant Fred's first-ever Christmas present would rank high on my own list of best Christmas presents ever.

—

Nancy's sister sent Grace's sons wristwatches that arrived as belated Christmas presents. The day after Grace took the watches home, I asked if her boys liked the gifts. Her mile-wide smile was punctuated with an emphatic, "Oooh, yes," as only Grace could say it.

She went on to describe the reaction of her youngest. When she showed Martin his watch, he wouldn't even take it from her. He first had to run outside and jump and holler. Then he came back in and started to reach for it, but had to run outside again. The same thing happened a third time. Martin's joy was just too vast to be contained in the house; the gift was overwhelming, so wonderful, that to begin with he couldn't receive it.

Nancy and I laughed at Grace's story, thoroughly enjoying her description of Martin's reaction, and sharing vicariously in his excitement and joy. Later I stopped and thought, *How different Martin's response had been from the usual way most of us Westerners receive gifts,* a real thought-provoker for me about how I receive the incredible gifts God gives me.

Truly, I'd never had a Christmas like this one before.

—

It wasn't just our interactions with nationals that broadened my perspective during the holidays. As I wrote in yet another weekly email early in January:

All the RVA students are now back from our December break, and like most kids, they have been comparing their Christmas haul. Do you know what was evidently the gift of choice for missionary kids in Africa this year? Heinz catsup! *I am not making this up. Perhaps it's because the local Kenyan brand, Peptang (I'm not making that up either), tastes as unpleasant as it sounds (imagine the flavor of red Elmer's Glue). Or maybe Heinz is just a reminder of home.*

Whatever the reason, kids here on campus were recounting the opening of real catsup on Christmas morning with the same level of excitement that the latest video game might elicit back in the States. Walking across campus, I actually saw two MKs high-five each other after one of them exclaimed, "I couldn't believe it: sixty-four ounces!"

—

Early in January, Grace invited our family to her house for lunch. After an hour of walking to get there, which involved lots of steep, uphill climbing, Matthew said, "Dad, she does this every day!"

Grace and Peter's house had a breathtaking view. It was a small home, but had two glass windows, considered a real luxury in Kenya. The house also had a poured cement floor, which is even more rare. Our boys brought a Nerf football, and both families had fun tossing it around. None of them had ever thrown an American football, so the passing techniques varied greatly.

Grace served us a wonderful lunch, the highlight of which was a mixture of potato and beans, the dish's green coloring enhanced by pumpkin leaves used for flavoring. Following the meal, as is Kenyan tradition when guests visit, we played games. After which Grace and Peter's family sang and danced for our entertainment. Then, for perhaps the only time on earth, the Peifer family was asked, "Do you have a song to sing for us?"

It probably needs to be said: the Peifers will never be mistaken for the von Trapps. Or anything close. (I was kicked out of our church choir back home because I could make a whole section go flat.) So we managed to stumble and mumble our way through one song, "Give Thanks with a Grateful Heart," which was received graciously by our hosts. But there was no call for an encore.

—

As soon as we got back to the campus late that afternoon, Nancy and I hurriedly cleaned up and dressed to go with five carloads of RVA folks for a night out in Nairobi. The occasion: a special staff dinner at the Inter-Continental Hotel, with crisp linens and a pianist playing in the background. It didn't seem much like Africa.

We were saying goodbye to a couple who had worked at our school for twenty years. The fine, multicourse meal for both Nancy and me — tip included, plus a little extra to help cover the evening for the retiring couple —set me back a whopping eleven dollars. Fancy hotels and concrete slabs are each part of Kenya, but we didn't often get to live in both worlds on the same day.

The thrill ride home that evening made for an unforgettable ending to an already memorable day. There are few streetlights in Africa and many Kenyans who believe that using headlights wears down the battery. So every night drive is an adventure, some more than others. We made it back to Kijabe safely that evening, but after-dark traveling in Africa is not for the faint of heart.

—

The Peifers' social calendar filled up fast that first month of the new millennium. When friends invited us out to Nairobi for dinner again, the restaurant featured zebra on the menu. Several of us were game (pun intended) enough to order it. We all laughed when the waiter asked, "How do you like your zebra cooked?" I can tell you it was very tasty. But I'm afraid I still don't know the answer to that last question.

Which brings me to another interesting difference when eating out in Kenya: In any but a handful of the more exclusive restaurants catering to a wealthy clientele, when you order something to drink, your server will ask, "Baridi or moto?" (Swahili for "Cold or warm?") This even if you are ordering a Coke. Two reasons: One, most Kenyans don't have refrigerators, so they are not used to chilled drinks. Two, many Kenyans have terrible teeth with multiple cavities, and ice-cold liquids hurt too much.

—

With all the eating out we did that January, we needed a little extra exercise. We got more than a little one Saturday when the Peifer clan climbed nearby Mount Longonot, which we could see from the windows of our dorm's family living quarters. At 9,120 feet, the peak of this dormant volcano is only fifteen hundred feet higher than RVA. But the mountain rises several thousand feet into the sky from its base on the floor of the Rift Valley.

The hiking trail from the entrance gate of the national park located high on the side of the mountain, up to and around the crater rim, was a bit less than ten kilometers, but with a difference in elevation of more than two thousand feet. More than steep enough to suit a couple of middle-aged, gravity-challenged Texans. The hike to Grace's house (just as long, though not nearly so steep) had been a good warm-up.

Giraffe, buffalo, and hartebeest roamed this mountainside park. When, at one point, the trail took us within twenty feet of a herd of grazing zebras, I decided I much preferred mine *uncooked* and free-ranging in their natural habitat. So it was a good thing we'd already packed a lunch to eat when we reached the top. Mount Longonot was a long climb, but one of the most wonderful and rewarding experiences I've ever had as a father. Any dad hopes someday his children will go beyond, accomplish more, and achieve greater heights than he ever did. And I got a graphic visual image of how I might feel on that future someday every time I looked up that trail to see my two sons high and higher above us, already forging ahead.

When we finally caught up with JT and Matthew at the rim, we decided that would be the perfect place to picnic and enjoy the spectacular views. Peering over the rocky rim and deep into the mountain, we were surprised to see verdant treetops where a forest has grown and covered the crater's floor in the century and a half since the volcano's last reported eruption. More impressive was the 360-degree panorama stretching out and over, up and down the Great Rift Valley to where it disappeared in a notch at the horizon, continuing its three-thousand-mile course, which started from Syria in the Middle East and cut like some long, partially healed geological scar, nearly the length of the African continent.

Following lunch, and after hiking around the rim's circumference, JT and Matthew proceeded to run down the trail that we'd all trudged up that morning. The boys beat us down, by who knows how long. For me, what was more than three hours up took just less than two hours down. But I did not run.

By the time we rejoined our boys in the parking lot at the bottom of the trail, I'd thought up a potentially lucrative business idea. I remembered seeing tourists strolling down sidewalks in Nairobi wearing souvenir T-shirts that bragged, "I Climbed Mount Longonot." I figured I could market one saying, "I Fell Off Mount Longonot."

Okay, full disclosure. I didn't fall off the mountain, nor did I ever create and sell a shirt making that claim. But given my athletic and marketing aptitude, I certainly could have. And when I tried to get out of bed the next morning, I definitely felt like I had.

—

We soon discovered that the second term can be harder than the first, at least for some dorm residents in a boarding school hundreds, maybe even thousands, of miles from their families. Because you should have gotten over homesickness by this time, the tears that sometimes come at night to even the toughest of fifth grade males can seem particularly humiliating.

I spent a lot of time patting boys on the back, letting them know it was okay to cry, and assuring them that their parents missed them just as much as they missed their parents, probably more. But I could never say or do enough.

—

I had adjustments of my own to make when school started again in January. As I reported to the folks back home:

In addition to the tasks assigned me last semester, I've been given two new responsibilities this term.

1. I am teaching kindergarteners computer. I have already discovered the difference between teaching first graders and my new kindergarten class. It's volume. As in decibels, not in class size.

Five-year-olds may be little, but they are loud: "WHAT DO I DO NEXT?" "WHAT IS THIS FOR?" And the most popular of all: "WHY?"

2. I know many people thought it funny that I would go to Africa. A lot more of you thought it was even funnier that I was asked to sing in a Kenyan home. But I can't think of any clearer proof of God's great sense of humor than the following: I am going to coach basketball.

Even I have to admit there is just something amazingly amusing about a white guy going to Africa and being asked to coach basketball. It's even funnier if you know the only real skill I developed in basketball growing up was fouling. When a game was getting out of hand, I was the guy, the hatchet man, the coach sent in to guard the opponents' best player, using any and every means necessary to stop him from getting any more points. I'd elbow my man in the gut under the boards. And clobber him hard every time he went up for a shot. The intent was letting the other team's star know he was going to pay a price to do anything. Hopefully discouraging him from trying. And if he had to go to the bench to cool down or recover from the battering, so much the better.

That was and is pretty much the extent of my roundball skills. And something tells me my fouling techniques would probably be inappropriate to teach a team of young and impressionable missionary kids. But since I can't — and never could — dribble, shoot, pass, or do much of anything else to contribute to any team I ever played on, this promises to be an interesting basketball season. I start coaching fourth to sixth grade boys and girls next week.

Despite the adjustments required by my new duties, overall I feel much more comfortable this term because I'm already familiar with most of the basic daily routine, which has allowed me, in the words of my British colleagues, the opportunity to be a little cheeky.

Thoughtful, loving husband that I am, I wracked my brain for something special I might be able to do for my bride to brighten each and every day for Nancy this semester. So I have already trained this term's class of driving students to always greet Nancy every time and anywhere they see her on campus — no matter the hour, no matter who she's with, no matter what she's doing, and no matter what she is wearing — with the following greeting (best delivered in a halting monotone): "Good morning, Mrs. Peifer! My, what a lovely dress!"

Mrs. Peifer is truly enjoying her greetings. And my shins should recover by midterm.

—

Later in January, I went to a computer show in Nairobi. The last trade show I had attended in the States was held in a massive convention hall crammed with high-tech sales booths representing all the world's biggest company names in computing and information technology. Top executives and company reps demonstrated and sometimes handed out samples of their latest products. And the organizers booked the rock group Chicago and The Pointer Sisters for entertainment.

This Kenyan computer show was a little less extravagant. Twelve exhibitors set up folding tables in one of Nairobi's first indoor shopping malls. Every booth had its own power backup, because if you don't count on the electricity going off a dozen or so times a day, you are fooling yourself.

I found about half of the salespeople knowledgeable, and the other half full of wind, which may be a better ratio than trade shows in the US.

That Nairobi experience made me think: How hard it must be to run a computer company in a country with irregular power and unreliable phone lines. But what an opportunity! India built a middle class in a generation by leapfrogging technology. Could that happen in Africa? Would the nation of Kenya get its shot?

I hoped so.

8

Of Toys, Boys, Spears, and the WWF

THE TOYS WE'D BEEN WAITING FOR FINALLY CLEARED CUSTOMS. BUT before I tell you the end of that story, let me recount the beginning.

In October, a couple of months after we arrived in Kenya, we received four emails in one day asking us what we wanted for Christmas. We responded in our weekly email that our family didn't want or need anything, but that we would love to get some small toys we could distribute to children in our local hospitals and at a nearby orphanage. I'd mentioned that I thought Magna Doodles would make nice gifts. When we got a couple of boxes of toys that included a few Magna Doodles in November, we had a great time distributing them.

We'd mentioned toys in only that one email. But by the time the first boxes arrived, we started to receive regular notices from AIM headquarters in Pearl River, New York (where we had asked people to send any donated gifts so that they could be sent by a more secure means than ordinary mail). They were starting to get lots and lots of packages. And they wanted to make sure I realized that it was my responsibility to pay for the freight and customs.

I had budgeted money for that, but an amount based on the couple of boxes we'd already received, not the boxes and boxes of toys stacking up in Pearl River. So I hadn't been sure what to do.

When someone in our home church offered to use his corporate discount with Federal Express, AIM headquarters shipped all the boxes to Dallas. Our church in Texas took up a collection to help pay for it. My old company, Oracle, sent money. An old friend sent a huge check. And now in January we received our shipment. More than seventy-five Magna Doodles, dozens of coloring books and crayons, and almost one hundred Matchbox cars along with games, balls, and dolls. We opened the shipping container and wanted to weep for the generosity of our friends.

And we were informed that more was coming in another shipment. Which was a good thing. Because we knew there was no shortage of needy children who would love these toys. Word was Kenya would need ten thousand additional orphanages over the next couple of years. AIDS was devastating the country; in some villages, 90 percent of all adults had tested positive for HIV.

My next email home thanked our friends for the toys and the funds to get them to us. The abundance of gifts we'd received would cheer up lots of kids who hadn't seen much good news lately:

Kenya is in such a hard place. The headmasters of many neighboring schools have come to us and reported that they are out of food. Some of the students are fainting during the day because they are weak from hunger. The rains have not come, and the gardens have not produced, and the desperation grows. Even the grocery stores in Nairobi are putting limits on how much maize and beans you may purchase.

Electricity is now shut off twelve hours a day in Kenya. Many people get their water through an electric pump, and without power, they cannot get water half the day. The power system here is water generated; without water, there is no power. Imagine running a business with no power half the day.

With all that is happening here, the spirits of the people continue to move me. In the hospital this morning, I gave a beautiful homemade doll someone sent us to a little girl without fingers, a cast on one leg, and some kind of eye condition. You have never seen a face light up like hers did, and for the hour we were there, she carried it everywhere. As I was leaving, she walked over to me and I assumed she was going to give me a hug. But instead, she tried to hand me the dolly. When I asked her mama if the girl understood that I meant for her to keep it, the woman nodded and said, "She just wanted to give something to you, and that is all she had."

I persuaded the child to keep the doll, but she epitomizes Africa to me: people with so little who try to share all they have.

—

One thing I was learning in Kenya is that dreams can come true.

Later that week, our family had the privilege of delivering a supply of toys to the orphanage nearest us. The children gathered in a common area where we demonstrated how a Magna Doodle works. And then we handed out one of those toys to every child.

One little girl told me, "I have never had a new toy before." That was probably true for the vast majority of those kids. Some may never have had a toy of any kind they could call their own.

The Magna Doodles came in their original packaging, and one little guy kept hugging his box to his chest. When I finally walked over and asked if I could help him open it, the boy shook his head and told me, "I just want to hold it for a while."

Whenever I gave a gift in Kenya, I always tried to say, "This is from people in the United States who love you." After I made that announcement at the orphanage that day, several kids told Matthew and JT, "We are saying that we are very happy."

I can't adequately describe the sad conditions in that orphanage, and you wouldn't believe it if I could: the old smelly mattresses they slept on at night, the little food they were served in their one meal a day. But as they drew and wrote on their Magna Doodles, a real sense of joy filled that place.

—

On Sunday, January 30, I sent out a weekly email that included a family milestone:

JT turned eleven today, and it was a memorable birthday in lots of ways. Last year, his party was at Laser Quest; he and his friends shot each other with laser guns. No Laser Quest in Africa, but lots of stars, so he and five of his buddies camped out last night. It gets chilly here after dark this time of year, and the winds were blowing strong. But when you are in fifth grade, camping out for the first time without the parents, the thrill is so great you forget the cold. Or (probably closer to the truth) the chill is part of the thrill. They stayed up late planning future adventures, and came in this morning shivering, tired, and exhilarated. A perfect birthday.

—

Every evening, we had devotions with the boys in our dorm. We often invited different people from the RVA community to come and share. On one particularly memorable evening, one of the single women on RVA's staff brought a video she made when she bungee-jumped off the bridge hundreds of feet over the gorge at Victoria Falls on the Zambia-Zimbabwe border. The video was dramatic, and after showing it, she gave a wonderful talk about trust and faith.

What did fifth grade boys get out of the talk? More than you would think, it turned out.

The next morning, I discovered three different guys had tied their socks together, and then knotted one end of their sock ropes to a top bunk and the other end around their ankles, trying to see what it feels like to bungee jump. I can't tell you how well their experience equated to the real thing, but I have a vivid memory of many unkind opinions about what it was like to help three dorm daredevils untie dirty, smelly socks used in that manner.

—

A weekend or two after JT's camping adventure with his pals, our eight-year-old, Matthew, walked a mile in the dark with another eight-year-old to his friend's home, something I cannot imagine allowing in the States but didn't worry about in Kijabe, Kenya. The boys spent the next day together and had fun swimming and playing outdoors.

Matthew came home sunburned, and as his mother rubbed some first-aid cream on him before bedtime that night, he wondered aloud if his friend, Josh, had gotten sunburned and was hurting as much as he was. We told him, "Probably not!" because Josh is a Kenyan with dark skin. His reply was classic Matthew: "I wish *my* skin was black."

One of the unexpected benefits of living in Africa is the perspective on race it has given my sons. It's not that color doesn't matter to them; they don't even seem to notice it.

—

A couple of weeks later, I began my weekly report to family, friends, and supporters in what was for me an unusual way:

Usually, the title of each week's email is pretty easy to come up with. But this has been a wild week, so please vote for what you think would be the most appropriate of these titles after you read the entire email:

1. *"The Worst Valentine Ever Written"*
2. *"God Knows"*
3. *"Matthew and I Claimed the Eyeball"*
4. *"I Already Got to Touch the Intestines"*
5. *"We Put the Eyeball in the Fire"*
6. *"Redneck Hunting in Africa"*

I must also insert a disclaimer this week: none of this is made up. None of it ever is, but this week I need to make it clear; believe it or not, I didn't make any of this up.

To begin with, Happy Valentine's Day! Be glad that you didn't get this valentine, handwritten by my elder son to a girl in his fifth grade class (duplicated here with no corrections made): Hannah, no offence but it really embarreses me when you start coversations with me. Frankly this speaks out for all boys, but your still my friend. Your friend, JT.

Nancy and I convinced him this missive was not appropriate to send to a girl. But I think it is as close to a real valentine as JT will send for a few more years.

RVA dismissed early last Friday for a midterm break, and our family had the opportunity to visit a remote Masai village and camp in the African bush for the long weekend. Our adventure began on Friday afternoon when we traveled with our friends the Jacksons (the family with whom we'd gone to Mombasa back in December) to a school for disabled kids an hour's drive south of Nairobi in the town of Kajiado.

—

Our friends, Bill and Carol, had tried to prepare us for what we would see, but they couldn't. Not because conditions were so bad or because these hand-icapped kids were so deformed that it was tough to look at them, but because by the time we'd been there a few minutes, it was easy to forget that these happy, vivacious kids had any disabilities at all. Their motto at the school is "No wheelchairs," and they succeed. One of the first boys we saw was about eight and had no feet—just stumps. Yet he walked and ran, and even played soccer like anybody else. We saw kids with a broad variety of disabilities, but they were all smiling and crowding around to welcome us.

Bill, who is a physical therapist, was well known to many of the children. So they ran to him first and hugged him tightly. But they quickly accepted the rest of us as well. Nancy was soon walking around with a little girl on each hand and a third trying to get in. After several of the kids rubbed our curiously white skin, I realized we were probably the first white people some of them had ever seen in person.

One of the men who worked at the school had planted maize, and it was drying up. We expressed our sadness over this, and his response was telling: "God knows. He knows what we need, and we trust him."

I panic when little things don't go right, and I needed to hear that perspective.

With every strike against its students, somehow this residential school for disabled children was the happiest place I had seen since we had been in Africa. No doubt, much of the credit for that belonged to the director, Daniel, who has to be one of the greatest human beings I've met on this planet. And I'll tell you more about him. The biggest factor of all was the grace of God. Whatever the explanation for the spirit and atmosphere of this special place, it was wonderful to be around those children.

We were able to give each student a Magna Doodle, a coloring book and crayons, and a Matchbox car. One of the little guys was unable to thank me because he exhaled so deeply when I handed him his toys that he couldn't talk.

But the best part for me was that someone had sent us a stomp rocket, which is what it sounds like — a rocket that is launched by the air pressure created when you stomp on the launching pad. Watching kids without legs flinging themselves onto the pad to launch the rocket is something I will not soon forget.

After a delicious dinner of chapatis and stew, we visited with and got to know Daniel and his wife, Lydia, our hosts for the weekend. Daniel is a member of the Masai tribe, the eldest son of the second of his father's five wives. As a child, he had polio, which left him with severe physical disabilities. He can walk, but with a limp that severely slows and limits his mobility. Traditionally, and to this day, the Masai are herders of cows, goats, and sheep. So as a boy growing up, Daniel felt worthless because he couldn't help with tending the family herds. Frustrated that he couldn't do what other boys did, he angrily blamed God for his disabilities.

Then the Kenyan government passed a law requiring that at least one child from each Masai family go to school. Because Daniel was unable to help with the animals, his father selected him to be educated. At the school, a special one for disabled students, several things happened. He received an education; he met the young woman who would become his wife; he heard the gospel for the first time; and he decided to become a follower of Jesus. Daniel became a changed man as he began to see that he did indeed have a purpose, that his handicap was part of that purpose, and that he was created for a reason. He learned to be grateful to God for his disability, because it shaped him and his life in so many ways.

Now he is a respected elder in the community, and the opportunity we had to witness the impact of his work with these kids was one of the greatest privileges and blessings we had during that year in Africa.

Daniel and Lydia, who faces some physical challenges of her own, are both gracious and humble people who love God and the work he has called them to do at this residential school for disabled children. Not only do they teach and work with children, but Daniel also has been trained in making braces and prostheses.

After spending the night in the school's guesthouse, we were all scheduled to leave with Daniel and Lydia for his homeplace to spend the remainder of the weekend in Daniel's family compound, or manyatta, in a small Masai village two hours farther south of Kajiado. But before we could leave the school, Bill, the physical therapist, first had an appointment to put casts on a newborn patient whose feet turned inward. The baby's mama couldn't bear to watch, so Bill asked me to assist by holding the child's legs still and trying to comfort him. This helpless baby reminded me so much of our son Stephen (whose second birthday would have been the following month) that I had a good cry afterward.

—

We left the school and headed for Daniel's home village. On the way, we stopped at an open market to buy a few potatoes. As I walked around, I wondered why everyone seemed to be staring. Then I realized that it was because those in our party were probably the only white people for miles around in that part of Kenya. It was an experience I think every person in America should have at least once in his or her life.

—

The bumpy two-hour drive to Daniel's family manyatta, most of it over dirt roads, took us past herds of zebra, Grant's gazelle, and ostrich. We came close enough to the Kenya-Tanzania border that we could see the snowcapped peak of Mount Kilimanjaro, Africa's highest mountain, in the distance.

Daniel grew up somewhere beyond the outskirts of the proverbial "middle of nowhere," surrounded by nothing. The little village blended so well into the dusty, brown, sepia-tone landscape that this Texas tenderfoot might have passed right on by without ever noticing any sign of human habitation.

Fortunately we had Daniel with us, because he was telling us where to pull off the road and stop before I even noticed the one visibly distinguishing feature of his family manyatta: the small home Daniel and Lydia had constructed for themselves out of mbati (a corrugated tinlike building material) in a cluster of traditional mud and dung huts. The entire compound was encircled and somewhat camouflaged by a high, formidable fence of tangled, dried thorn bushes to keep lions and other predators from attacking the livestock at night.

Daniel's family greeted and welcomed us to their home by offering a traditional tribal ceremonial drink called mala. The Masai make mala by using a small chunk of burning charcoal to cleanse and coat the insides of a drinking gourd, into which they pour fresh cow's milk (sometimes mixed with a little cow's blood) and then allow two or three days for the concoction to ferment and thicken. The resulting drink is a thick, sour liquid that reminded me of plain yogurt with something of a smoky, charcoal aftertaste. Interesting, but definitely an acquired taste.

Then we visited with Daniel while he gave us a guided tour of his man-yatta and the rest of the village, which consisted of a handful of other man-yattas scattered across the countryside nearby. His youngest brother, Ngelli, lived in one hut with his first wife. Daniel's mother lived in Daniel's home when he and Lydia were away at the boarding school where they worked; on the occasions they came home, his mother moved into the second nearby hut. And a cousin of Daniel's lived in a third hut. Ngelli's second wife was only fourteen, so she lived with a younger sister in a nearby manyatta. Eventually she also would have a hut in this manyatta.

We met some of Daniel's neighbors and had chai (tea boiled with milk) together. And we drove several miles to see the pump where the village gets its water. That was another reminder of how tough life can be here. The people living in many Masai villages walk several miles a day to obtain enough water for their family and animals, and I was startled to realize how much time and energy they spend in pursuit of this one, essential life requirement.

Arriving back at the manyatta after the pump trip, we were greeted by Matthew and a friend, who enthusiastically announced, "We're having a goat roast for supper tonight, and Matthew and I claimed the eyeballs!" Matthew added, "I already got to touch the intestines." Sure enough, later on Matthew proudly displayed his goat eyeball to all who wanted to see it, and to many of us who did not. Later yet, when asked where his goat eye was, he informed us, "We put it in the fire for flavoring."

While we waited for the rest of dinner to finish cooking, the family's goats and sheep and cows were brought back into the manyatta for the night. And it was milking time. Nancy got to milk one of the goats. She later con-fessed that she'd always wanted to milk a cow, but she thought a goat was close enough to check that off her bucket list.

I was more excited about the goat roast, a traditional Masai celebration for guests. The roasted meat (nyama choma) was the appetizer, while the main course was goat stew over rice. I also discovered that goat liver is delicious. But I worried about developing a taste for it. Where might one find goat liver in Dallas?

We ate our feast inside Daniel and Lydia's home, which was not only built out of metal but had a poured cement floor. The house had something else that was even more unusual in Masai territory. On the roof of his home, Daniel had installed a solar panel hooked to a battery, and a small antenna. So after our meal, the men of the family and a number of male neighbors gath-ered in the little "living room" in front of a fourteen-inch portable television.

You need to understand that Kenya had only three broadcast channels at the time, one of which was the government station, perhaps the world's most effective cure for insomnia. So on another channel we watched a soccer match—in a Masai manyatta just beyond the outskirts of the middle of nowhere, on a black-and-white TV. Talk about surreal.

But that was not the biggest surprise for me. Guess what the most popular TV show in Africa (or at least that part of Masailand) was? If you guessed *Masterpiece Theater*, you would be wrong. *Frazier*, one of the top-rated shows in the US at the time? Not even on the radar screen, let alone the picture tube.

The correct answer is WWF—the World Wrestling Federation.

Evidently Africans love professional wrestling. When Daniel told me how much he liked watching wrestling, all the other Masai men who had crowded into that tiny room, none of whom spoke English, immediately turned their attention away from the soccer game and began an animated discussion of their favorite wrestlers and the things they liked best about the sport. They seemed particularly enamored with the old clothesline move.

I couldn't believe my ears. There I sat in a tiny tin home in the middle of an African wilderness, listening to Masai men speaking a tribal language unknown to me, and yet I could distinctly and repeatedly pick out the word *clothesline*. I swear I am not making this up; it was definitely the most surreal moment I'd had in my first seven months in Africa.

But that top ranking was not to last long.

When we turned off the TV, fourteen fearless fellows (and I) piled into one four-wheel-drive vehicle with a spotlight and set out to do what I can only describe (with all due respect to my Southern friends) as redneck hunting.

The strategy my new friends favored was different from any hunting I'd ever done or even heard tell of in the States. We drove in the dark, back and forth, over and through the wilds of a countryside populated by lions, zebras, leopards, pythons, cobras, ostriches, gazelles, and who knows what else. And we kept driving until someone noticed movement in the moonlight, and we shined the spotlight on the animal, hoping the glare would freeze the creature in its tracks. Then two of the Masai jumped out of the van and ran barefoot—across the savannah or dodging in and out of trees and brush in the dead of night—carrying hefty, six-foot spears and attempting to circle the animal and get close enough to hurl their weapons at it.

We never managed to kill anything, but the longer the hunt went on, the funnier it got. Have you ever golfed with someone who had to recount every stroke for you in agonizingly tedious detail? "First hole, the wind was coming out of the east, so the ball hooked a little; I had to play a five iron out of the rough. Second hole, I used a seven; overshot the green." You know the type?

Well, these Masai hunters were a lot like that. Every time they launched their spears and missed, they raced back to the vehicle and explained, in detail, every little thing they had done, just how close they had come, and why they had missed. Since they knew I didn't speak their language, they then acted out the whole thing for my benefit. Which seemed appropriate, since words could never adequately describe how hilarious this all became the later and longer this futile "hunt" lasted. I don't know when I'd ever laughed so hard or so enjoyed the great outdoors as I did playing cross-cultural charades that night, in the dark, in the African wild.

By the time we finally got back to the village, Nancy and the boys had retired to our tent, which we'd set up inside the manyatta. But I stayed awake another hour, lying on the luggage rack atop our vehicle, staring up at the heavens and contemplating the cosmos. I counted a dozen shooting stars in a night sky glittered with more, brighter, and seemingly closer stars than I'd ever seen in my life.

A fitting end to a memorable day, and yet another wonderful reminder that God knows and has a purpose in everything and for every person he has ever created.

9

Bunny Hops and Ostrich Runs

How do you motivate young children to learn computer skills? A real teacher could tell you. But I'm not a real teacher, so I had to figure it out on my own. By halfway through that second term, I had discovered and perfected three principles that worked for me:

1. *Empathy.* One of the cutest first grade girls of all time, Joy, had come in to computer class and told me that she was sad because her parents would not be coming for midterm break. Then she started to cry. I can't stand little girls crying. I have sons, so I have developed immunity to boy tears. But I just can't handle girl tears. As we sat there and I tried to think of something helpful to say, I started crying too, which caused Joy to stop crying so she could comfort me.

2. *Negative encouragement.* I think I am a natural encourager, but that gets old fast. So I first told my sixth grade class that they would get a treat if they were able to master some database problems. Then I told them that I didn't want to spend money on *them*; I wanted to spend it on *me*. So anytime they made a mistake, I praised them, and anytime they did something right, I yelled at them. I knew I was on to something when one kid bragged, "Mr. Peifer yelled at me *four* times today!"

3. *Humiliation.* For third graders, I learned one thing that always works is to give them an opportunity to humiliate the teacher. I discovered this after assigning a practice exercise introducing a new program they needed to master. I was getting absolutely nowhere with them until I announced that for anyone who could do it perfectly, I would bunny-hop around the class. Six minutes later, every kid had the exercise down pat. In fact, when three kids demanded retroactive bunny hops,

I was forced to say something I never in my life expected to say: "Don't get greedy with bunny hops!"

———

Nancy went to a women's retreat one weekend in March, leaving me alone with ten boys. This gave me a wonderful opportunity to put into practice all I had learned in seven months as a dorm parent. Of course, the weekend also showed me how much more I needed to know.

But I was encouraged to realize I had grown in one important way: I knew how to handle sick kids now. During our first months at RVA, if one of the boys came into our room in the middle of the night to announce that he thought he was going to get sick, I leaped out of bed in a panic, yelling, "Not here! Go to the toilet. NOT HERE!" Often the shock of being so loudly instructed resulted in an undesirable consequence.

But on that Friday night, when I was the lone adult on dorm duty, a kid came into my room and announced he was going to get sick. Having learned from experience that my role should be more like that of a hostage negotiator, I rose slowly and calmly from the bed before responding in the most soothing tones, "I am so sorry; where does it hurt?" even as I gently but firmly and steadily guided him out of my room, down the hall, into the bathroom, and over to the toilet. Some middle-of-the-night discussions work better in bathrooms than in bedrooms.

———

The drought had been ferocious for months by that point. And since Nancy was gone, I met with some of the vegetable ladies who peddled their produce door-to-door at RVA every Saturday. But when I asked one woman how her garden was doing, she started crying. I patted her on the back and tried to empathize. But I've never been truly hungry, and my life and that of my family don't hinge on whether my garden comes in. I didn't want to offer her empty words, but that is all I felt I had. My entire life I have always been so glib, but Africa often leaves me with nothing to say.

———

Matthew chose to be baptized one Sunday during that second term, and he asked me if I would baptize him. A group of RVA kids got baptized that day in what was a moving service. Each kid shared why they were choosing to be baptized, and then a friend they had recruited read a Scripture passage they had chosen. Then after they were baptized, a song of their choosing was sung. The service was conducted outside with the entire school present.

Of course, it couldn't be a Peifer family event without something a little different occurring. The girl who got baptized right before Matthew selected Psalm 23 to be read by her friend. So it prompted a few giggles when Matthew's friend read the same passage. But that wasn't nearly as distracting as when Jessie, our increasingly codependent dorm dog, tried to jump in after me when I stepped down into the baptismal pool.

But nothing could detract from the joyous meaning of the day. Here again, I didn't have much to say, but I didn't need to. Baptism is such a gift! All I said was, "Matthew, some things are like really good ice cream. You don't have to add anything to them; they are wonderful all by themselves."

—

Nancy and I accompanied the Titchie School kids on a field trip to an ostrich farm one day in March. After a long and loud bus ride with dozens of young children singing "ninety-nine bottles of pop on the wall" at full throttle, we arrived. By the time we finished what I thought was the full tour of the place, I figured we'd learned all we would ever need to know, and more than some of us had ever wanted to know, about ostriches. But I was wrong.

Who knew that people could ride an ostrich? Which pretty much everyone decided we had to do. One of the funniest things I've ever witnessed is Nancy clinging to the back of a big ugly bird, yelling, "But I don't *want* to go for a second lap!"

Then it was my turn.

How do you ride an ostrich? Trust me when I say it's harder than it looks. There is no saddle, so four men had to firmly hold their fine-feathered friend in place while I climbed aboard Big Bird as gracefully as I could. Little kids can sit high on the bird's back and grab hold about anywhere. Adults must straddle the creatures while holding on to the wings with each hand and trying to maintain balance.

I managed to stay aboard my bird for the entire ride in a distinctive style. I am from Texas, after all, so this was hardly my first rodeo. The four ostrich wranglers who led my mount around the track informed me in a tone of great admiration that I was the first rider in the long history of that ostrich ranch who had ever sung "Rhinestone Cowboy" as he rode an ornery ostrich.

—

A bunch of us got together for a Super Bowl party to watch a tape of the big game. In March. Making the strange time factor seem surreal was the fact that all the adults at RVA had already filled out their brackets for the NCAA tournament pool.

You have to understand that I love the NCAA. Back in the States, I would read everything I could find on it, watch as many of the games as possible, submit my predictions with the utmost confidence, and then invariably lose in the first round. But as I filled out my brackets for March Madness 2000, I realized I had not seen one game or read one article about college basketball all season long. Of course that did not stop me from being passionate about my picks, nor did it stop anyone else from loudly disagreeing with everyone else, although no one at RVA had seen a regular season game either.

I guess it's a guy thing, perhaps the quintessential guy thing. But what humbled me about the whole NCAA experience that year in Africa was ranking second (against forty-four other pool participants) with my predictions. Such unprecedented success forced me to realize an important truth: *I do better when I don't know nothin'* (which probably could be a hit song for Alan Jackson someday).

—

Speaking of basketball, when the RVA intramural basketball season ended, I remained undefeated against the other three coaches on our campus. Because of that, I got to pick and coach an RVA all-star team to play against two other schools. Unfortunately, when the first opposing team swaggered into our gym, it looked to me as if several members of their seventh grade squad were in need of a shave. I don't think it was my imagination that a couple of them had sets of car keys clipped on the outside of their duffel bags.

That game was not pretty; we lost 29-6. I tried everything and used every imaginable combination of players. Our overgrown opponents proved too much for us. But we soon got another opportunity against our second rival school. I was the only coach who had both boys and girls on his team, because (1) I believe in equal opportunity, and (2) sixth grade girls are a foot taller than sixth grade boys. The other team still had a height advantage, but my guys and gals played great right from the start. We were doing so well that at the half, we were winning 20-0, and I had played every player.

Starting the second half, I did the opposite of what any self-respecting coach would ever do. I looked around at my players in the huddle and thought, *He can't dribble, she can't pass, and he won't shoot; I'll put them all in at the same time and give the other team a sporting chance.* And wouldn't you know it, the guy who wouldn't shoot dribbled, the guy who couldn't dribble passed, and the gal who couldn't pass shot, and we scored—time after time. Which I guess proved once and for all what they always say: great coaching shows.

By all rights, I should have been thrilled by my team's play. Instead I worried that it looked like I was running up the score on our opponents. So I started shouting instructions, encouraging my team: "Slow down; take it easy out there now." "Drop back; don't pressure the man with the ball." My players were probably even more confused that I groaned every time we hauled down another rebound or scored another bucket. I know they looked at me funny when the other team finally scored and I cheered louder than anyone else in the gym.

We won 35-2, and during the postgame celebration, I decided to retire from coaching basketball forever. Not just because I wanted to go out on top, but because I realized that my coaching career would never get any better than this. Besides, I wanted to give some other coaches a chance for glory.

—

I tried not to brag too much in my first postseason email home. Instead I chose to report about another aspect of my RVA experience:

I have taught an eighth and ninth grade Sunday school class this term at RVA, and it has been a challenge. It is somehow comforting that even teens in Africa grow sullen and self-absorbed. But how you reach past that has been my question. And I haven't had a good answer.

But today, on the last Sunday of the term, I brought my class down to the hospital. There are several children with hydrocephalous, which can cause a baby's head to be three times its normal size. I've found it to be one of the hardest things to look at that I have seen since I have been here in Africa. The week before we went, I asked the class to read these two Scripture verses:

Seek first the Kingdom of God and the wealth of his righteousness.

Wherever your treasure lies there will you find your heart.

My class played well with the children and obviously enjoyed the experience. But two of my girls were crying at the end, and when I asked why, one of them said, "I think I found my heart." There are good tears, you know.

—

Our family had the opportunity to go to another game park the first week after the term ended. Samburu is known for the river that runs through the park. But at the time of our visit, it was dry. You could walk across the river bottom, which is why there was a staff member whose job was to pace back and forth all night to make sure none of the leopards came across to the "people side." Whenever you think you have a bad job, remember, you could be walking back and forth with a flashlight making sure leopards don't eat the guests.

I am not sure how to make this next point, except to say that when animals are out in the wild, you see things you don't see at the Fort Worth Zoo. Compared with the birds and the bees, elephants and zebras leave nothing to the imagination, which leads to interesting discussions in the car with young children.

But a visit to a game park is a great opportunity to marvel at the wonder of creation, and marvel I did, until our truck got stuck and I had to get out and push. Pushing a motor vehicle in an African game park ten minutes after you watched a prowling leopard leap from a tree is an altogether different adventure. After many minutes of middle-aged huffing and puffing, we managed to get the car out of the mud, just in time for one of the rangers to drive up and scold me severely for being out of the vehicle.

When I asked him if he was concerned about the leopards, he shook his head and told me, "They kill only at night. But the Cape buffalo were starting to snort." That was when I first noticed a nearby herd of black buffalo studying me with anger in their eyes, which brought to mind stories I'd heard about buffaloes attacking Range Rovers—and winning. So I obediently got back in the car, wishing for a little less marvel.

―

Later that same week, we had a different kind of unsettling experience when we took the boys into Nairobi for a couple of days. We went bowling in a modern twelve-lane alley, complete with automatic scoring, the only such venue in Nairobi.

Looking around at one point, I realized the only people bowling were Indians and wazungus (Swahili plural for Europeans, Westerners, white people). Not a single African bowled the whole time we were there. We'd gone thinking it was time to start reacclimating our kids, reminding them of life in the States. But I left there feeling, for the first time since I had been in Africa, ashamed of myself for what I had done.

―

Later we went to the movies, the first movie we had seen since we had been in Africa. Playing at a triple-screen theater in Nairobi were such first-run features as *The Matrix*, *You've Got Mail*, and the one we saw, *Toy Story 2*. Before every movie shown in a Kenyan theater, they run a government newsreel that is so bad it is quite amusing. The one we saw was of the president of Kenya watching the military troops proudly marching back and forth in several different arenas, each time to "the thrill of the spectators." Spin city was not an art form yet in Kenya.

—

The following Sunday, we went with Grace to her family's church for the first time. To get there, we traveled in common Kenyan style, by matatu. That's a Swahili term for a public conveyance consisting of a privately owned vehicle, often some sort of minivan that is crammed to the gills with paying customers who are charged seemingly arbitrary amounts, depending on the distance they are going and how badly they want to get there.

Our Sunday morning matatu was a Nissan minivan, probably fifteen years old. The driver managed to get eighteen people in it. I sat in the front seat with Matthew on my lap, with someone sitting over the gearshift between us and the driver. Nan and JT were somewhere in the back. I couldn't see them. But Grace told us later that it seemed to her a comfortable ride.

Her church had metal siding, a rather rough and uneven cement floor, and narrow wooden benches with no backs for the congregation. We arrived there just as the ten o'clock morning service started; it lasted until two in the afternoon. Nancy, our boys, and I were the only non-Kenyans there. The two Kikuyu kids on the bench in front of us were so fascinated by me that they turned around and faced me the whole service. This made it a challenge for me to enter into the spirit of worship. I didn't help matters by making faces to get them giggling, which naturally prompted other kids to wander over so I would make faces at them, something I am sure the pastor appreciated.

He must not have been too offended, because after the service, we were invited to lunch with him in the back of the church. He apologized that we would have to eat with our hands because the church could not afford knives and forks. The boys were thrilled. But the meal was a humbling and disconcerting experience for Nancy and me.

Following lunch, we walked a mile back to catch the matatu. It was then we realized that we had enjoyed a cushy ride before. Because this time, we climbed in and waited. And waited. Matatus seldom, if ever, go until they are full—and *full* is a relative term. Or "in the eye of the beholder." Or something. While we were waiting, we noticed an older gentleman sitting in the seat in front of us. He appeared to be ill and was going to a nearby hospital. But that did not speed things up. The driver waited until we had thirty people on that minivan.

Kids sat on laps, and we had seven people packed in per bench. The last four potential riders were pushed, prodded, and pried into the van, until screams indicated that doors were closing on people. The solution? *Not* to close the side door, leaving four people standing on the running board, clinging to the outside of the van for dear life as we pulled away. Nancy and I couldn't tell whether we smelled antifreeze, transmission fluid, or brake fluid, but some distinct, overheated automotive odor hung in the air as we drove. And after we'd gone only a short way, we stopped and let two people off. Incredibly, four replacements climbed on.

We all reached our destinations safe and sound. But as I climbed stiffly out of that van back in Kijabe, it struck me: Matatus are the primary mode of transportation for most of the people of Kenya. It's this or walking. I knew I'd often groused about my daily commute in Dallas—with air-conditioning, a comfortable seat all to myself, and a great sound system.

I hoped someone would slap me if I ever complained about it again.

10

Nature's Nightsongs
and the Negative Tense

D URING OUR MONTHLONG APRIL BREAK BETWEEN TERMS, THE PEIFERS
spent three days and two nights on safari in the Masai Mara, Africa's
most famous and the world's largest remaining game reserve. We camped
just outside the park at the family home of a sixth grade girl in one of my
computer classes. We didn't really know the rest of the Russell family before
that. But in a spirit we'd found common among the missionary population in
Kenya, they welcomed us with an open-armed generosity you'd expect from
lifelong friends. And by the time we left, it felt like they were.

All year I'd heard teaching colleagues say that if we had the chance to visit
any of our students in their family homes, we should seize that opportunity,
because it's the best way to understand and appreciate our RVA students. And
that proved true.

Caylan and her family lived in a small house sided and roofed with sheets
of tin nailed to a rough wooden frame. The parents and their three daughters
used an outhouse every day, year round, because their home had no indoor
facilities or flush toilets. They did have running water for a shower and sinks,
but that water could not be drunk, used in preparing or cooking food, or
even used for brushing teeth without first being filtered, treated, and heated
to a boil. The Russell family generated their own electricity a few hours each
day—as long as they had enough gas to run the generator.

Their only human neighbors for miles in any direction were the Masai
families living in a handful of manyattas scattered around and sharing the
same hillside with the Russell home. Those traditional tribal compounds
consisted of a cluster of extended-family hutlike dwellings encircled by a

crude but effective woven thorn-bush barrier to protect them and their live-stock from carnivorous creatures roaming the night.

The Russell kids had no English-speaking friends and few neighbors at all their age to play with. Their basketball court was hard-packed earth. They washed clothes by hand each week. The days we were there, Caylan, her old-est sister, Cristen, and their mother, Terri, kept busy trying to smooth and improve the long, rough drive from the main road up the hill to their house by removing the biggest and potentially most damaging stones by hand.

Yet I never heard this twelve-year-old, either at school or during our visit, complain about her living situation. The entire family felt called of God to share the story and teachings of Jesus with the Masai people, and so that's what they were doing and why they were willing to live as twenty-first century pioneers. But consider a few of the benefits: Their family home sits on a hillside with an incredible view. They live on the edge of the most famous wild-game park in the world. They fall asleep each night listening to an ancient African soundtrack featuring the night songs of a mixed ensemble of lions, hyenas, and elephants. Television and radio can't dictate what they should want or "need."

Everyday life is an adventure. And these folks are in the enviable position of knowing they need to trust God daily for things we all really need God for, but often do not recognize that we do.

—

From the Russells' place, it was only a five-minute drive to the Sekeni Gate to the Masai Mara National Reserve, which was everything I ever pic-tured when I thought of Kenya—more than eight hundred square miles of untamed African wilderness, home to hundreds of different animal species, all of which roam free and can sometimes get up close and personal.

None of the "roads" are paved; in fact, they give new meaning to the word *rough*. But that just adds to the thrill and makes it essential that you drive a car you know to be reliable. If it breaks down, you need to be pre-pared to sit in your vehicle for hours waiting for someone to happen by, because if you get out to go for help, you could soon become the daily special on someone's not-fast-enough-food menu.

We had heard tales of an unfortunate few visitors who had spent days in the park and never seen much wildlife. Happily for us, our first game drive late in the afternoon of our first day removed all worry that we might be in that number. Even before we entered the park, we spotted gazelle, hartebeest, and wildebeest. Once inside the park, we enjoyed a brief shower, which settled the dust and seemed to bring out the animals. Within the first half hour, we encountered zebra, giraffe, elephants, and large herds of other grazing animals. We drove quite close to the elephants, stopping within twelve to fifteen feet of them. Lots of little guys too. Our two guys were thrilled to just sit and watch.

Unfortunately, the rain resumed as we headed back to camp, and it fell even harder as we attempted to make dinner. Only the Peifers could arrange a wet camping trip in the middle of a drought. We managed to get some food into our stomachs, then abandoned our dirty dishes to nature's rinse cycle and headed for bed. Fortunately, everything in the tents was dry, so after peeling off wet clothes, we snuggled into our warm sleeping bags and settled down for a good night's sleep. At least the boys and I did.

My gifting in life is to be able to fall asleep within moments of closing my eyes, and that rainy night was no exception. Nancy, on the other hand, stayed awake for hours listening to strange, loud, and unsettling wild animal sounds. Next morning, Nancy told me she was pretty sure the first sound she had heard was a hyena, a kind of wailing howl. Then came a noise she said sounded a bit like an elephant's trumpet, but ended with a big, snorty sort of *woof, woof, woof*. She assured me she hadn't felt afraid, knowing the Russells' property had a high, heavy fence all around it. However, she did admit the rather loud and uncommon noises were so hard to sleep through that she hadn't finally dozed off until after 1:00 a.m.

The next morning, Terri Russell told Nancy that the second sounds she'd heard were definitely lions. They prowl around the neighboring manyattas at night, growling, roaring ferociously, trying to get the enclosed livestock so terrified that they panic, break out of the manyattas, and run right into the waiting jaws of the lions.

When Nancy told her the boys and I had somehow slept through the racket, Terry laughed and said that wouldn't have happened if we were there on one of the *really* noisy nights when the lions and elephants got into it together.

Our second day on safari started out damp, but it didn't rain during breakfast, and for that we were grateful. When we finished cleaning up around camp, we took another longer game drive on which we covered more of the park and saw the animals we'd seen the prior evening, plus a lot more, including lions and hippos. The hippos were probably my favorites. We saw dozens of them in a river, all but their big snouts, bulging eyes, and broad gray backs submerged in muddy brown water. Admittedly, they were not much to look at. But what intrigued me most was how vociferously and frequently wild hippos bellow, snort, belch, and toot. Which, I'm sad to say, reminded me of fifth grade dorm boys, though the hippos were a little louder and a lot less huggable. And I also learned these roly-poly pachyderms are not the gentle, innocuous, and silly creatures they pretend to be. They attack and kill more people in Africa each year than lions do, or any other of the big cats.

It rained again, but by the time we returned to camp, the downpour was over. We enjoyed a dry night and had a wonderful time around the campfire and stargazing. If you've never done it, someday you really need to treat yourself to stargazing somewhere remote — maybe not Africa, but somewhere far from civilization's lights. Nancy exclaimed that she never knew there were that many stars.

When we finally went to bed that second evening, Nancy was the one so exhausted she dropped right off to sleep. But I made myself stay awake and listen for the creature concert she'd attended to the night before. I didn't have to wait long for the return performance of a very impressive, far-off-Broadway production, featuring the vocal talents of a local band of hyenas and what sounded like an entire pride of prowling lions.

At one point, when I thought I heard the soft-padded footfalls of one of the king of the beasts passing by only twenty yards or so away, I felt grateful for the high, sturdy chain-link fence between us, and that it was not just a jumble of prickly thorn bushes. I tried not to think about how futile any fence might be in the face of a rampaging rogue elephant or an unhappy hippo.

I have to say, it was an unexpected but gratifying reward for staying awake, truly a thrill to lie there and listen to the night sounds of so many wild animals. We camp lots in Texas, but armadillos just don't inspire the same, uh, *exhilaration*.

The next day, we took one last, early-morning game drive and were all rewarded with sightings of a jackal, cheetah, and, last but not least, a leopard in a tree with its fresh kill. After which we returned to the Russells' to break camp, pack up, and thank our hosts for their great hospitality before heading back to Kijabe.

All in all, our safari proved a wonderful time for the whole Peifer family. One of those pinch-me-I-must-be-dreaming experiences none of us will ever forget. And which we topped off when we got back to civilization (or at least to the edge of it at RVA) by sitting down with our sons and watching the newest Disney video version of *Tarzan*. Surely I wasn't the only one on the couch whose irony detector went off even before Nancy commented that it was fun now to be able to name all of the different species of animals shown.

—

On one of my April emails home, I gave the headline, "This Time I Was Determined."

During this term break, we had one final opportunity to take Swahili. Since I had made such a fool of myself in our first class, I was determined not to make my instructor laugh this time.

In general, Kenyans are a very polite folk, and would think it the height of rudeness to laugh at any inept, earnest American. And yet last term I managed to make them laugh quite often. Which was why I vowed this class was going to be different. I did okay the first two days, which were mostly review. But on the third day, we learned to speak in what I can only describe as the negative tense. (The fact that I don't know what else to call it probably tells you English teachers out there all you need to know about my language aptitude.)

Since my innate ability to say negative things in my native language has gotten me in trouble on many an occasion, I was thrilled at the idea of being able to be negative, but more discreetly, in my second language. When our instructor asked each student to give one example, a complete sentence about something we "were not," I was so excited to have grasped this new language principle that I enthusiastically volunteered and launched into my sample sentence (in perfect Swahili, of course) to say "I am not . . . uh . . . uh" before it hit me that I didn't know what I wasn't. So I improvised.

At the end of my complete sentence, my teacher punctuated me with a shocked expression, and then held his hand to his face. I realized in that instant I was in trouble. You know how, when someone is determined not to laugh, then loses it, he loses it big time. Well, that's what happened. Minutes later, between gales of laughter, my instructor managed to gasp out, "You . . . just said . . . you are not . . . a toilet!" Then he tried to regain composure, but before he could, he evidently had to repeat himself, loudly: "YOU SAID . . . YOU ARE NOT . . . A TOILET!" I didn't know why he felt he had to do that. I heard him the first time. And I understand English. Even better than I speak it.

Thankfully it was the class's chai time—Kenya's version of a coffee break, but with Kenyan tea—and I went to run a quick errand across campus. When I returned and stepped into the break room, the instructor looked up at me over his teacup and lost it once again. I thought he was going to spew hot beverage everywhere, like those spit-takes you see in old slapstick comedies. But he somehow managed to gulp down his last swallow before he burst out laughing, pointed at me, and told his wife, who was the other instructor, "HE SAID HE IS NOT A TOILET!"

It was a long week in Swahili class. But at the end of it, that instructor called me a mzee, which he told me means elder, and to which he quickly added, "I know this is an insult to white people, but Africans like to be called elders; it means that we are beginning to be respected." I chose to feel honored by his words, in part because I now realized that when I return to the States and get lip from younger friends about how old I am, I will have a retort.

—

The good news was that we received eight more large boxes of toys in the middle of April. The bad news was that the customs officials in Nairobi called to tell us they couldn't release the shipment to us until we paid them a fee of thirty-five thousand shillings (about five hundred dollars US). I knew they just wanted a bribe, so we began to negotiate. It got pretty fierce.

Customs: You will pay thirty-five thousand shillings.

Me: These are donated toys, given to orphans free of charge. And you want to charge me thirty-five thousand shillings?

Customs: Yes.

Me: Send them back.

Customs: Send them back?

Me: If you aren't going to clear them, SEND THEM BACK.

Customs: Okay, twenty-nine thousand.

Me: SEND THEM BACK. And by the way, I am writing a letter to *The Nation* newspaper about what you are doing. HOW DO I SPELL YOUR NAME?

Customs: What will you pay?

Me: ONE THOUSAND SHILLINGS. NO MORE.

Customs: We will send them back.

Me: DO IT.

Customs: Fifteen thousand.

Me: I said I will pay only ONE THOUSAND!

Customs: Will you pay 2,100?

Me: Okay.

Even though I had all the necessary, signed documentation from the hospital, the school, and the orphanages involved, even before I talked to customs, I still had to negotiate the bribe down from five hundred dollars to thirty dollars. That's the price of business as usual in Kenya, and the ugly underside of so much government in Africa, where too many public officials routinely use their power to their own advantage. If a few orphans didn't get toys? Tough. And that attitude made me spitting mad.

—

A lot of experiences and realities still caught me by surprise, even after nine months in Africa. Some make you stop and realize what a slow learner you are, a few irritate the stuffing out of you, but most of the time you just have to shake your head and accept the fact that things are different here. Here are a few reminders of that fact from a few of my surprising experiences that April:

The butcher came by one Saturday when I was the only one home, so I received our order. As I took the meat and carried it into the kitchen, I noticed how warm the package was, which was a surprise, since it was a cool day. Then it struck me: the butcher's shop has no electricity and no refrigeration, so as soon as the animal is killed, he must deliver the meat. It cured me from ever ordering anything rare.

Someone gave us a subscription to *Time* magazine when we left the States the previous July. We had received five copies of it to date. In Kenya, magazines were routinely stolen out of the mail and sold on the streets. There was a guy at RVA who subscribed to a woodworking magazine. Driving into town one day, he saw someone hawking the latest issue of his favorite periodical. Since he hadn't received his for several months, he stopped and bought the copy, only to find his own name and address on the subscription sticker affixed to the back of the magazine. Another friend received a box of chocolates in the mail from her fiancé back in America. When she opened it, she found tooth marks in the candy.

This whole matter of "mailfeasance" became a personal Peifer issue when we learned a check JT's grandfather had sent him for his birthday had been stolen and the amount changed to say twenty-five hundred dollars—quite a difference from the twenty-five dollars it had been originally. Fortunately, the bank caught it, and there won't be any charge to Papa. But imagine the challenges of doing business in a country where the mail is not secure. It is sad, and incredibly frustrating. But what's even worse is the government's official response when confronted by a recent newspaper expose about the scandalous amount of lost and stolen mail. They simply shrugged and said, "It could be a lot worse."

In my next email home, I listed a few other *different* things from my Kenyan experience that probably wouldn't happen in the United States:

• *A friend is buying a car and is having it delivered to his home. The car does not arrive when promised. He finds out it was damaged when it ran into a giraffe.*

• *Some Kenyans are talking to a medical doctor from the States. They ask him about his wife, and he informs them he is single. They are shocked by this, since he is still a young man. He asks why. Their response: "Your bottom is too big for a single man."*

• *I am wandering around a craft fair when a guard hands me a brochure for the event. Since this is the third time the same guard has tried to give me the same brochure, I hold up the first brochure and tell him, "You already gave me one!" He smiles at me and says, "Sorry, it is because you are white. You all look alike to me." This is at least the third time a Kenyan has said that to me.*

• *We buy our eggs from a gentleman who goes door-to-door delivering them. They are good and fresh, but they are very brown. How do you dye a brown Easter egg?*

• *We didn't hide any eggs outside the night before Easter because we didn't want the baboons to get them.*

As I keep learning, a lot of things are different here!

But I closed that same email on a couple of different, and more serious, notes:

You may have read about the recent bombings in Sudan. We have friends who work in a hospital there; they and their medical facilities are targets because it is a Christian hospital in a Muslim area, which for some reason is enough to convince at least one group of Islamic radicals that blowing up the only hospital in hundreds of miles would be a neat idea. Leaders of the Western mission that founded and still staffs that hospital have been talking about evacuating the personnel, because conditions in the country have deteriorated over recent months. After a bomb went off less than a thousand yards from the hospital last week, the mission strongly suggested their people consider leaving. The hospital staff, almost to the person, declined the offer. They say they want to stay and help, because they know if they leave, there will be no one there to help or provide much-needed medical care to tens of thousands of desperate Sudanese people.

After hearing about their story, I read a quote just this week about a young kid who was killed in World War I. When his journal was found, one of his last entries said, "I will work, I will sacrifice, I will endure, I will fight cheerfully, and do my utmost, as if the issue of the whole struggle depended on me alone."

I know I will never be asked to fight or face death, like that young soldier, on a military battlefield. Nor will I ever serve as a medical professional in the midst of a brutal civil war. But I want to live my life like they do. With that kind of commitment. Whether I am in Kenya, or Grapevine, Texas.

—

And finally I reported to those family and friends whose support and prayers had enabled us to spend a sabbatical year living and healing in Kenya:

We went to the hospital today and saw the usual sad cases. We have seen the most brutal things in Africa. There is so much poverty, so much illness, so much despera-tion. And when you leave home for a year, you find out who your friends are, and who they aren't. That too is a hard thing to see. The economic cost has been great, the effort rewarding, and yet you have so many goals you realize you won't achieve in your last few months.

But a little boy in the children's ward today just couldn't stop grinning at the truck you gave him, and his father's eyes filled with tears. A little girl got her first baby doll, and promised me she would take very, very good care of her. Then, as we left the hospital, Matthew told me, "Dad, I know this will sound crazy, but every time I go to the hospital and play with those kids, I feel like I'm changing the whole world."

No, it has not been an easy year, but it has been worth it all.

11

Flying Ants and SATs

BEFORE THE SECOND TERM BEGAN BACK IN JANUARY, I HAD RECONFIGURED all the computers in my Titchie School classroom. I had cleaned them, updated the operating systems, and installed a bundle of new programs. In contrast to the trepidation with which I'd approached my initiation into the unknown world of education at the start of the school year, I felt calm, collected, and confident. I was more than ready for round two—long before the students arrived back on campus after their Christmas break.

A day or two prior to the resumption of classes, my principal walked by the computer lab. I was standing in the middle of the room, admiring all my handiwork and feeling rather proud, prepared, and almost professional. A kindly, gentle, soft-spoken man, Don Schuit stepped into the room to ask how things were going. I gave him a quick rundown on all that I'd done in that classroom over break, and assured him that both his elementary school computer lab and I were up to snuff and ready to go for term two. Don nodded and surveyed the room before gently suggesting, "I think perhaps you may have forgotten something." I asked him what. He motioned toward one of the classroom walls and said, "I think it's probably time you change the bulletin board."

I started to remind Mr. Schuit that it wasn't *my* board; I'd inherited it as is from the teacher who'd taught in that classroom the previous year. I hadn't referenced the bulletin board one time during the first term. I wasn't personally into bulletin boards, and frankly, I thought they were too old school for a computer lab anyway. But I realized he was well aware of all that.

So I kept my mouth shut and hurriedly put together a new bulletin board before classes started the next day. But I confess I paid no more attention to it that second term than I had during the first.

One day near the end of our April break, Mr. Schuit again dropped by the computer lab for a little visit. He began the conversation in his usual, kind, gentle, tactful, and affirming manner: "Thanks for changing the bulletin board last term, Steve."

I just knew there was a *but* coming. I was wrong. *However* was the word he used as he turned his gaze from me toward *my* bulletin board: "Black-and-white advertisements for Arthur Anderson Accounting culled from a *Wall Street Journal* issue on ecommerce are *probably* not age-appropriate for first grade children."

He *probably* had a point. He clearly expected yet another new bulletin board for this third term.

I don't know if you have ever tried to create a classroom bulletin board that an educator with a twenty-three-year career as an elementary school principal would deem appropriate for kids in kindergarten through sixth grade. That is much harder than it looks.

I found some tattered old magazines from 1991 that still had most of their pages with photos intact. I tore out a stack of pictures and cut apart a big bunch of headlines so that I could mix and match the words and visual artwork to create—*ta-da*—an exceedingly eclectic and (hopefully) *acceptable* educational masterpiece.

I felt a little disappointed about my students' lack of response to my efforts; I'm not sure they even noticed the change. But my handiwork clearly made an impression on my professional colleagues. One afternoon at the end of the first week of classes, a teacher with a classroom at the other end of the building came by after school and stuck her head in the computer lab to get a look at what evidently had become the talk of the teachers' lounge. I invited her into my room so she could get the full effect. She promptly burst out laughing. "I always thought *my* bulletin board skills were weak!" she informed me. "Thanks, Steve!" She exited the room laughing gleefully.

There was a time (okay, lots of times) earlier in my life when I would have been embarrassed, insulted, and perhaps even infuriated by that. However, I chose to see this experience from a different, more mature perspective. I knew I wasn't and never would be a real teacher, but I found consolation in knowing I could still be a real source of encouragement to those who are.

~

I decided to start my first email of our last term in the RVA school year with something of an apology to the folks back home:

I've been a rude host—please forgive me. I've not properly introduced you to the Dorm Boys, but I can do a much better job of doing so now than I could have earlier, since I've slowly been getting to know them myself all year:

• Joseph Kim, aka Eating Machine: Joseph is a Korean who is quiet, a good athlete, a diligent student, and great on the clarinet. His nickname is due to the determination displayed during mealtimes—he puts his head down and shovels. I have seen champion eaters in my time, and I would put him against all comers.

• Seth Shaffer, aka Tarzan: Seth is an American from Michigan who has a great smile, natural athletic talent, and the ability to walk on his knuckles—hence the nickname. Tarzan is, of course, the favorite movie of this fifth grade boy's dorm. And Seth has gone the farthest in his emulation of their hero.

• Joo-Young, aka Tan Man: Joo-Young is another Korean, a gifted student, a terrific singer, and the kind of kid who thoroughly enjoys sports, without any athletic gifting. He earned his moniker for the incredible effects he achieved evidently spending his entire spring break lying out in the sun.

• Gun-Woo, aka Basketball Jones: Gun-Woo (pronounced Gun-new) is a Korean who loves junk food, sports, and seems to be the first and only one of our prepubescent charges to be aware that not all girls have cooties. An interesting combination of kindhearted and mischievous. Struggles with his English, but understands much more than he can say. So he tends to speak in one-word sentences, often quite effectively. Some of the other guys were giving him a hard time one day recently; he came running to me enraged and just shouted, with eloquent expression, "Teasing!"

• Joey Speichinger, aka French Toast: Although Joseph is the eating machine, he defers to Joey as French Toast, who, even though he is the youngest and shortest of our boys, has no match when it comes to consuming FT. Seth has a great smile, but Joey has the ultimate smile. He is also one of those kids who has to pause and think when you ask him, "Where are you from?" Because he's lived in Africa longer than he has in the US, that simple question doesn't have a simple answer for Joey. He is the epitome of what many educators and child psychologists have started referring to not as MKs but as third-culture kids.

• Dae Han, aka Mystery Man: Dae Han, another Korean, is a master politician, or a master manipulator, depending on the day. Capable of strolling into a room where three guys are wrapped up in a quilt, yelling, "I've got dibs on the blanket," and somehow ending up with it a few minutes later. Earned the Mystery Man moniker for making a habit of hiding when it's time to go to bed. He's also convinced that Michael Jordan will be the next US president.

• Daniel Orner, aka Lego Man Dan: An American who is perhaps the brightest

and hardest working of all our boys. Named LMD for his talent at tuning out the entire world when working on Legos. Uncanny ability to turn any and every conversation toward himself and his own personal experiences; i.e. three of the Korean guys were talking about their homeland when Dan walked up to join in and immediately hijacked the conversation by saying, "I've never been to Korea," and promptly proceeded to list all the places he has never been.

• *Manraj Brar, aka Fast Feet. An Indian, he likes to ride his bike and is an excellent math student. Known for being able to run down the stairs so rapidly that the whole house shakes.*

• *Alfred Aseka, aka Batman: New to our dorm this term, Alfred is a Kenyan who is also a great singer, a good basketball player, and sharp on the computer. Alfred has been with us only for a week, so we are still getting to know him.*

• *And then there is Jessie, aka the codependent dog: The dorm's only female, other than Nancy, of course, Jessie started out as JT's dog and for a time followed him everywhere on campus. Including to his classes. Until we made it his responsibility to regularly groom and bathe her. The fickle canine so despises water (except evidently and inexplicably in the form of baptismal pools) that she immediately transferred all of her allegiance to me and has followed me constantly ever since. To the point where, if I don't lock the bathroom door behind me, she will manage to get the door open, then lie on the floor to watch and wait while I am using the facilities.*

―

When Nancy and I volunteered to be dorm parents at a boarding school for missionary kids in Africa for a year, we had no idea what we were getting ourselves into, or what it would be like to live with a bunch of ten-year-old boys. We thought our experience with our own two sons, JT even being the age of the other dorm boys, would serve us well in the role. After ten years of boy-raising, Nancy and I felt we'd developed a pretty effective tag-team parenting routine. Two of *us* more than equaled two of *them*.

Two-on-ten proved a different equation. But it certainly made life interesting.

One room had the following nightly ritual throughout much of the third term:

Me: Goodnight. *(leave, turn off light, close door)*
              Five minutes later:
Them 1: Shut up! Uncle Steve will hear you.
Them 2: But watch my flashlight blow up your dresser.
Them 3: SHUT UP! HE'LL HEAR YOU.

Them 1: WHAT?

Them 2 & 3: SHUT UP! HE'LL HEAR YOU!

Them 1: HEY! I'M NOT THE ONE YELLING!

Me: *(opening door)* Goodnight. *(leave, turn off light, close door)*
Repeat

You gotta love fifth grade guys, even when they make you wonder how they can twist and turn ordinary dorm life into an alternate reality of their own creation. As happened one night when one of the guys in another room asked me about who ran against President Clinton back in 1996. (I have no idea why.) So I told them about Bob Dole and how he was wounded during World War II. I told them I had shaken his hand once and that he'd extended the left hand upside down because of his injury. And I demonstrated how he did it.

When I put the guys to bed, I always shook their hands as I bid them each goodnight. But from that evening on, the guys in this particular room insisted on shaking hands like Mr. Dole does. So every night, when I extended my right hand to say goodnight, they each said, "Bob Dole," (as if introducing themselves) and extended their left hands turned backward and upside down to grasp mine.

Night. After. Night. After. Night. As if I was caught in some kind of a crazy time warp, like in the movie *Groundhog Day*. No matter how many different things happened during my day, every night Bob Dole reappeared to cast a rather strange shadow over my reality. I'm not superstitious, but I could take that to mean only one thing: six more weeks and silliness season would be over, just about the time school let out and we headed home to Texas.

Our time in Africa was growing short.

—

Something interesting happens when you find yourself living in a different culture, in a foreign country, on another continent, half a world away from any member of your family, every friend you've ever had, any familiar face you've ever known. It tends to give you a new, deeper appreciation of the value and character of your human relationships. You miss those relationships you left behind, and you begin new ones to fill that void and meet the universal need we have as relational beings. Living in a place where new relationships are the only kind you can hope to have, hospitality also plays a bigger, richer role in your life—both the receiving and the sharing of it—than it ever did back home.

We had three new friends visit us in our home at Rift Valley Academy the early part of our third term there. Our paths probably never would have crossed back in America. If they had, we might never have thought we had enough in common to pursue a friendship. But each of those good folks impacted and challenged me to look at life and its meaning in a fresh and different way.

Stacy was a young nurse who, because of health issues, could not get approval from her sending agency to come to Africa as a full-time missionary. She had arthritis, asthma, and a host of other serious problems. But she kept applying, pleading, and pressing her case until she persuaded the organization and its board to allow her to do a three-month volunteer stint in Kenya. Since she'd arrived in country, Stacy had bounced (often literally) all over Kenya, taking health care out into the bush and working under the most primitive and grueling conditions to provide basic yet life-saving medical treatment for desperately poor and needy people. But in doing so, she endured great pain herself.

When you realized what the experience was costing her—physically and emotionally, as well as financially—you couldn't help wondering, *Why in the world would anyone put themselves through that?* But the answer to that question was as clear as her motivation. She loved God so much that she wanted to serve him by helping and loving other hurting people in any way she could.

Another couple, Ron and Rhonda, had arrived only months before. In their short time in Kenya, they both had been seriously ill, had many of their possessions stolen, and struggled to adjust from small-town life in the American Midwest to the unimaginable poverty and urban sprawl of Nairobi and its huddled masses of multimillions. Yet both Rhonda and Ron had maintained the most amazing attitude through all that had happened to them. They too just wanted to demonstrate and share the love of God by helping meet the basic needs of others.

These three new friends helped me, giving me new insight into myself. After their visits, I admitted to Nancy that I used to struggle to relate to people like Stacy, Rhonda, and Ron. Probably because I had envied the strength of their commitment. But during our sojourn in Africa, I was beginning to understand the role that people like them, and so many of our colleagues at RVA, could and should play in my life. I need people around me who are already living at the next level, to remind me who and where I want to be. For too much of life, my goal had been to get to, and be on, the top. But that didn't really matter anymore. Now I just wanted to keep climbing.

—

Have you ever made a really stupid promise to your kids? Well, that's what I did. And I'll get to the gory details soon enough. I always hate to give away the crucial plot twist of a story too soon. But I'm hoping the title of an email I sent home in early May of 2000 will intrigue you enough to read the whole story: "Eating Flying Ants: A Gourmet's Guide."

Kenya is the only place I have lived where I could see dust clouds in the middle of a downpour. It has finally started raining here, and the children at RVA and around Kijabe have been running outside rejoicing. If you have never been in a place where life and death depend on rain, count it as a wonderful blessing.

The other side of rain is that it brings out the flying ants. My really stupid promise was to tell my dorm kids that if they caught and cooked it, I would eat one of these supposedly edible delicacies, and tonight I did. The boys caught many of them, fried them to a crisp in oil, and the countdown began. "Three, two, one; eat it, Uncle Steve!" It was tasty enough to eat another. And like many dreaded things in life, the anticipation was worse than the reality (or unreality). Although, when we get the pictures back and you see the look on Nancy's face as she ate one, you might not believe me.

—

What is your worst memory of high school? For me, taking the SAT is in my top ten.

One Saturday in May, RVA administered the SAT on campus, and I was recruited to be a proctor. I was instructed to "just walk the aisles and look grim," which I have never found to be a hard thing to do when hanging around high school juniors. The fear in the room before the exam felt almost solid enough to reach out and touch. The power of this test to impact their lives made normally confident kids nearly quiver in their seats. But once the test began, you could see a physical and emotional change pass through the kids when they suddenly realized, "Hey, I know this stuff." By the end of the test, some of them were practically strutting in their chairs, which seems hard to do and probably would hurt a guy my age to try.

Some aspects of high school life at Rift Valley Academy, such as the dreaded SAT, are not that much different from what kids might experience in any high school back in the States. But there are also a lot of distinct differences. Five hundred students were enrolled at RVA that year. But because it is a boarding situation, faculty and staff get to know them in a way that is much different than in most other places. Some of the differences are fun and add to the experience; an intramural basketball game where you know all the kids playing takes on a different dimension. When one of the kids got accepted at a big college in the States, it was a victory for all of us.

But the other side of it is that you see many deep and private hurts that kids can often hide in a less intimate setting. When senior girls didn't get invited to the senior banquet, there was no mistaking the disappointment and pain on their faces. I saw a kid who practiced every day for months still not make the varsity rugby team, and his sadness was palpable. Those kinds of things happen everywhere, I know. But you notice them and feel them so much more when everyone is living on campus and you're with those kids all day long.

For a lot of students at RVA whose passports say their home is the United States but who've lived much more of their lives in Africa than in America, the specter of graduation looming in the near future foretells a different and more difficult rite of passage than it did for most of us. Yes, it is an anticipated milestone, marking an exciting entry point onto the road to adulthood, a cherished memory you will share with your best friends in life. But an RVA graduation also promises to be as much an ending as a beginning—a sudden, painful, perhaps even permanent parting of ways. Many of our seniors had boarded since sixth grade; by May of their final term, they were all aware that in a couple of months, they would graduate and leave not only high school but also Africa as they headed off for college, some of them never to return.

When I graduated from high school in suburban Chicagoland, I knew my circle of friends and everyone we'd gone to school with would all still be living in the same town the next day. When kids graduate from Rift Valley Academy, they and their families head for the airport and scatter around the world the next day. They will be lucky if their best friends end up living in the same country or even on the same continent they do.

How do you deal with that reality when you are eighteen years old?

I was confident these great kids would find the grace and strength they needed to do it, because they were some of the brightest, most well-adjusted young people I had ever known. Still, I wished I could somehow make what was coming better, or at least easier, for them. Yet I knew I couldn't.

12

Broccoli and Carnivore Parties, Hold the Donkey Meat

AS WE APPROACHED THE END OF OUR YEAR OF SERVICE IN KENYA, I surprised myself with the realization that teaching spreadsheets to elementary school children at RVA had been one of the most unexpectedly rewarding things I had ever done. It certainly hadn't started out well the previous September. I hadn't known how to communicate even basic principles of computer technology to first through third graders.

The challenge of my IT work for the school's business department had been interesting and fun. I'd even enjoyed my high school students and my role as their driver's ed instructor, in a strange, masochistic sort of way.

But I had truly dreaded classes with my youngest computer students.

I've known many people who are gifted at working with young children. A number of them teach at RVA. I never was in that number. I tried. I tried just about anything over the course of that school year. Don't forget my creative use of empathy, negative encouragement, and bunny hops. (I never will.) But as anyone who has taught elementary school (or been a parent) knows, kids can be frustrating. Fortunately, they can be cute and funny enough to make up for that—sometimes. Like the second grader who insisted, "Mr. Peifer, there is no *S* on my computer." When I showed it to her, she exclaimed, "How did *that* get there?"

But the day I introduced spreadsheets to second and third graders was not a bit funny. It may have been my most discouraging day ever as a would-be teacher. I no sooner mentioned the concepts of columns and cells than these energetic kids, who'd practically bounced in and ricocheted around the lab before the bell rang to start class, instantly took on this zombie look.

For the longest time, no teaching technique I tried seemed to work with my youngest students. Until I finally learned to reach them the way I taught my friend Fred, the young Kenyan man who had chopped our firewood and done other odd jobs for us in and around our dorm and yard all year. Fred had never lived in a home with electricity. Just turning on the computer was a frightening thing for him at the beginning. If I could make the technology make sense for Fred, maybe I could translate it for these young missionary kids.

I'm sure it took me more time than it would have taken a real teacher. But within the first couple of months after I started working with him in the computer lab, Fred was keeping track of his paycheck on a ClarisWorks spreadsheet. He had never before had a savings account; he didn't know what one was. I explained it to him and promised to start a matching gift account (whatever amount he could save, we would match), starting as soon as he learned how to set it up as a spreadsheet with a formula. He figured it out in a day. And by those last months of the school year, Fred had accumulated, by Kenyan standards, a sizeable savings account.

The first principle I'd learned with Fred was the importance of starting at ground zero. We moved on to something new only when I got the "all clear" and knew he'd mastered the most recent material. We picked up speed only after Fred started pushing for more. In surprisingly short order, Fred could load software, reformat drives, and even help kids in my youngest computer classes print their reports. He soon gained confidence with computers and regularly surprised me with the things he was learning about them.

I had been so encouraged by my success with Fred that I tried spreadsheets again that last term with my younger students. I discovered that those same principles worked with them; the results were gratifying. I have won million-dollar accounts before in my corporate career, but watching third graders high-five each other because they learned how to sort on a spreadsheet was every bit as satisfying.

Most of the days that school was in session, I kept the computer lab open for the kids during the lunch hour. By spring term, I routinely left Fred in charge. One day nearing the end of the school year, when I stopped by to check on it, nine students were in the lab playing with spreadsheets, some of them using the program for purposes I doubt any software creator ever could have imagined—like the Baboon Sighting spreadsheet, complete with times, dates, head counts, and sizes. And there was Fred, leaning over a computer terminal in the middle of the lab, helping one of the kids with a problem.

I slipped out of the room before they noticed me. I didn't want anyone to see me cry.

—

At the beginning of our final term, the school administrators had split my fifth grade computer class between girls and boys; they were doing a health section and did not want the kids to giggle during it. This inspired me to set up an interesting competition of my own to see if we could discover the difference between girls and boys (so to speak) in computer skill. Each class had to do a series of problems with database, spreadsheet, and typing trials. I announced that the winning group would get a year-end ice-cream party.

The losers would get a *broccoli* party.

For sheer motivation, I don't know that I have ever seen anything (not even bunny hops) that works quite as well as broccoli. When one kid exclaimed, "Do we have to *eat* it?" I answered, "Buckets and buckets worth." Even the thrill of the end of the year cannot equal the horror of broccoli to preadolescent children. So I got unprecedented focus and tremendous results from them all term.

I used a different motivation with Fred. I had been trying to teach him how to type all year, and he'd kept telling me he would never get it. I finally told him he was probably right, but if he could manage to type just twenty words a minute before I went back to America at the end of that term, I would give him a cash bonus. He was soon typing fifty-five words per minute.

—

But no matter how much progress I felt I was making with my students, or how well I felt I was learning and adapting as a teacher in Kenya, challenging cross-cultural moments had a way of popping up when I least expected them.

For example, as an end-of-the-school-year project to show what they'd learned, my first graders created a slide show on the computer. I asked them to make pictures of their parents, their pets, their teacher, and so forth. Then I suggested they draw the seasons.

Them: Which one is the cold one?
Me: What do you mean?
Them: Which season is the one that gets cold?
Me: Winter.
Them: Which one is the dry one?

Then it hit me: Kenya, straddling the equator as it does, has a wet season and a dry season. There is no winter and no real change of seasons as North Americans count them. And since most of my first graders had lived in Africa the better part of their lives, winter was a foreign concept, which led to some interesting pictures.

—

I'd had a few cross-cultural challenges of my own over the years. And as I confessed in one of my emails home in May, before that year in Africa, *I have always felt a measure of disdain when people from another culture could not figure out American football in ten minutes. It seemed so easy to me that I figured any ongoing confusion suggested a lack of moral character. At least I felt that way until yesterday, when I watched my very first rugby match between RVA and another nearby school.*

The game made no sense to me at all. Someone next to me tried to explain it, but I kept trying to understand it in the context of football, so the more he talked, the more confused and lost I got. Evidently the solution was to quit trying so hard to understand it and just give myself over to the brutality of the sport. When I did that, I can honestly say, although I still didn't quite get it, and some of it just looked like doggy-piling, I kinda enjoyed it. But it did make me wish I could watch the Cubs play a doubleheader instead. And I am sure that by the time we get home the end of July, they will have sewed up the division race and be ready to roll through the postseason as they go on to win the World Series in four games and then begin a dynasty that . . .

(Sorry! I got off the track there.)

I do think that from now on I will have more grace for people who don't get football and baseball. And I will work to understand the finer points of rugby. But this multi-culturalism business has its limits: there is no Wrigley Field in Africa.

On another note: the Economist *magazine came out this week, and it was depressing to all of us here. Maybe you saw the cover story: "Africa — The Hopeless Continent." It identified and addressed a number of the problems here. Many of them are getting worse and worse: poverty, AIDS, corruption, tribalism. I could write for a week. But the more I've thought about it, the more I am grateful to be in a place where the intellectuals and the capitalists have given up. Because that means the truth is clear: there is only one Hope. And when Africa turns around, it won't be the intellectuals and the capitalists who will get the credit.*

I gave a black Barbie to a little girl in a wheelchair at the hospital this morning. She had casts on both feet, and she was so excited, she clicked her casts together. She made the doll walk, then turned to me, and said, "I will walk like her someday."

So will Africa, I pray.

—

Not only did I wish Africa well, I wished the people of Africa well, one person at a time, as I continued to put my Swahili to good use. The greeting,

"Hello, how are you?" in Swahili is "Habari yako?" (Hah–BAR–ee YAH–ko). The most common response to that is, "Mzuri sana" (Mah–ZUR–ee SAH–nah), which I assume means something close to "Very well" or "Very fine," another boring everyday exchange that to me seemed somehow unworthy of a language as exotic and beautiful as Swahili. Which was why, by the third term, I'd gotten to the point that whenever I encountered Kenyans on the RVA campus, I sang them my greetings to the tune of the *Hallelujah Chorus*:

> Habari yako
> Habari yako
> Habari yako, habari yako
> Habari yako!

When I first started this creative cross-cultural custom, I got rather piercing stares. But by that third term (perhaps I'd learned more in my April Swahili class than I or my teacher had thought), it was becoming common to have Kenyans respond by singing:

> Mzuri sana
> Mzuri sana
> Mzuri sana, mzuri sana
> Mzuri sana!

No matter how well I was adapting to cross-cultural living (or *not*), I couldn't help being startled from time to time by the constant reminders that I was in Africa. Like the headline I spotted in a Kenyan newspaper one day in May. And I promise you that I am not making this up: "Alert As Police Seize More Donkey Meat."

Authorities had discovered that someone was selling donkey meat all over Nairobi. It was illegal to sell donkey meat and call it beef, because donkey meat was not inspected. I doubt that could ever happen in America; there is no doubt it happens often in Kenya. The only question is how often.

———

How do you celebrate your bride's birthday in Africa? Even in rural Kenya, there was one tradition that I determined not to deviate from—the annual birthday cheesecake.

I venture to bake only once a year, so the pressure is always on. Will this cheesecake slope to the right? Will it somehow be crunchy like the famous 1990 model?

This year (2000) we had a new and unique variable: Grace, our cook and house-helper, was in the kitchen watching. Kenyan men, at least in the Kikuyu tribe, do not cook. So she was amazed and amused that I was attempting to bake. And Grace hates cheese (you would too if Kenyan cheese was the only cheese you had eaten), which made her doubly skeptical that my efforts might result in an edible treat.

If I do say so myself, the cheesecake came out fine. I found even greater satisfaction in the fact that Grace agreed to taste a small bite and exclaimed in shock, "IS GOOOOOD!" I don't know if it was my culinary prowess or the cheese that surprised her the most, but I take what I can get.

Celebrating Nancy's birthday with nine adopted dorm sons was also interesting. They made her cards and asked her to reveal her age. When she told them, they exclaimed in such loud unison and disbelief, "FORTY-THREE?" that I am sure she will cherish the memory forever.

The following weekend, Nancy and I and our two boys went with some good friends who share a birthday to the Carnivore, a popular Nairobi restaurant famous for its menu boasting enough different game to please the palate of any hungry meat-eater. You pay one price, and the waiters keep bringing platters around until you raise the surrender flag on the table to indicate that you have given up and can eat no more. JT was determined to eat as much as our friends' seventeen-year-old, six-foot-four-and-still-growing son. And while he fell short of achieving that goal, JT had that teenager worried for a while. And Matthew nearly kept pace, which struck fear in this father's heart as I imagined future food bills as my boys got older.

Among the different meats offered that evening were ostrich, zebra, impala, and crocodile. They were all quite good, although Kenya needs a little help with its barbeque sauce. And the evening finale was amazing. I've heard a lot of different renditions of "Happy Birthday" sung in restaurants over the years. But nothing like this. With the addition of African drums, our Carnivore waiters gave "Happy Birthday" a beat it has never achieved in the States.

—

I worked all that year with a guy in the business office who had arrived in Kenya about the same time we did and did a remarkable job working on our systems. He was an accountant and a programmer, and had a real "let's fix it" attitude. Duane was fifty-nine, and back in the States he had been the manager of information services for a major international hotel chain. He could have commanded big bucks in retirement as a consultant. Instead he came to work at RVA.

But what impressed me most about him was finding out that he visited the junior high boys' dorm at least one evening every week to give their dorm parents a break, and to reach out to kids who were struggling being boarding students. With all due respect to Duane, he may have been the least likely guy on that campus to relate to junior high kids. With more due respect to my programming and accounting friends, people skills are not always the words that spring to mind when you think of those professions.

But in his own way, Duane was reaching out and making friends with kids who aren't the easiest to reach. And watching him do it convicted me; I was struck by the realization that all too often in life, I wait until I think all conditions are right before I try to help someone, and I often lose the opportunity. Duane didn't wait until he was cool; he just tried. And as much as his work ethic and computer skills had impressed me, his determination to try to help impacted me the most, and made me want to change the way I am.

I had read lots of magazine stories and books about people who do brave and heroic things. But Duane helped me realize that stepping out of your comfort zone sometimes is the most courageous thing of all. I usually miss stuff like that because I don't pay attention; I'm glad I got to see it this time. I wish you could meet Duane; he was a true inspiration to me.

—

Speaking of comfort zones, Africa had a way of forcing me out of mine. Only to discover that in some cases my comfort zone proved to be bigger than I'd thought. As in this case I wrote home about just a few weeks before our scheduled return home:

Did you ever have a dream that you didn't even know you had until it came true? When I was in high school, I had a gym teacher who began every class period with the command, "Line up, maggots!"

RVA is a kind of place where you might be asked to do different things at different times. As our time here draws to an end, I have come to a place where I have been asked to use my special skills in a unique way.

I am now a gym teacher. And I am teaching badminton.

I have friends from the adolescent era of my life who read those two previous sentences and are now wiping off their screens because they just spit tea at their monitors, because they recall my athletic ability. Add to that the fact that I have not played the sport ... game ... whatever ... of badminton in twenty-five years, and you have a recipe for excellence unmatched by anything I have previously attempted here in Africa.

But after the first day of teaching PE, what startled me most about the experience was how easily and how naturally "Line up, maggots!" came back to me. It was then

I realized that I had always wanted to yell "Line up, maggots!" at a group of impressionable young people. And now I had the opportunity.

⁓

The previous year, on our fourteenth wedding anniversary, I had taken Nancy to the vending machine at the dorm we stayed in during orientation school just weeks before we'd left for Africa. And I'd told her, "Honey, anything you want here you can have." We'd had meetings morning, noon, and night, and we had no opportunity to do anything else. But on our fifteenth anniversary, I felt I ought to do something even *more* special. So with the help of some friends who agreed to stay at our dorm, we booked a weekend getaway to the Mount Kenya Safari Club. Normally, there would be little chance we could afford such a special place. Prices were high and, especially as a missionary, you don't usually have extra money. But because we were in Kenya for a year, we were considered legal residents, which qualified us for residential rates that were only a sixth of what tourists pay.

American actor William Holden founded the MKSC in 1959, and it is lovely, with beautiful gardens, wild forests, and spectacular views right at the foot of Mount Kenya. Some friends we went with were birders, and they spotted more than seventy different species. MKSC has an animal orphanage, and we fed ostriches, monkeys, golden crested cranes, and bongos out of our hands. At one point, a monkey was leaning on Nan and holding her hand to get more food. He later jumped on the back of a 125-year-old tortoise named Speedy, no doubt planning to ride off into the sunset, if only the sun wouldn't set for another, oh, say, 125 years.

We visited a nearby game park one afternoon, where we watched a herd of elephants wander to a water hole to drink and bathe, toured a chimp conservatory started by Jane Goodall, and petted a live rhinoceros. A poacher had orphaned this rhino when he was six months old, so he had lived around humans his whole life and was considered tame. To reach him, we walked about a mile through a forest and then out onto an open grassland where we suddenly found ourselves standing in front of a one-and-a-half-ton rhinoceros. He seemed a lot like a big dog; he ate out of our hands and let us pet him. It was one of those experiences you never expect to have in life.

A guard with a large caliber rifle attends this rhino twenty-four hours a day because poachers are such a problem in Kenya. As our guide told us, "We shoot first, and then ask questions." Africa's rhino and elephant populations have been decimated by poachers for their horns and tusks in recent decades.

And if the economy continues to deteriorate, many fear the poaching will get worse.

As I wrote friends and family after that weekend outing, *I never expected to celebrate fifteen years of marriage in Africa, but it will be an anniversary we will never forget. The secret of a happy marriage is to marry Nancy Peifer. Since she is already taken, I wish for you that you would experience all the joys of the covenant that I have. It has been a rich and wonderful fifteen years.*

I think we both felt the fifteenth year had been one of the richest and most wonderful yet.

13

This Close to a Clean Getaway

THE CLOSER WE GOT TO OUR TIME TO HEAD HOME, THE MORE WE reflected on the memories and experiences of what had been a life-changing year for our family. As I began to do that, I realized the biggest reason our African adventure had been such a great one for me was that I had Nancy there, sharing it with me.

I know I've already talked about Nancy and our boys quite a bit (though not nearly as much as I should have). But at this point in the Peifer family saga, it strikes me that you haven't heard enough of her voice to know that I'm not exaggerating when I tell you what a beautiful, smart, loving, thoughtful, and spiritually sensitive woman my wife truly is. So I decided to let you hear, in Nancy's own words, how she summarized our African year in the last weekly report she sent to all the family, friends, and supporters on our email list just a couple of weeks before the end of our third and final term.

7/4/2000—How do you sum up a year like this?

I don't even know where to start! In some ways, I feel like a teenage boy who grew eight inches in one year and nothing fits anymore. I've seen so much that I've never seen before. I've done so many things that I've never done before. And some that I didn't think I could do. I've changed many of my ideas about myself, my family, my country, the world, and God. So how exactly do I summarize all this?

I'll start with God. I have encountered him as bigger than ever by seeing, firsthand, more of his incredible creation. The awesome grandeur of the Rift Valley and Mount Kenya, the beauty of calla lilies that grow wild here, the humor and even absurdity of some animals—like the marabou stork and the warthog! I've understood more of God's fathomless love, care, and faithfulness by meeting people who have a fraction of what I have in tangible things, but twice what I have in faith in our heavenly Father, and who are not at all disappointed by life.

I've experienced more of God's forgiveness and grace (which is new every morning) when I come to him with a worn out, complaining spirit and find he doesn't turn me away. Instead, he supplies me with what I need from his abundance by allowing me to see others as he sees and loves them, and then by pouring his own love over and into me.

The world has become a lot smaller to me this year. Smaller and more personal. I now know people I can visit in Canada, England, Holland, Belgium, Kenya, Uganda, Tanzania, Zambia, South Africa, South Korea, and Congo (not to mention almost all of the fifty states).

People dying from famine here in Kenya have names and families. I've met people who care for refugees in southern Sudan at the risk of their own lives. I know people who live without running water or electricity, by choice, in order to serve others. Yes, it's much, much more personal. I see America as so incredibly blessed, and yet so ignorant of that fact. I was ignorant before this year. America has so much more than other countries do.

I was gratified to hear a Brit say she considered Americans very generous people. Then I had a Kenyan friend I buy baskets from teach me about true generosity. This woman is now the sole supporter of her family of seven children. A loving mother whose fourth-born had to drop out of school for lack of funds when the family couldn't come up with the fifteen dollars needed. Despite her own need, she gave me one of her handmade baskets as a going-away gift, to bless me. Because she knows there are worse things than being poor. It is far worse to be selfish.

My own family, both immediate and extended, has become dearer to me. Scarcely hearing the voice of my sister, father, nieces, and in-laws this past year has made me realize more fully the treasure they are to me. They love, encourage, give balance and perspective, hold me accountable — and are just plain fun. I've seen my husband and my children change and grow in ways that wouldn't have happened had we not come to Africa this past year. My boys have shouldered more responsibilities, borne inconvenience, and made do with a lot less "stuff," without complaint and with a great spirit of adventure.

My husband has grown in his gift of encouragement; his heart has been broken, in love, by the orphans and disadvantaged children here. He has become more and more the one who not only completes me but also helps me be more than I dreamed I could be. (And he recently whisked me off for a two-day, fifteenth-anniversary getaway in the highlands of Kenya, which will refresh us for years to come just by remembering it.)

And as for myself: God told me earlier this year that I should get out of the box I had created for myself. As I've attempted to do that, I've discovered that I can do a lot more than I thought I could! I feel like a kid again in some ways—the whole world lying ahead of me, full of boundless opportunities and adventures! Whatever God has in mind for my family and me, we can all say with our whole hearts, Yes!

So the next step of our adventure leads us back to America, back to Texas, back to Grapevine, back to home on Willowood Drive, but not back to the same old thing. Whatever God has in store for us there will be new and fresh and exciting. We look forward to continuing to share with all of you—our friends and family—all that is yet to come!

Thanks for sharing in this year with us. Thank you for your emails, cards, and letters, gifts, toys for the kids, prayers, financial support, and most of all your love and friendship. We pray that God will bless you with a relationship with himself, just as he has us. Jesus summed it up well when he said, "And this is eternal life, to know the Father, and Christ Jesus whom he has sent" (John 17:3).

Love to each of you, Nancy

After reading such beautiful and thoughtful reflections from my better half, you're going to be thinking she's my much, much better half when I tell you what I couldn't help doing during our last week of school at Rift Valley Academy.

Our final week of classes coincided with the school's annual alumni week, when grads return from all over the world to see relatives graduate, participate in class reunions, or just to visit the old campus for a few days. There seemed to be quite an attachment between RVA students and the campus that was not merely a school but a home to most of them for years. So it was easy to spot the visiting alumni.

Just for fun I would surreptitiously discover the name of an alum I'd never even met and then I'd walk right up to him or her, react with pleasure to see them, and exclaim something like this: "*Mike!* How the heck are you? How long has it been?" The reactions were pretty much what you'd expect: stuttering, stammering, and deep gazes trying to determine or remember who in the dickens I was. When I didn't blow it by laughing, I could string them along for a good long time.

A varsity versus alumni soccer game was scheduled. The halftime show was performed by the first through sixth graders, who marched onto the field, formed a wobbly RVA, and then played "When the Saints Go Marching In" on kazoos and recorders. It was pretty cute, and some in the crowd even recognized the tune without being told what it was.

The yearbooks also came out that week, a huge annual event at RVA. We all went into the main auditorium to see the unveiling. School tradition calls for each issue of the yearbook to be dedicated to a staff member or couple in an elaborate ceremony, which that year included flashing lights, rapping, and a skit to introduce the couple being honored. It was both hokey and touching and altogether uplifting and refreshing. And I walked back to the dorm after the program that night thinking this might be yet one more area where Africa has it over the States.

I was definitely approaching the last of our days in Kenya with many mixed emotions. But I knew things were stirring deeply within me when two of my badminton students put their arms around me and said, "Mr. Peifer, we're proud to be maggots."

—

I've heard lots of teachers, parents, and students make the sweeping claim that "no one learns anything on the last day of school." But I think I proved them all wrong, once and forever. The final day of our school year at Rift Valley Academy began for me like so many others before it. I rushed out of the dorm right after breakfast and was hurrying across the already bustling campus, heading for my office to get an early start on my daily to-do list, when I heard their sweet pleas. "Mr. Peifer, Mr. Peifer, can you come over here and help us?" Two of my youngest computer students, both second grade girls, stood beneath a small tree a few feet off the sidewalk.

I'm an experienced father of boys. By this point, I'd also spent an entire school year as dorm parent to another nine, count them, preadolescent males. I'd mastered the art of ignoring and saying no (whichever is required) to boys in almost any scenario imaginable. But I was still an absolute pushover for girls. Immediately stopping and turning my full attention toward these two sweet little girls, I noticed they were alternately smiling sweetly at me and furtively glancing up into the tree above their heads. "What's happening?" I asked.

"Could you pleeeaze help us, Mr. Peifer? There's an awesome lizard up in this tree. He'd make a cool pet. But we can't reach him. Can you help us get him down?" I walked over to see what they were talking about. Sure enough, I spotted a rather imposing, foot-long reptile peacefully perched in one of the tree's lower branches. "I don't think I can reach him either," I told the girls. And frankly, I didn't much want to. But when they begged me to lift one of them up to try to capture the creature, I agreed. I boosted one eight-year-old girl onto my shoulders and the two of us had the following conversation:

Me: Do you have him yet?

Her: Can you lift me a little higher?

Me: *(trying to stand on tiptoe)* I don't think so. Do you have him yet?

Her: Can you move a little to the right?

Me: *(tiptoeing right)* Do you have him yet?

Her: I'm so close.

Me: Do you have him yet?

Her: Oops.

Me: What do you mean, "oops"?

Her: I had him, but he tickled my finger and I dropped him on your shoulder.

Me: WHAT?

Her: He is crawling around your neck and I hope he doesn't go down your shirt.

Me: GET HIM! GET HIM!

She got him. Thankfully, before he found his way inside my clothes. I am sure he made some missionary family a fine pet. But that's how I learned —on the last day of that school year at Rift Valley Academy, no less—that hoisting little girls onto your shoulders to catch lizards is a *fine* way to make certain you are fully awake first thing in the morning. *Any* morning.

—

I told that last-day-of-school lizard story in the final report I sent out to the people who had prayerfully and financially supported us during our family's yearlong mission venture. The lizard helped lighten the mood of what was an otherwise rather serious and reflective e-missive, which I concluded by opening my heart to thank and tell our faithful family and friends, *I came to Africa to serve, but it gave me so much more than I could ever return. Because I grew up in the suburbs of America, the poverty of the third world has been so much worse than I ever imagined it could be. The hardships that the people endure here are staggering. But the people here are so astonishing. They have been so kind, and so giving, and so fun to be with. The fact that they continue to persevere overwhelms me; I don't think I could do it.*

We had Grace and her family over for lunch this week and made pizza. When we explained how people in the States just pick up their phones, order a pizza, and one is delivered, their response was astonishment. They couldn't imagine it. The idea of buying new clothes is beyond the hope of many of the people here. To my knowledge, except for RVA and the hospital, there is no running water in the town of Kijabe.

Seeing the immense poverty and illness has to make you look at your own life differently. I've always been grateful for a wonderful family life, but I took so much of what America has for granted. Worse than that, I've taken it as an entitlement. I hope that I never forget the lessons learned here.

To all of you who helped us this year with financial support, with toys, and with kind emails, I wish I had words for what you have meant to us and how much we appreciate you. If you have never been away from almost everyone you know for a year, you might not understand how important email is, and how grateful we are for old and new friends who kept in touch.

The only way I can think to describe my life after Stephen died is that it was like driving a car that had slipped into neutral. I had my foot on the gas, but it didn't go anywhere. The engine roared, but nothing else worked anymore. Then we came here for this year, which has shown me the truth in one of my favorite Scriptures: "He who seeks to find his own life will lose it. He who seeks to lose his own life will find it."

When Stephen died, I felt like I lost my own life. Africa helped me find it again. I'm ready to go home.

—

Less than a week before our flight out of Nairobi, I took a day off from packing and went out with a bunch of RVA colleagues to deliver food to the families of kids at an elementary school in the Karima community down in the valley. I'd made a handful of these relief jaunts over the course of the year. But this one last trip made me realize I hadn't taken the opportunity to venture off the RVA campus nearly as often as I should have.

To be honest, most of my previous food distribution experiences had felt a little too much like drive-by relief work. I'd gone mostly because I felt like I ought to do something. I hadn't gotten to really know any of the people we were trying help. I'd simply unloaded the food and left. I told myself part of the reason was that it's difficult and time-consuming for Westerners to learn to see past the dust and dirt and rundown facilities that are merely the surface of poverty in Africa. And that's true. But the greater truth is that the process of getting to know the people can be uncomfortable, perhaps even painful. On some level, I think that scared me.

But something happened this day at the Karima school. After we unloaded the food, I visited a third grade classroom. The first thing I noticed when I walked in was that most of the students were sitting or lying on the dirt floor while the teacher addressed her class. I thought, *This is strange.* But I assumed this teacher was using a new and unusual discipline technique. I'd heard enough stories to know Kenyan classroom discipline can be harsh.

My young Kikuyu friend Fred had once told me, "When I was in school, I would never have respected any teacher who didn't carry a discipline stick and use it often."

So I hadn't known whether to be amused or horrified by the disciplinary instruction provided by way of an official Education Ministry poster hanging on the walls of other Kenyan government schools I'd visited. The large posterized drawing of a student came with a prominent warning and a graphic arrow indicating where on the head educators should *not* strike students with a stick, for fear of causing serious, permanent hearing loss. But numerous other arrows pointed out areas on the body where teachers could and should apply firm discipline without reservation or risk.

So I kept watching those children on the floor, looking for clues that might tell me what was going on. But they exhibited none of the tell-tale restlessness, resentment, or defiance I'd expect from kids being punished. The required school uniforms they wore—red sweaters over white shirts or blouses with dark blue pants or skirts—looked worn and frayed. And lying in the dirt wouldn't help the condition of those outfits, which I suspected were the only set of clothes many of these students owned.

Though I couldn't spot a single pair of shoes in the entire class, I didn't see any protruding bellies that would have indicated a history of severe malnutrition. However, I did notice a hollow-eyed emptiness on enough faces to realize these kids were missing something. There wasn't much learning (or anything else) going on while I was in the classroom that day. I guess the unsettling passiveness in those children should have been my clue. But it wasn't. Instead, I had to ask the teacher just before I left her room, "Why are so many of your students lying on the floor?"

She smiled politely at me, but her eyes and the rest of her facial expression conveyed pure sadness. The teacher pursed her lips and glanced out over her classroom. Then she turned back toward me and lowered her voice to say, "This is Thursday. Most of these children haven't eaten since Monday. If they try to stand, or even sit up, they will faint." I noted the matter-of-factness in her words, as if maybe she was tired of picking up the children who'd fainted. Not that she no longer cared, but more likely because the grinding hopelessness had worn down and broken her spirit.

My mind searched but could find no adequate words of response. There was no way I could have articulated my reaction to her. It was simply too strange. Because the feeling that came over me in that classroom brought to mind a cinematic Jack Nicholson quote from what was even by that time an old movie.

Albeit honored with an Oscar for Best Picture for 1983, *Terms of Endearment* (starring both Nicholson and Shirley MacLaine in their own Oscar-winning roles) is a troubling movie, centered around the loves and lusts of four morally and relationally challenged characters engaged in unhealthy marital and extramarital pairings.

It's not a movie I'd recommend to anyone as a great source of wisdom. But the pertinent quote came when Nicholson, playing a philandering, commitment-leery, retired astronaut, is literally and figuratively walking away after a fling with Shirley MacLaine's character. He's reaching for the doorknob on his way out of the room (and out of her life) when she freezes him in his shoes by asking what response he might have to the fact that she loves him. Nicholson knows he's caught. And he conveys multiple layers of meaning and understanding of that fact when he concedes that he was "just inches away from a clean getaway."

There I was, less than a week from the end of my African commitment. All that was left to do was to finish packing what few possessions we'd brought with us, plus a wonderful, healing, year's worth of memories we were taking home. I'd seen all I'd come to see and done all I'd come to do in Kenya. And more. Now I was going back to the future in the land of baseball, to resume a promising and lucrative business career in the high-tech world. I too was just inches away from a clean getaway when that teacher brought me up short by telling me, "This is Thursday. Most of these children haven't eaten since Monday. If they try to stand, or even sit up, they will faint."

The moment I heard those words, I knew my life could never be the same again. That was as clear as a light clicking on in a dark room. Deep in my heart, I understood right then that I could never walk away from Africa. But it would take a little more time to get that message through my head.

14

Lamborghinis Don't Matter

I HAD NO DOUBT ABOUT WHERE THE REST OF THE FAMILY STOOD WHEN IT came to life in Africa. One day, maybe two-thirds of the way through our volunteer year, our family—just JT, Matthew, Nancy, and I—had been sitting around our table at mealtime. I don't even remember what prompted my words; maybe we'd all had a great day, maybe one of the boys commented on something he loved about being in Kenya. Whatever created the positive mood of the moment, as I looked around the table at my happy family, I said (not at all in a tone of resignation but in a tone of simple acceptance), "We're gonna come back here, aren't we?"

I may have posed it as a question, but the boys didn't take it that way. Or maybe they did, and they were just giving their answer when they responded by leaping to their feet with celebratory cheers and then dancing around the room. Nancy just smiled and watched our sons' reaction. I knew what she would want to do if given a choice. Not that she'd said anything to pressure me to consider anything beyond the twelve-month commitment I'd made. But she didn't have to; I'd seen that she'd been at home in Kijabe from the start.

Later she told me that for months she'd been asking God, "Why is my heart totally lost to this place and these people, when we both know this is just a one-year gig for Steve?" So to sit at that dinner table and hear me concede even the possibility of coming back would have thrilled her soul. But she wisely avoided pressing me more about the idea at the time. She and the boys waited patiently, or at least not too impatiently, for me to come around. I knew they wanted to be there; a father knows his family. I wasn't trying to be mean or to disregard their feelings. Nor was I being disobedient to what

I was beginning to think God might be calling us to do. I merely wanted some time to make peace with the implications and the reality of the major decision this would be.

Looking back, I don't know exactly why I needed that time. It may have been a feeling that I still had something to prove in business. Perhaps the way I'd struggled and seen my productivity lag after Stephen's death added some motivation to show myself, as much as anyone else, that I still had what it takes to make it in the fast-paced, high-pressure technology world. I can't explain why that seemed like such a compelling need at that point in my life. But it was.

I'd assumed that I'd rejoin Oracle; a number of the managers there had indicated they'd have a place for me when I returned from Africa. But between the time we landed back in Dallas and when I checked with folks at Oracle, I was by contacted an Oracle consulting company and offered a director-level position that would pay me considerably more than I'd ever made before.

Out of a sense of obligation, I let my Oracle friends know I'd gladly work there again if they wanted me, but when I told them about my unsolicited offer from the other company and its accompanying salary package, my former boss at Oracle congratulated me and encouraged me to take the deal. It did seem to be one of those too-good-to-refuse opportunities that I simply could not pass up. In addition to more responsibility and income, working for a different company offered a fresh start, for while I had good relationships from my time working for the software giant, there were also difficult memories at Oracle, especially my last year there in the wake of Stephen's death.

The new job offer was a strong affirmation for me because it was such a major step up the corporate ladder. As a project manager at Oracle, I'd overseen the work of a lot of people—outside consultants and consulting companies Oracle contracted to implement our products all over North America. But I answered to a number of higher-ups within Oracle. This new company would be one of those outside consulting firms I used to contract with. But my director-level position (and pay) meant I was in charge and could run my part of the company. As director of our company's Oracle Financial Implementations division, I was responsible for all the consulting and contracting our firm did to help client companies implement (install, convert to, train on, use efficiently, update, and maintain) Oracle software and systems with which they operated the financial side of their businesses.

I immediately embraced the challenges that came with the greater responsibilities, and I soon convinced myself I was up to the job. I enjoyed being back near old friends in the Dallas area, and quickly settled into a familiar suburban American family routine. Whenever I found myself thinking about Africa, the needs there, and the possibility of going back, I had only to look at my paycheck and tell myself, *A couple of years of doing this and I can pay off the house, provide some financial security for our family, and be in a much better position to think about that.* I said much the same thing to Nancy, who I knew (though she still wasn't voicing the desire out loud) wanted nothing more than to return to Kenya and gladly would have done so at a moment's notice.

Meantime, my own plan seemed to be going well. The Oracle Financial division of our new company did well. And the people at the top let me know they recognized and appreciated my contributions. I received further affirmation from the fact that people outside our company seemed to notice what we were doing. Headhunter firms started calling to feel out my potential interest in positions with other companies. I even got invited to be a keynote speaker at a big regional Oracle Users Group conference in Las Vegas early that winter of 2001.

I'd never been to Vegas before, and I've not felt the need to return since. But my one and only visit to the Gambling Capital of the World was a heady, humbling, and ultimately life-changing experience, and not in any stereotypical Sin City way. What happened to me in Vegas doesn't need to stay in Vegas. I'm more than happy to explain.

The heady part started the moment I arrived and discovered what it is like to be treated in a manner to which I was not accustomed. Because I was a keynote speaker for this big industry shindig, the conference had booked an entire suite just for me. The place was so swank and so huge that I had to call home to tell Nancy I wished she and the boys could see it. Or better yet, I wished they had all been able to come with me.

Then my keynote went as well as I could have hoped, and I sensed it was well received by the audience of three thousand or so. The tech boom may have plateaued, but few if any at the conference believed that that was more than a temporary pause for an industry destined to continue to surge on into the twenty-first century. Indeed, the expert leading one session I sat in on told all of us who came to his seminar that we needed to "go ahead and order your Lamborghinis now, because in the next ten years, you are going to become wealthier than you ever imagined was possible." That comment certainly created a buzz throughout the room, although it set my teeth on edge.

Despite my reaction to such a blatant appeal to the materialistic motives of his eager-to-believe audience, I soon had my own reasons to think that optimism about the future of the IT industry might be warranted. Because, before that conference ended, I had four job offers and landed a multi-million-dollar consulting deal for my company. Talk about being affirmed.

All by myself, walking back to my hotel after getting verbal confirmation on that deal, I felt like I was on top of the world—at the top of my game, anyway, both personally and professionally. But as I strolled past the "glitter gulch" that is Fremont Street, soaking in the sights and sounds of the city, my mood shifted and my thoughts changed. I looked around me as if with new eyes, at the blinding, color-changing neon nonsense promising food, fun, females, financial windfalls, and the fulfillment of all your fantasies.

I wondered how much electricity it took to create such an illusion of lights and lies. I thought of all the Kenyans I knew, entire villages I'd visited that had no electrical power. How could both—such contrasting—places exist on the same planet? Maybe they didn't, really. It struck me as I continued walking that Africa was the real world. What I saw around me in Vegas was a neon mirage, its emptiness reflected on so many lonely faces in the crowds. None of it was real. None of it mattered.

Back at my hotel, walking into my suite and looking around, it hit me again. *None of this is real. None of this matters. I don't need a Lamborghini. I'm not where I belong.* But I knew where I did belong. So I picked up the phone and called Nancy to tell her what had just happened in Vegas. The big deal I'd signed. The long walk I'd taken. The bright lights and the empty faces I'd seen. The deep insights I'd had into what is meaningless and what is real in life. And the easy decision I'd just come to. I told my wife what I'd already told God: "I'm ready to go back to Africa."

Nancy wasn't surprised by the decision I'd made. She knew better than I did that eventually we were going back. But she was surprised by the suddenness and the certainty I had about the decision, because I'd seemed so motivated to pay off the house and provide a measure of financial security. But I was ready to go now. And that prospect thrilled her and the boys.

Once again, as soon as our decision was made, the plans fell into place. And they needed to if we were going to make it back to Kenya in time for the start of the next school year at RVA in September of 2001.

AIM quickly accepted our application to become full-time missionaries. Then it was time to raise financial support again—a larger amount this time, since we'd be going for a four-year term. I gave notice to my company. They wished me well, although some of my colleagues no doubt questioned my sanity. Those who knew me best may have been doing that for a while already.

Nancy and I quickly decided that if we were going to be living in Africa for the long term, it made sense to go ahead and sell most of our household possessions rather than pay for four years of storage. We also put a "For Sale by Owner" sign in our yard and gave ourselves a few months to sell it before we listed it with a realtor.

The quick decision to sell our home and most of our belongings probably seemed rash to many people who knew us. But I felt so much more clear that I was doing what I was supposed to do this time than I had two years previously, that letting go of our *stuff* seemed surprisingly easy. Saying goodbye to friends and family was much harder.

In many ways, I felt like my life had been split in two when Stephen died. My old life ended, and no matter what I'd done for three years, I'd been unable to get it back. There was still a big part of me that loved being a suburban dad, doing lots of normal, fun stuff with my kids. And I knew that going back to Africa this time meant leaving behind a life that I'd loved —for good. That part wasn't so easy. But when we sold our house two days before the date we'd set to list it with a realtor, I took that as one more sign (and there had been numerous others by then) that we were doing what we needed, and were called, to do.

—

The entire Peifer family returned to RVA life in Kijabe, Kenya, in August of 2001, with a different mindset and, for me, a deeper level of commitment than when we'd arrived there the first time just two years earlier. We thought we knew what to expect this time. But Africa continued to surprise us (we found a family of baboons in our yard when we arrived at our new dorm) and confront us with some of its greatest needs. And ours.

—

Researchers have traced the spread of AIDS throughout Africa by way of major truck stops scattered around the continent. Considerable evidence suggests that the propagation of this deadly epidemic began for Africa in Mahi Maihu, a Kenyan truck-stop community at a major crossroads in the Rift Valley just below Kijabe, which has been absolutely devastated by AIDS. Hundreds of orphans were in this one town, so we went there with some other RVA staff to deliver food and play with the kids at an orphanage on one of our first Saturdays back in Kenya.

Before we visited the orphanage, we distributed food and clothes to several widows in the area. Nowhere in America can prepare you for this level of poverty. One woman lived in a home roughly the size of two small office cubicles. It had dirt floors and mud walls and was furnished with two crude chairs. She and her six children lived there. None of them had shoes. What little clothing they owned, they wore—all donated hand-me-downs. This mother told us that she managed to get her children fed. Their one meal of rice or maize a day was served without plates, knives, or forks; the kids grabbed handfuls of it and ate standing up.

Her biggest concern was school fees. (There was still no free public education in Kenya. I have been at a school where a child whose family could not afford school fees was beaten with a stick for sneaking into class without paying.) This mother could barely afford to feed her family one meal a day (the average for Kenyans); school fees were beyond her. Yet she knew that without education, her children would never have much of an opportunity in life.

To live in that kind of poverty has to be overwhelming; to know that your children will also have to live like that must be one of the most painful things any parent could endure.

—

From there we went to the orphanage, where we watched some women cooking a massive kettle of stew over an open fire. Kenyan cooks are so used to being around flames they evidently don't notice the heat. Because when I asked if the fifty-pound cooking pots were hot, they assured me they were not. But believe me, when I grabbed the handles of one to help load the food into a van, it was all I could do not to scream, drop the pot, spill the food, and risk a host of orphans not getting anything to eat that day. The highly amused cooks told me my problem was that I had "white hands." All I could think to say (without actually saying it) was, *Someday I will have you ladies over for some authentic Mexican food; then we will see who can handle the* heat.

I felt honored to be remembered at this orphanage because the last time I had been there, we were able to deliver hundreds of toys our supporters had sent for the children. So many of the kids greeted me warmly this time, and some ran to get their Magna Doodles to show me their latest drawings. Although English was their second language, I did manage to teach a group of fifty kids to shout "I love Texas" at the top of their lungs. Which I'm sure was educational for them. Without words, I also managed to lose in six races, a hopping contest, a hold-your-breath competition, and a you–can't–smile game.

Then the director showed me the dorms; those little kids lived in tough circumstances. One big problem was how many of them wet their beds. Eighteen to twenty-four children slept in a single room on foam mattresses;

the odor was more than I could bear. Some of those spongy pads were more than five years old; there just wasn't any money to buy replacements. And the orphanage "dining hall" was in real need of new tables. We tried to repair the old ones, but the wood was rotting and they were just breaking down. A lot of the kids had to stand when they ate.

As we were leaving, many of the children clung to us. The dedicated orphanage staff worked hard, but there were so few of them and so many orphans. Children need adult attention, and these kids got so little of it. The director noticed the tears in my eyes as I told his kids goodbye. He grabbed my hands, looked right into my face, and smiled sadly as he said approvingly, "You are one of us."

It was the nicest thing anyone had ever said to me during the time I'd been in Kenya.

—

But what meant even more was something Nancy told me shortly after we returned to RVA. One day as she had walked through the seventh grade boys dorm past the huge window looking out over the valley thousands of feet below, Nancy explained, "It hit me like a ton of bricks; my dreams were all met! The big one, of course, was the fact that I was on the mission field in Africa where I'd always felt called to be. And not just for another twelve-month short-term volunteer assignment, but with my husband and family as full-time missionaries. What's more, I'd always wanted to live on a hill [the side of the Great Rift Valley is *quite* a hill!]. Growing up, I imagined someday living in a house with a white picket fence [which Twiga dorm had, plus a beautifully landscaped yard with walks lined with colorful flower beds]. And I'd always thought how nice it would be to live somewhere my family could walk to church, which we do.

"I know those last three dreams were just little things I never really expected to amount to anything," Nancy admitted. "But today, looking out our window and suddenly realizing I had all those things, I broke down and wept at a God so great and magnificent, yet so personal and detailed."

Her words took me back more than two years before, in the wake of Stephen's death, when we were both drowning in grief and cried out to God for help and I heard, *Make your wife's dreams come true.* I was so glad I did.

—

We went to the New Life Home one Sunday. It's an orphanage for abandoned infants. One baby girl had somehow survived being left down in a latrine for several days. By the time she was found, ants had eaten much of the skin off her face. But she had recovered and was doing fine.

As we toured the beautiful facility (the absolute nicest we had seen anywhere in Kenya), we were informed that of thirty million people in this country, more than one and a half million are orphans. You do the math. One out of every twenty Kenyans is orphaned.

—

You know how in the US everyone will greet you by asking, "How you are?" and you are expected simply to say, "Fine"? And how that gets old? I took it as a sign of my personal progress in mastering my second language that once we were back in Kenya for the long haul, I even grew tired of singing my greetings to the tune of the *Hallelujah Chorus*. So as a change of pace, I decided to enliven many of my greetings with an interesting change of inflection. I continued saying "habari" in a normal voice, but then, on the last syllable of "yako," I would sound like my underwear just bunched up. It never failed to get a somewhat surprised and what I would argue was also an appreciative response from Kenyans. In the spirit of trying to learn a new word a day, I also began answering "Habari yako" by responding "Baridi sana." Roughly translated: "I am very cool."

Ironically, Kenyans tried to correct me every time I said this by informing me, "No, it is very warm." The irony is this: I have never been cool one day in my life. But it fell on me to try to explain what cool is. I think you can make a case that Africa invented cool, and Africans are so cool they don't know it and don't even know what it means.

Having me explain cool to Africans is probably a great argument for why they need *more* missionaries in Africa, preferably some cool ones.

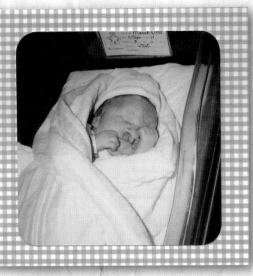

Stephen Wrigley Peifer,
whose purpose in life was
to change our lives

The only family photo we have of all of us with Stephen,
March 1998

The Peifer family at the top of Mount Longonot, near our home, December 2009

The Peifer family with children home from college at our home in Kijabe, December 2009. From left to right: Nancy, Steve, Matthew, JT, Katie, Ben

*Steve, Nancy, Ben, and Katie
in Bedford, Texas*

*Steve and Nancy at the
2007 CNN Heroes Awards
Show in New York City*

Steve in front of one of the schools where lunch is provided

The whole Peifer family, December 2010.
From left to right: Katie, Matthew, Ben, Steve, Nancy, JT, Janelle

The lighter side of the Peifer Family, December 2010 in Fort Worth, Texas

Graduation at Rift Valley Academy

Chip Carter

The annual Multicultural Day at Rift Valley Academy,
celebrating both unity and diversity

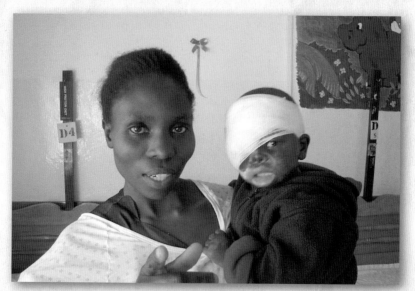

*A child who was treated at the CURE hospital we visit every Sunday
with a group of students from Rift Valley Academy*

Another child who was treated at the CURE hospital

A baby elephant that charged our vehicle in Masai Mara

One of the better roads traveled in visiting the various schools

Maize delivery at the beginning of the school term

Sorting the maize to remove any stones or grass before it is cooked

Margaret at Nyondia, standing by the cooking fat

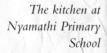

The kitchen at Nyamathi Primary School

Students lined up for lunch, the one meal they can depend on, at Kiriko Primary School in Kenton

Students awaiting lunch at Nyakinyua Primary School, in Masailand

The kitchen at Nyondia Primary School

Steve trying his hand at cooking lunch at Nyondia

Kiriko Primary School

Kinungi Primary School

Kinungi Primary School

Young girls at Nyondia Primary School jumping rope during the lunch break with a rope made from tied-together grass

One of the youngest students enjoying her lunch

Kinungi Primary School

Kiriko Primary School

A boy walking in front of his school,
Kamuyu Primary School

A parent addressing the
school at Awards Day at
Ewaso, a Masai school

Awards Day at Ewaso, one of the three Masai schools we work with

*A classroom
at Nyamathi
Primary School*

*Grade 8 students in
a typical classroom at
Kinungi Primary School*

Students at Muchorui Primary School

The dedication of the first solar-powered computer training center at Karima

The computer center at Munengi

The computer teacher at Muchourue Primary School

Lucy Wanjiru, the head teacher for all of the computer centers

Student at the computer center in Kenton

Steve having fun with the children at Nyondia Primary School

Steve visiting the students at Kiriko Primary School

15

No One Plays Dumb
Better Than I Do

BACK IN TEXAS, A FEW WEEKS BEFORE WE HAD HEADED BACK TO AFRICA, another missionary called to inform us he was shipping a freight container by boat. But it was only 75 percent full and he wanted to fill it up. He wondered if we might want to send some stuff in his container and share the cost proportionately. Until that point, we hadn't thought we could justify the expense of our own shipping container, but this offer made the price affordable.

The biggest things we'd wished we could take but hadn't thought possible were our mattresses. Real mattresses are hard to come by in Kenya. You could get a foam pad, which was fine for young Turks, but not for an *elder* with a white beard like mine. So we were thrilled that our mattresses could go after all. Turns out, 25 percent of a freight container was more space than we imagined; we were able to fit in lots of other stuff we had been thinking we'd have to leave behind. Some friends helped us crate up our piano and mattresses and more. Then another friend drove everything on a truck to Houston, where it all was loaded into a container that would be loaded onto a cargo ship heading for Africa.

Several months after we got back to Kijabe, we received an email saying our container had arrived in Nairobi, and that we should be there for the opening. I went into the city and found the freight yard, which had hundreds of containers. Some were as large as a railcar, and since they were spread out for several miles, I had a two-mile hike just to get to our container. The procedure was this: Our shipping company had our lock. My role was to be there to watch them unlock it to witness customs inspecting the container and to make sure nothing got stolen. And I was ready to fulfill that duty, except that when we unlocked and opened that heavy steel shipping container, a large piece of lumber prevented our access to anything inside.

The Kenyans' limited hand tools were no match for the machine-driven nails pounded into that lumber back in Houston. After an hour, with no real progress, I took a crowbar from one of the men and pried the top of the crate up just enough to get a handgrip. Then I pulled myself up to the top and bounced up and down on what looked to be a thick and sturdy sheet of plywood, hoping my weight would cause it to buckle. After several minutes, two Kenyan men climbed up to add their weight to mine.

It soon became evident our strategy would work, though it might take some time. So what does one do in the middle of a freight yard in Kenya, standing high atop a shipping container with two other men, trying to break down plywood?

I had to sing the perfect song: "Surfing Safari."

Teaching two non-English speaking Africans to sing the refrain "Surfing safari, yeah surfing safari" while balancing and bouncing atop a huge container had to be the most surreal moment of my life to date. After about ten minutes without a wipeout, and two *Sing again*'s from my enthusiastic co-riders, the wood finally gave in. We then hauled out about twenty pieces of the container. Almost forty different people came by to look, to ask questions, or, most likely, hoping to hear more singing. After almost three hours, we were instructed to return the pieces to the container.

While we were waiting for the inspection to be completed, I talked with a young man named Moses. He told me he was a newlywed and made a fair living at the freight yard, but lived in one of the worst slums in Kenya. It had almost one million people, according to some estimates, and I accepted his invitation to visit him in December when school was out, if we could borrow a vehicle. I liked Moses and was curious to know why he lived where he did. He explained that because he was the eldest son in his family, it was his duty to help his younger brothers and sisters complete their education. Because he was currently paying his younger brother's school tuition, he could not afford any housing except the slum.

I'd driven by that place, and it was truly horrible. To choose to live there to help your brother had to be one of the most remarkable sacrifices I ever knew of.

—

The freight company eventually delivered everything to our place at RVA in two separate shipments which came several days apart.

We brought over lots of CDs this time. I'd told all my Kenyan friends, "I will learn your customs and attempt to learn your language, but by the time I am done with you, I guarantee you will know Motown well. I have high expectations that by the time I leave Kenya, all my Kenyan friends will know the difference between Martha Reeves and Junior Walker." I would show them what it truly means to be cool. It seemed the least I could do.

Our family's experience returning to Kenya reminded me of the old joke: guy goes to Vegas in a fifty thousand dollar car and returns home in a three hundred thousand dollar bus. After all, we had a four-bedroom, two-and-a-half-bathroom home in Texas, and now we had six showers and four toilets in the dorm. JT, Matthew, Nancy, and I shared a bathroom, which was fine; we knew running water was a luxury in Kenya. And we could take *hot* showers if we went outside and built a fire under a water tank. So life in the junior high boys' dorm was surprisingly cozy, except for one thing.

Our sons would dry themselves on whatever was available. The thought that it might not be *theirs* never seemed to cross their minds; I was convinced that if the original copy of the Magna Carta had hung in our bathroom, one or both of them would have dried off with that. Which created a measure of suspense every time I got out of the shower and wondered, *Did they get my towel today?* I'm afraid I didn't do well in towel bingo.

It often seemed so easy to get caught up in the busyness of school and the minor inconveniences and frustrations of RVA life that you forgot some of the extraordinary experiences some of our students had gone through.

In the weeks after 9/11, people from the American embassy were on the RVA campus because there had been death threats against the parents of two of our students. Their parents were working in a Muslim area, and some people evidently were unhappy with them. The kids were shaken up because it wasn't safe for them to go home to be with their parents, so they had a couple of scary days. The parents believed that if they left at the first sign of trouble, they would be sending the wrong message. So they stayed and continued their work. I admired their courage and conviction, and I prayed for their kids.

Some of my students had seen so much in their short lives. One of my students was camping when a horde of rhinos charged her tent. Her family was able to get on top of a car and stayed there until morning. More than a dozen of our students' families had been evacuated from the areas they were serving. One kid and his parents fled just thirty minutes before there was a slaughter in their compound. Another girl talked about her friend being murdered—after that friend had to witness her own mother and father being killed before her eyes.

It so grieved me that children had to know the horrors of war. And it especially hurt me to hear what had happened in New York City and around the United States on and after September 11. Weeks later and eight thousand miles away from home, there was still no way I could truly comprehend what had happened, how life had been changed forever in America. Even in Africa, Americans felt violated by the impact of those four hijacked airplanes.

Kenya doesn't let you forget you are an American either. For weeks there was an anti-American march every Friday in Nairobi. Although most Kenyans remained supportive of America and friendly to Americans, many Muslims in Kenya were militantly anti-American.

⸻

Returning to Africa offered yet another surprise: I found I was no longer bothered by what had given me the shakes two years earlier. I could now go into the hospital and see the most horrible deformities and not react to them.

Evidently human beings can get used to anything. While I didn't want to get jaded or be uncaring, I don't think that was what was going on. It's just that to be effective, you've got to move past the shock, and I think I had finally passed that point. Our first year in Kenya, I sometimes left a room and got physically sick after I'd seen kids who'd come to our hospital. This time I could go to the worst cases and hold those kids. I was grateful for the change. But I was still surprised.

⸻

I was convinced that the person who will get the largest crown in heaven is the woman who taught the combined first and second grade class in the Titchie School that fall term of 2001. I had them for forty-five minutes a week in the computer lab, and their comments would range from "I don't want to use a mouse; I'm afraid of mice" to "Why can't we upgrade the operating system?" I never knew how she did it, but I was so glad I wasn't their classroom teacher that there weren't enough words in an English/Swahili dictionary to express my gratitude. Those kids consumed the longest forty-five minutes of my week.

⸻

We had to begin the alien registration process the second week of November. Although we had a passport and a visa to come *into* Kenya, we also had to register as aliens in order to stay in Kenya. It seems like it would be a fast and simple process, but it wasn't. You don't just go to the capital and register. You have to go to Nairobi (one hour each way) and fill out paperwork and pay your fee. This enables you to return the following week to begin the process. Why it can't be done the same day is a question without an answer, for they do nothing with your paperwork during the intervening week.

We arrived when the offices opened at 8:30 a.m. There were four windows, none of which were labeled. We stood in one line for a period of time, while people sitting in the back of the office stared at us. Finally, one of them came out and collected paperwork from people who had appointments for the current week, and then that person disappeared for forty-five minutes. When I looked in the back, files were everywhere: on the floor, in the chairs, in no order that I could discern.

We sat and waited. Finally, they started to call names. Thirty minutes passed before our name was called. We stood and approached the counter. There wasn't a line, just a cluster of people hovering around a window. The woman behind the counter glanced at our forms and asked us to sign our names. At one point, she said "chai," the word for a common drink that is also a euphemism for a bribe. But she didn't know with whom she was dealing, because:

1. I can't pay a bribe; I'm a missionary.
2. I've negotiated contracts worth millions of dollars.
3. No one can play dumb more naturally or better than I can. Whenever she mentioned chai, I kept thanking her and saying, "I'm not thirsty." Until, after another twenty minutes, we were given back our forms and instructed to go to another room for fingerprinting.

I'd never been fingerprinted before, but I don't believe it is like this anywhere else. First they took prints of all my fingers, and then a handprint of each hand. Afterward, they pointed to a pile of yarn and told us that we could wipe our hands on that. As we did so, they told us we could return in a month to pick up our form. We left more than three hours after we'd arrived.

The sad part of this is that the Kenyan government didn't seem to understand what such inefficient bureaucracy cost them. Taking up so much of my day for no good reason wasted the time and energy I could have used to help orphans and visit sick kids in the hospital. I saw a doctor in that office, and all I could think about was how many sick people wouldn't see him that day because he had to wait in a stupid line to get one simple sheet of paper.

Kenya's governmental bureaucrats had recently decided they would no longer allow short-term doctors to practice medicine in our area. For decades the hospital in Kijabe had attracted surgeons who came at their own expense for short periods to do extensive numbers of surgeries in their specialties. It allowed us to find kids with special problems and let them know when a surgeon with the special skills to treat them was coming. Then they would be operated on for free.

Kenya was now saying that if they didn't come for a whole year, doctors couldn't use their medical skills. What was the point of such a ruling? To encourage doctors to stay longer?

I'd been amazed at how many doctors found time and money to come. This new regulation would make health care around the country worse, far worse. Spending several hours of my life in a pointless line is one thing; preventing doctors from helping sick and dying children is quite another. Both are symptoms of the same problem: a government bureaucracy gone so awry that it no longer thinks through anything or considers the consequences; it just does what it does and what it has always done, because it can.

In the end, the banality of evil is what exhausts you. You can battle against an evil terrorist; how do you fight an underpaid clerk following stupid orders?

I was beginning to understand why many people felt so hopeless that they just gave up. I never had to fight city hall in the States, but living in Africa, I quickly gained a greater empathy for those who do.

—

I addressed some other cross-cultural differences in the email I sent home the week of American Thanksgiving:

This week will be unusual; Thursday will be just another workday here in Kenya. I'm sure it is the ugly American in me that is still shocked that Africans don't celebrate Thanksgiving. But it will be business as usual here. Since we are full up on our schedule, a kind friend has invited us over for a turkey dinner. Don't feel sorry for us, though; did you get Moi Day off?

The cultural differences here are still striking to us. Nan has written about how taboo it is to ask someone if they are pregnant. Contrast that with the States, where everyone who is pregnant tells everybody that they are. Our friend Grace told us that if we ever asked her if she was pregnant, she could slap us!

I experienced the other side of it this week. Some of you might remember my telling you about Charles, the man who carved salad spoons and bowls as a demonstration for our dorm boys when we were here before. He has since died, but his son and an older friend came by yesterday to try to sell some of their wares. After showing us what they had, the older friend informed me that Charles's son was sixteen and was soon going to become a mature man.

I thought about the States and what that might mean; the only thing that came to mind was getting your driver's license. Here it means something quite different. The way you become a man in the local tribe is to get circumcised when you are seventeen. And you have to do it without showing fear. And it was perfectly permissible to talk openly about it. I'm afraid I would not make a good African. I showed fear just talking about this custom. And the way I flinched as we did so suggested I could never be a brave tribe member. I admit I've always been kind of a rude guy, but I can't quite imagine even on my worst day going up to some sixteen-year-old kid and asking, "Yo, you been circumcised yet?"

Have a happy Thanksgiving. And if you are a guy, I trust I gave you one more thing to be thankful for.

—

With all due respect to Nancy, after sixteen years of marriage, birthing and mothering her own sons for more than a dozen years, and serving as surrogate dorm mom to ten-to-twelve sons of other mothers, my poor wife still didn't understand males. At the end of each term, we had a day of dorm cleanup, and we wrote down a list of tasks our charges needed to do. On the list she was going to give to junior high boys, she had written, "Wash walls if necessary."

Sadly, it came to me to inform her that I was forty-six years old and had *never* felt like it was necessary to wash a wall. If the walls were bleeding, I would bet money that there wasn't a seventh grade boy on the planet who would take that as a clue to wash them. So we changed the suggestion to a requirement and made the boys pass inspection before they could go home for a month.

But this year, before the boys headed home for Christmas, we had to have a contingency planning meeting. Because the US embassy had been bombed in Kenya a few years earlier, and 9/11 had heightened tensions all over the globe, our school administration decided we needed to have a contingency plan in case of emergency. Every staff member and student was expected to pack, and keep ready at all times, one carry-on bag containing passports, clothing, and a few other necessary personal items. I asked our dorm guys what they thought they should have in that bag. They listed things such as:

Hockey stick
Poster of favorite soccer player
Candy

And as I told our friends and family in our end-of-semester email home, "Not one of them thought that a change of underwear was a necessity. Which I think gives us all reason beyond the obvious to pray for peace on earth this year."

Then I went on in that same email to suggest the biggest reason the Peifer family was in special need of prayer that holiday season.

16

So Obvious, So Right

THE REST OF THAT DECEMBER 3RD EMAIL MAY HAVE COME AS A SURPRISE to some of our friends and family. I told them we'd made a huge decision, perhaps the toughest one Nancy and I had ever made. We wanted to assure people that it was by no means a spur-of-the-moment decision. In fact, it made our decision to come to Kenya the first time, and then to come back to Kenya for the long haul, seem like a walk in the park.

Having said that, I went on to explain:

I have always, always, always wanted a daughter. I would not trade my sons for anything, but I have wanted a daughter badly.

My brother also had three sons. And before the youngest was born, he threatened that whatever the baby's gender, his third kid would wear a dress. Fortunately, he didn't follow through on that threat; his son Jon is a very handsome young man who never would have looked right in that kind of attire. My brother eventually had two beautiful granddaughters and has found his peace.

But it had been on my heart for a long time to consider adopting. There are so many Kenyan children who need homes that it is hard not to consider it. But our first year here was too soon after Stephen's death for Nancy, so it was something we put on the shelf.

When we returned to Kenya this time, Nancy started to consider the possibility of adopting. As she prayed and weighed the pros and cons, she came to realize that the cons were mostly fears, and she told me she didn't want to be ruled by fear.

Then a Dutch missionary friend of ours who lives in Nairobi stopped by RVA for a visit and told us he had adopted a child. Nancy asked him, "With so many orphans out there, wasn't it hard to choose which one?"

His response changed our lives. He said, "It was so obvious." Later, when Nancy told me what he'd said, we both wept.

The moment Nancy heard about twins at the New Life Home, an orphanage for abandoned babies, her heart leaped. She knew they were for us. When she told me, I immediately wondered, Who is this woman? During all three of her pregnancies, any time I so much as mentioned how neat I thought it would be to have twins, my wife actually hit me! Now she is talking about adopting twins?

We talked to our boys about the idea. One was very pro adoption. The other was very leery; he didn't think any baby could or should take the place of his little brother Stephen. Which is one reason we all went to the orphanage together, knowing it had to be a family decision.

There is so much need in this country. But you shouldn't adopt children out of a sense of need. The decision requires more than that, especially when you already have a family. So I talked to African-American friends back in the United States about the idea; I know how controversial a white family adopting black children can be. I know how many issues we may face as a family. And we have had three children as infants; I'm very realistic about how much work and sacrifice it will take to adopt four-month-old twins, especially at my age.

But as we walked out of that orphanage after our first visit, our reticent son said, "Let's get them both!" A truth that I still don't quite understand made itself clear, and we knew: they were supposed to be ours; they were our children.

We've begun the process of adopting Katherine (who will fulfill a longtime dream of mine to have a daughter) and Casey (her twin brother). These twins were abandoned at three days of age and have been in the orphanage since that time.

The bureaucratic adoption process can take a long time here, so we ask for your prayers. We have already committed to go to northern Kenya for a ten-day trip starting Thursday, so we will be out of touch for the next few days. We expect to get the twins soon after we return, hopefully before Christmas. But whether that will occur is an open question right now. We will begin as foster parents, with the goal of adopting after a six-month period.

I wouldn't be honest if I didn't tell you there have been times of high anxiety and sheer panic as we made the decision to adopt these children. Half the time we have been thrilled, and half the time we have been terrified. But in the end, it wasn't a hard decision at all. As our friend had told us, it was so obvious.

⌣

Three days after writing that e-missive, we packed up and headed for northern Kenya to visit some of the most remote areas on the planet. This wasn't going to be a tourist trip but a once-in-a-lifetime opportunity to experience a number of different cultures few outsiders ever get a chance to observe.

We rented a game tracker, a big rugged truck that can roll through or over almost anything, which would come in handy on the non-roads of Kenya. In addition to our truck, eight carloads of friends and acquaintances caravanned with us. We camped the entire time, spent four days without access to showers, and went for seven straight days without seeing another motorized vehicle that wasn't with our party. We're talkin' beyond the boonies and a rare opportunity to experience the *real* Africa.

Day One: We drove seven hours to Mugie Ranch, which has lions, giraffes, and elephants. On the way, we stopped for a bathroom break, except there was no bathroom. I walked about a half mile away from the caravan and felt self-conscious. I realized that I had not squatted since I was a junior in high school, and my squatter is not what it once was.

Day Two: We went to Kurungu, another eight hours away. When we arrived, we were treated to a wonderful outside shower. Nowhere else I've ever been has the night sky seemed so spectacularly bright as it is in Kenya. So looking up at the stars while taking a shower after traveling all day over dusty roads in an open-air vehicle was a glorious experience I will never forget.

Day Three: In the morning, we visited a nearby village where families share their mud huts with the infant animals they raise. Most of the children wore little, if any, clothing, and many of the women wore no tops. Several thoughts came to mind:

- It is amazing how easily and rapidly you can get used to nudity. I went from being embarrassed to blasé in less than fifteen minutes.
- Without being crude, national women without support garments who do hard work all their lives could end America's fixation on the mammary glands in about fifteen minutes.
- Poverty is a relative term. You would certainly call these people poor by American standards, but they live in beautiful surroundings in a close, caring community.

We were invited to watch the Samburu warriors dance, and it was quite the production. When they asked if any of us would like to participate in the festivities, I thought, *This is my big chance.* I joined a large group of Samburu warriors for three dances, which from what I could tell consisted mostly of jumping up and down and yelling. You'd think it would be hard to mess up that kind of choreography, but judging from the rather loud gales of laughter,

I managed to do so. My reputation for being the whitest person on the planet remains unchallenged.

Day Four: We went to an open-air church for their Sunday morning service, where we saw dozens of wooden walking sticks lying on the ground outside the entrance to the building. The Samburu are traditional herdsmen, so their distinctive walking sticks were sort of a cross between a shepherd's staff and the marungu we'd seen in other parts of Kenya—a carved, wooden, clublike weapon with one hard, rounded, baseball-size end, which could be thrown at or used to clobber predators. Worship is always interesting in another language, but the sincerity and wonderful singing carried the day. After church, we drove to Korr, which was another four hours away. We were getting good at setting up our tents. JT and Matthew had theirs up in no time; unfortunately they didn't zip it closed until later that evening.

Day Five: Matthew woke up the next morning with more than sixty mosquito bites on his face, and even more on each arm. We don't think these were malaria-carrying bugs. But we were glad we'd been taking precautionary doses of antimalaria drugs in preparation for this trip. Better safe than sorry.

From Korr we visited the Rendille tribe, a seminomadic pastoral people that migrated down into Kenya generations ago from the southern desert regions of Ethiopia. A gregarious people, the Rendilles are sometimes referred to as the Italians of Africa. I shook so many hands I felt like I was running for mayor in the first village we stopped in.

When I shook hands with the children, I would jump up and down, and was amazed again to realize that in every culture, little kids love to giggle. These people raise camels and live in such harsh desert conditions that much of the liquid they consume is cow's blood. It was truly amazing to see how they could survive in such a brutal environment.

Day Six: As much as I was learning to appreciate the beauty and distinctiveness of different cultures, I was impressed by how important reading is, and distressed by the power of illiteracy to keep a people down. The missionaries living and working among the Rendille people were doing an amazing job of teaching adults how to read and working on translating the Bible into the Rendille language at the same time. Many of the adults had no schooling at all, so it was a daunting task. But to see the determination of the people trying to learn would encourage anyone to soldier on.

Day Seven: We headed for Kalacha, which is on the edge of the Chalbi Desert. I saw my first mirage and understood how easy it would be to be fooled. After driving for many hours, we arrived at the home of one of our

RVA students, who was spending the December break with his parents. He wanted to show me the deadly black mamba snake he had caught right near the campground where we would be staying. He had it in a jar, and I was grateful for glass in a way I had never been before.

Day Eight: There is a pool of sorts at this campground, set up by creative missionaries. Matthew was so thrilled that he spent the whole day in the water. I was the adult who watched the kids. Besides his grandparents, his friends, and his dog, the only thing Matthew really misses about America is swimming. So he made the most of it.

Day Nine: We headed back to Kurungu. But because it had rained, the roads were tough to navigate on our return trip. At one point, going up an unpaved "road," our truck lurched so violently to the right that I thought we might tip over. We got everyone out of the truck, and after several minutes of pushing and spinning of wheels, we were grateful to finally escape the mud. The African bush is not a good place to be stranded.

Day Ten: We stayed overnight in a campground where lions roamed unrestricted. Nan and I were taking a walk when another couple started yelling for us to run because there were lions just ahead. So we ran, only to find out what they'd heard in the bush nearby were elands, not lions. But we did see several lions later.

Day Eleven: When I started this trip, I found it embarrassing to squat. By the end, I was convinced I could drop trou in the middle of Macy's the day after Thanksgiving and not think a thing of it. But I wasn't sure whether that was progress or regression.

A few random thoughts and questions floated through my mind at the end of our trip:

How can you help without damaging what is precious in a culture? Some of the children we saw wore no clothing at night, and so pneumonia was common. The custom of one tribe was that by leaving his spears in front of any hut, a warrior could claim the privilege of sleeping that night with any woman (or women) who lived therein. Besides the obvious subjugation of women, this traditional practice was one reason that AIDS was sweeping through the region. Other serious health problems stemmed from horrific sanitary conditions and chronic hunger among the children.

Yet we witnessed so many wonderful, admirable things in the cultures of the various tribes we visited: close, caring communities, strong family ties, an understanding, appreciation, and respect of nature few of us in our twenty-first century world will ever have. How can you keep the good in a culture, while working to help eliminate what is harmful? That's not an easy question, and I'm not sure there is one formula that fits every circumstance. But I came away from our adventure enjoying the different cultures and longing to help change what is harmful and deadly.

Much has been made of the cultural imperialism that colonialists, and too many missionaries, once practiced. But what I saw in those ministering among the remote tribes of northern Kenya at the outset of a new millennium were sensitive, committed, caring folks who looked to see and understand what was in the local culture that they could learn from and build upon. They helped convince me that pure Christianity, divorced from cultural influences, is the one thing that could truly change this country and all of Africa for the better. These were what I call "heavy lifting" missionaries. Like one couple working in a community of twenty thousand, who handled all the famine relief in their area during the drought. At the same time, they had to expend tremendous time and energy just trying to survive and stay alive themselves. I walked away in awe of their sacrifice and their love of the people.

—

When we got back to RVA, we received word that we should be able to get the twins on the 23rd, less than a week away. But before that could happen, we had to have a home visit from a Kenyan social worker, who was responsible for hundreds of adoptions. She had already failed to make several appointments before we realized the problem: she didn't own a car and couldn't find transportation to Kijabe. We had imagined a lot of reasons for the missed meetings. But never once had we considered the possibility that the head social worker for Kenya couldn't get to Kijabe from Nairobi because she didn't have a car. When she did finally make it, we learned a lot more from her about the twins since she was from the same tribe.

—

The night before we were to get the babies was a long one for Nancy and me, full of excitement and anxiety. *Are we doing the right thing? Will it hurt JT and Matthew? Can we really do diapers and late nights at our age?* But once we got to the orphanage to pick them up and held them in our arms, all the fears and uncertainties melted away.

Until the first night and the first diaper. When you haven't been awakened by a screaming infant in years, it is a jarringly disorienting development. The first few days were nerve-racking. It took me several diapers to get back in the swing of things; on more than one occasion, I violated the NRA's golden rule of diaper duty: always assume every gun is loaded. But within just a couple of days, the babies started to adapt to a new setting and routine. Once they figured out they didn't have to wait in line with sixty-three other infants to be fed, they really seemed to settle down.

JT and Matthew adjusted to their new roles much quicker than Nancy and I did. Matthew immediately assumed the duties and title of chief bottle maker. JT would feed the babies and put them in the Johnny Jump Up. The twins loved their big brothers from the start, which made our Christmas the sweetest ever.

We ended up keeping the orphanage's name for our new son. He was such a gentle bear of a kid that *Ben* just seemed to suit him better than *Casey*.

Several old friends wondered if Ben would be ignored because I now had a daughter. Frankly, I had the same concern at first. But Ben was the cuddliest guy in the world, the kind of bouncing baby boy you couldn't help but want to hold and be with. Katie was a delicate flower, who any objective observer could instantly see was obviously the most beautiful girl in the world. And who sounded just like Chewbacca, and those were her *happy* noises.

A couple of nights after Christmas, Katie woke up and started crying. After I changed her diaper and fed her, I sat on the couch and let her fall asleep on me. It just felt so right.

17

It's Just Not Right

M Y CORPORATE PHILOSOPHY IN AMERICA WAS "ALWAYS FOLLOW A schmuck." With that strategy I never worried about matching up job descriptions to skill sets and personality profiles. I just figured if I followed a loser, I could be mediocre and still look good by comparison in any position. However, I hadn't done that in my last job, and it was embarrassing. My boss was a genius tech who by some amazing accident was also cool, and I was a dwarf by comparison.

The same thing happened to me our second term back in Kenya. RVA's director of finance was a force of nature. An ace programmer with twenty years of IT experience, he routinely spotted potential glitches no one else noticed and fixed them before they became problems. Definitely not the guy you want to follow. But when he took temporary leave to go back to the States for his daughter's wedding, I was assigned the role of acting director of finance. Fortunately, his second in command knew the ropes and was pretty much expected to do everything. In all honesty, I'm guessing I was supposed to be a figurehead for four months, so people would appreciate the real boss *lots* more when he returned. I didn't think I would do anything but attend a few meetings.

Then our bank got bought out. So I had to go to Nairobi to represent RVA to meet the officials at the new bank. We had called several times to make an appointment with our representative, but he was never available. We finally talked to someone who told us to just come in and he would see us.

When the friend who went with me and I pulled into the bank parking lot, guards with mirrors on long poles examined the underside of our car to make sure we didn't have a bomb down there. I was even more disconcerted when we went into the bank and were informed that our representative had been out of town for ten days and wouldn't be back for another week. They could have told us that on the phone. But in Kenyan culture, if you care about a relationship, it's often considered impolite to tell someone something you know they don't want to hear. So it's thought best not to be too direct.

One of the bank employees ushered us into a waiting room and assured us someone else would come by in a moment to help us. After five minutes, I asked my friend how long he thought we would have to wait for that someone. He said, "Five minutes." I told him, "A Coke says forty-five minutes." Forty-five minutes later, I was tempted to go double or nothing. But I was tired of waiting. So I walked back out into the lobby, approached the first person I saw who looked like a bank employee, politely introduced myself, explained I was with Rift Valley Academy, and informed him, "We were one of the largest depositors in the other bank; might someone want to see us?"

Moments later, we had lots of company. Of course, the new checkbook was still not ready. And everything we were promised would be grandfathered in from our previous bank wasn't. So it looked like I would have some work to do after all.

—

Matthew and I climbed Mount Longonot on New Year's Day 2002. I was trying to do something special with each of the older boys so they wouldn't feel left out in the wake of the twins' arrival.

As we reached the top and sat down to rest, I thought of all the usual New Year's resolutions: lose weight, exercise more, read Proust. But none of those seemed all that relevant to me as I sat looking out and over the great Rift Valley. I turned and tried in vain to make out the location of Kijabe and the RVA campus in the hazy distance, high on the edge of the valley's escarpment to the east. Then as I closed my eyes and thanked God for the incredible opportunity I'd been given to begin a new year of life, sitting on top of a mountain with my son in the middle of Africa, I suddenly knew the goal I was to have for that year: *Don't make peace with the fact that there are hungry children.*

The words weren't audible, but they were as clear as if they had been. And that same week, I wrote home telling our supporters what I planned to do about it:

What's on my heart for this year is a plan to go underground to provide lunches for schoolchildren. I should have more information about it soon, and hope you will consider helping me with it.

157

If 9/11 taught me anything, it's that it's time to put my cynicism away. I'm around hungry kids all the time, but I don't want to become jaded to it. I don't want to spend years of my life here and not try to effect a change. If I don't do something, I will have made peace with the fact that there are hungry children.

—

We could have used a little more peace at the Peifer house as the new year began. Our ongoing battle was with six-month-old twins who acted like they had just gone through a major life transition. So bed was the ultimate enemy. Getting them to sleep around the same time and then to sleep through the night was the challenge. The best we could manage for a while was a 5:30 a.m. wake-up call, which I could live with, since that was when I usually got up anyway.

Katie woke up happy—as soon as she was taken from the bed. Ben needed to be consoled for a while before he believed he would be set free. Katie was a good eater; Ben was voracious. The first time I fed him, he chugged his milk so fast I worried that once he downed the last swallow, he'd try to eat the bottle. They soon began to understand they were no longer at the orphanage, that there were only two babies in our house with four bigger people who were all eager, ready, and willing to meet their needs. So it was no longer necessary to scream with such urgency.

The biggest surprise to me was how dry African babies' skin is. After you change diapers, you usually put some oil on their bottoms. After a bath, they get oiled down all over. I had lots of African-American friends in the States, but I didn't remember this ever being a point of discussion. Which I guess makes sense: if one of those friends had ever come up to me and said, "Did you know our people suffer from dry skin?" that would have made for an unusual topic of conversation, even by my standards.

—

In addition to my other duties at the school, I had been asked to fill in as the eighth grade English lit teacher that year. Again, not exactly my strong suit, but it did provide daily interaction with students, which reminded me that the kids growing up at RVA have led very different lives than mine.

One kid's parents lived and worked in Yemen. He told me that he'd met John Walker Lindh (the twenty-year-old American who'd been in the news for months after being captured in Afghanistan fighting for the Taliban) when Lindh had been in Yemen studying multiculturalism. He said John Walker had tried to convert him to Islam.

One of the girls in my English class informed me that her father had been offered forty camels for her hand in marriage. The father turned down the offer, feeling that should be his daughter's decision to make, and that eighth grade was a bit too young to get married.

I asked a group of students how many of them had ever been evacuated because of war, and more than half indicated they had. I asked how many had seen someone starving to death, and virtually every student's hand went up.

⁓

On a less serious note, I was regularly reminded that I too was now living a very different life than I'd ever lived before. As evidenced in this email report:

Assuming that you are an adult reading this, I would also assume that if a large rat made its way into your bedroom, your response probably would not be, "Sweet!"

However, this was the reaction of my oldest son when he discovered the rat. The rest of the dorm quickly sprang into action, and Rat Wars began. They all got sticks and invented many different traps to catch the creature. Nothing has worked yet, but I think this is the moral equivalent of a new video game in the States.

⁓

A church back home sent us shoes to give away to Kenyans. We had planned to donate them to an orphanage, but there were so many adult sizes that we began looking for people around RVA to give them to.

We offered some to Grace, who still worked for us. Her husband was not working then, so she was the sole provider for her family. We showed her about three dozen pair to choose from, but after she studied them for a while, she excused herself. She was just so overwhelmed by the opportunity; she simply couldn't believe that each of her children would have a new pair of shoes and that she would be able to choose from so many. Almost every Kenyan I know buys used shoes from the side of the road, and the choices are pretty slim. Grace told us later her boys were so excited that they couldn't sleep that night.

I was reminded yet again how much I still took for granted.

⁓

It was the end of January by the time we got our holiday greetings sent to folks back home. But we waited till we could send our letters with someone going back to the States, since so much of the mail in this country gets stolen.

And there was more than one legitimate excuse that year, as we explained in the letter itself:

There is something just so darn special about being the last to get their holiday letter done. But there have been three major events for us this year:

1. *The decision to return to Africa—leaving a great church, a wonderful job, beloved friends and family—was so hard and so easy at the same time. We had a fantastic life in the States, but the bottom line is this: we are supposed to be in Africa. It has been confirmed to us in many ways that this is the place for us for a season.*

2. *September 11 changed everyone. For me, looking at pictures of those New York firemen setting their faces as they charged off to probable death or injury made me want to throw off the cynicism and apathy that I've ingested for so long. America's 9/11 heroes made me want to be better.*

3. *Those of you on our email list already know, but we were led to adopt six-month-old twins who had been abandoned at birth. Katie and Ben have been with us for a month, and it has been a wonderful time. It has changed everything for us, but the changes have been good ones (with the possible exception of sleep deprivation). What we've noticed the most in the last weeks is that our babies know they are home, and that they know we are Mom and Dad and big brothers. It's just the most wonderful experience to adopt, and it has brought all of us closer together.*

We've gotten permission to begin a project that we hope will make a difference in this country, and we have lots of duties and responsibilities on the campus. It should be a year that will be full of about everything.

—

In Jewish culture, you are declared a man when you are thirteen. In many African tribes, the rite of passage into manhood involves circumcision. I don't remember my thirteenth birthday, but I wanted JT's to be something he would always remember. And when he learned the African tradition about circumcision, he was grateful he would not remember *that* for his thirteenth. So he and I set our sights on Mount Kenya, the second highest peak in Africa —at 16,500 feet.

Seventeen of us were going, and we left school that Friday hoping to arrive at Mount Kenya by four o'clock, because then we had a two-hour hike to our base camp. We had hired a guide to provide transportation, food, and porters. This being Kenya, however, we'd been on the "road" only an hour when we had a blowout. It took two hours to repair, so we arrived too late to get to base camp and stayed the night in a little house near the gate.

I should pause here to say that my idea of a great vacation is a good book and a quiet beach. I'm not the adventurous type, and at forty-six, I was not in my best shape. I knew this would be a stretch.

We began our hike at 7:00 a.m. Mount Kenya is untouched; there are no clear trails in many areas, and without experienced guides, it would be easy to get lost. As the morning wore on, it became increasingly clear that this was going to be tough. There were two other seventh grade boys in addition to JT, and they were far ahead of the adults on the trip.

Around noon, we stopped at a glacier-fed stream, where I drank the most delicious water I have ever tasted. By about this time, reality had begun to sink in. We had at least five more hours of extremely challenging hiking to do, and it would get cold once the sun went down. When we arrived at the bunkhouse—altitude fourteen thousand feet—I was as tired as I had ever been. We ate some soup and stew and then went to bed. With 20 degree temperatures outside, and no electricity or fireplace in the bunkhouse, going to bed was the only way to get warm.

Our alarms sounded at 3:00 a.m. We planned to reach the summit in time to see the sun rise. As a father of seven-month-old twins, it was my opinion that sunrises are *vastly* overrated, but we had a full day ahead of us, so I needed to get going. We climbed for hours with flashlights, which did little to dispel the darkness and nothing for the cold. There were stretches when the only way to keep moving up was on hands and knees. The higher the altitude, the more you gasped for each breath. It was so much harder than the day before. Eight people dropped off before the last hour. But both JT and I made it. And when we reached the top, we embraced, and I cried from the incredible emotion of it all. JT cried because he hurt so bad; he had an altitude headache, he was exhausted, he was hungry, and we realized we still had to climb down.

I'd run some marathons in my younger days, but in a race, once you cross the finish line, you are done. You get in your car and drive home. But standing on that peak was the first time I had thought through the fact that I was going to have to retrace my steps down this mountain. The difference between a thirteen-year-old boy and his forty-six-year-old father after the three-hour descent to the bunkhouse where we'd overnighted was that JT ate breakfast, looked refreshed, and was eager to go, but I considered the five more hours of hard hiking still ahead of us and didn't know if I could make it.

We started down about 10:30 a.m. and finally reached base camp around 5:00 that afternoon after almost thirteen hours of hiking in one day. Sometime around two o'clock, my feet had stopped moving. When I gave them a command, they responded by saying something unkind about my mother. It was the most unusual I had ever felt; if my behind had caught fire, I would not have been able to run to a bucket of water. About that time, a Kenyan carrying a huge bag on his head ran past me with a cigarette in his mouth. I wanted to cry.

But after a good night's rest at base camp, the two-hour hike to the park gate the following morning felt good. This being Kenya, the van that was scheduled to arrive at 11:00 a.m. to take us back to Kijabe showed up at four that afternoon. Which meant the real adventure was to begin: another experience driving in Kenya at night.

A few final thoughts on our father-son endeavor:

1. Why didn't I take more pictures? The only explanation I can think of is that I was just too tired to do it.
2. Embracing my son on the summit, looking at JT and seeing the realization on his face that he had made it and had pushed past his limitations, is something I will never forget.
3. No one can take this experience away from me.
4. But I would gladly give it to anyone who asked.

———

We never tried to dress our twins alike. We just considered them such different and distinct individuals from the start. So it seemed more than a little ironic that when we took them in for their first doctor's appointment, they each had ear infections in the *same* ear.

Ben got his first haircut, and no longer looked like a detective from some '70s TV show. Once his ear infection cleared up, we started to see more of his personality. He liked to dismantle toys. Katie, except when facing the horror of bedtime, was happy and curious. She loved to go for walks and to look all around. My baby daughter was already maturing into the most beautiful girl in the universe, but before she did the deed, she would grunt in a manner that alerted people miles away to what she was doing, which also provided great inspiration for my English class.

In my experience, grammar is the most boring subject in the world to teach, and certainly to learn. So when we did drills in class to identify irregular verbs, what did I make those self-conscious eighth grade students do? They had to grunt before every irregular verb. I don't know that it made grammar any less boring, but it certainly made that eighth grade English lit class memorable.

—

By the end of February, Katie still wasn't sleeping well, and getting up with her most nights — on top of the rest of our schedule — had me exhausted. And then, as happened every couple of years, I threw my back out and couldn't get out of bed one morning.

At the Kijabe hospital, run by the same mission as RVA, the doctor who examined me was professional and thorough. Then it came time to prescribe my medication. Since the hospital depends a lot on donated medicine, he was handing me stuff and saying, "This hasn't been expired *that* long," and, "This will *probably* still work." Stuff you don't generally hear in the States.

It proved to be great medicine; I slept sixteen hours a day and it made me incoherent when I was awake. After five days, I stopped taking it and realized how truly tired I was. I hadn't gone into adoption naively, but nothing had prepared me for how much time twins would take. And I was still trying to do everything else.

I was too embarrassed to admit I couldn't do it all. But by the end of each day, I was ready to give up. When the principal of the school, a kind man, ran into Nancy one afternoon and asked how she was doing, she burst into tears. Another administrator came over to the house later and told us the school wanted to offer us the day off on Friday.

My response to that was, "I've really screwed up, haven't I?" He said, "This isn't about screwing up, Steve. It's about knowing that everyone needs a break sometimes, and we want to offer one to you."

My *big secret* had been exposed. But once it was out, it was so freeing. I certainly didn't like to admit that I am weak, but I am, and it was liberating to stop pretending I'm not. I was reminded of how little I can do in my own strength, and how God delights to be strong in my weakness. Suddenly the weight of the world was off my shoulders. Nancy and I were going away for a whole day by ourselves, and it was wonderful to realize that we needed it and could do it.

In the year since we'd come back to Africa, nothing had been easy. But everything had been worth it.

—

Our date was great. It's remarkable how being away for a day can refresh your perspective. It was the first time I had driven to Nairobi since we had returned to Kenya, and it was nothing at all like driving in Dallas. I dodged mule carts, sheep, matatus seemingly driven by escapees from the asylum for the criminally insane, and potholes so deep and so wide you couldn't do anything but bid farewell to certain parts of your car as you went through them.

Even so, we had a wonderful time eating alone in an Indian restaurant, shopping, and just bumming around, together and free of all other responsibilities for a whole day.

We went to one huge open-air market to stroll around and see what they were selling. There I had the following verifiable, I-am-not-making-this-up exchange:

Me: How much for that?

Vendor: One hundred thousand shillings. *(for an item I knew you could buy for fifty shillings)*

Me: You must think I'm rich and dumb.

Vendor: I did not think you were rich.

—

But that vendor was wrong, as I was reminded by a couple of incidents I wrote about in another email home:

Matthew and I went down to the hospital to deliver some gifts to the children. We haven't been able to go as often this term because of the twins, so it was special to be down there. We saw the usual sad cases, and I was reminded of what a friend of mine said about working in the African health care system: "This is the only place I've ever worked where malaria is a hopeful diagnosis, because at least it can be treated."

As we were leaving, we heard a small girl, about five, crying as she was being dismissed. I couldn't understand what she was saying, and I asked the nurse if she was still in pain. The nurse said no, she wasn't in pain. The little girl was crying because the hospital was the first place she had eaten three meals a day, and she didn't want to go home and be hungry again.

Last week a Kenyan friend stopped by to see the babies and was amazed at how big they are. She asked what we fed them. Nancy replied, "Fruit, vegetables, cereal, and formula." Our friend responded, "If you can give them all that, then they will be very healthy." Again, a reminder that a balanced diet is out of the reach of most Kenyans; once a baby is off breastmilk, it usually stops having a regular and balanced diet.

We are surrounded by people who do all they can and still can provide only one meal a day for their family. It's just not right.

18

The Wedding Crier

I WAS AMAZED HOW MUCH MY SPIRITS IMPROVED ONCE I ADMITTED I couldn't do everything and realized I didn't have to. I could notice more of the positives in life and not let the negatives drag me so far down.

For example, I was greatly heartened (that sounds so much better than *I gloated*) when both Ben's *and* Katie's first words were "Da-Da." But to be perfectly honest, I need to humbly acknowledge that for some time, *Da-Da* seemed to mean anything and everything from "I'm hungry" or "I would like to be carried" to *an irregular verb is coming forth to the world.* Even before they connected it with me, hearing the twins say *Da-Da* was a thrill.

Part of the fun of living and teaching at a school like RVA was that Nancy could so easily bring the kids by to see me at any time of the day, even when I was teaching. And what seemed neat to me was how, in the course of five minutes in that classroom, our African babies would be held by a Dutch kid, a Swiss student, a Korean, two Kenyans, four Canadians, a Brit, and even a couple of Americans.

It was interesting to note the differences between the twins' personalities in social interactions. Ben would go to anyone. Especially if he thought they might have food or something interesting he could take apart. Katie was a little more particular. Confronted by too many unfamiliar faces at once, she cried for her daddy to pick her up, which never hurt my feelings.

But truth be told, Nancy was always better than I was at noticing, understanding, and articulating her appreciation for all of the positive ways the twins continued to impact our lives, as I was powerfully reminded by an email she wrote to our supporters on March 4, a date that had taken on special meaning for us since Stephen's birth and death four years earlier:

So many people have said or written to us, "What a wonderful thing you are doing. Those babies are so blessed to have you as parents." But as is so often true with God, the total opposite is what is really true. Yes, there has been sacrifice involved in taking them into our family. We are more tired and more tied down, and it's more expensive. But the blessings we are receiving through them far exceed our sacrifice. Their smiles melt many cares and worries away. They, surprisingly enough, have drawn our family closer together in a special way.

But the most important thing they are doing for me is helping me see more as the Father sees. I am seeing others more as God sees them. We've mentioned how the missionary community has gladly and graciously given us clothes, diapers, toys, bottles, etc. But my Kenyan friends have helped me to understand a deeper level of generosity.

Several of the women I buy vegetables from will give me two bananas or three apples and say "Kwa watoto" ("for the babies") and not accept payment. Their gift just about nullifies any profit they make from my small purchases. And then today Grace brought to me a bag from a close friend of hers. I've been with her friend Emily only on four or five occasions; she is a sweet woman with a gracious spirit who lives without a husband in a one-room home and cares for three young grandchildren whose mother has abandoned them. In the bag Emily had given Grace to bring for my babies was a liter of milk and two eggs.

As I looked at that dirty bottle of milk and those two little eggs, I could only think of King David's response to an unexpected kindness in the second book of Samuel, chapter 23 — words I'd never really understood before: "Far be it from me, O Lord, that I should accept this."

I cried and knew I wasn't worthy of such a gift. How can I ever thank Emily enough for her gift, which so demonstrates the love of God? Perhaps by allowing the Father to work in me such selflessness and generosity, such trust in him to know that I too can give out of want, and yet have everything I need.

Ben and Katie are doing well — growing and eating. Katie is even beginning to sleep better. They can just about sit up by themselves. Katie has cut two teeth and Ben is about to. Katie aggressively and purposefully rolls everywhere, and Ben rolls occasionally. Both have smiles that just melt you. Ben's smile makes you think you are the most special person in the universe. Katie's is infectious and makes you think all is well with the world.

Yes, it is we who have been blessed in a very wonderful way by having Ben and Katie added to our family.

—

The end of the term was coming soon, and we always had a big dorm party, which prompted me to make what was, perhaps, the stupidest announcement in the history of my life to the *entire* dorm: "Friday night's dorm party will commence with a water balloon fight. After which, you may no longer address me as 'Uncle Steve.' I will be known as 'Mister Toast,' because I will be that dry at the end of the fight."

The gory details are best left to the imagination. A grand time was had by all but one.

—

A Kenyan friend asked me to help him purchase a cow. I agreed on the condition that I got to name her. He informed me that Kenyans do not name their cows. I asked if it was part of his tradition to borrow money to buy a cow. He asked me, "What do you want to name the cow?" And I thought, *Why should I get all the fun?*

So I announced a contest for the supporters on our email list. The person who submitted the best name for the cow would receive (1) an original batik from a local Kenyan artist, and (2) the thrill of knowing they were the first person ever to name a cow in Kijabe, Kenya. The outpouring of contest entries was so great that I was able to announce the winning name in our next weekly email, which began:

1. *Many of you have* way *too much time on your hands.*
2. *If someone is expecting a baby and I yelled, "Name it Steve or Stephanie," that would be* charming. *If you suggested the name Steve or Stephanie to name a cow, I consider that a sign of* immaturity *and* rudeness.
3. *Those of you who decided to use this contest as an opportunity to insult me severely hurt your chances of winning.*
4. *We had more response to this email than the one in which we announced we were adopting Katie and Ben. It has made us ponder if we should have adopted cows, or perhaps had a contest for naming the babies.*
5. *There were more than a hundred and fifty entries, and it was not easy to come up with a winner. But in the end, we picked the following: Kow-Jabe!*

We had invited some special Kenyan friends over for lunch and to help judge the contest. After we finished that, I told them, "I have tried to understand your culture, but you must join me in understanding my culture. You cannot truly do that unless you watch *Star Wars* and eat popcorn."

You haven't seen *Star Wars* until you have seen it with people outside your own culture. The Kenyan contingent liked Chewbacca the best; we suspected that was because Katie still sounded so much like Chewie when she was happy. Our guests also seemed to enjoy the refreshments; they all referred to it as "popcorns," which made Matthew giggle.

During that same lunch, we had asked all our Kenyan friends about Fred's wedding. Both JT and Matthew had been asked to be in it (JT as a grooms-man and Matthew playing the wedding march on the piano), and Fred had assured us it would last only an hour. I'd been in Kenya long enough not to believe that. So I took my own "national poll" around the lunch table that day and asked our guests how long they expected the wedding to take. Grace: "Five hours." Stephen: "All day." Cecilia: "At least five hours." Joel: "All day and some of the night." We decided to make plans accordingly.

Fred begged us to bring the twins. "It will only be one hour," he insisted again and again, saying it just wouldn't be the same if the whole family wasn't there. We were "this close" to bringing them, until JT and Matthew went to the rehearsal. Evidently it is traditional at Kenyan weddings for the bride to walk down the aisle V-E-R-Y, V-E-R-Y slowly to show how very, very sad she is to leave her parents. At the point in the rehearsal where Matthew had played through the processional for the *seventeenth* time and the bride still hadn't made it all the way down the aisle, we made a quick decision to engage a babysitter for the twins.

The wedding was to start at 10:00 a.m. The boys, since they had respon-sibilities, went early. When Nancy and I showed up at 9:45 a.m., the only people at the church were the groomsmen. We didn't yet know that in Kenyan tradition, the bride is always late to her wedding. So about 10:45, the bride's car showed up, escorted and surrounded by three dozen women singing and dancing and having a big time. Every bride should get a greeting like that on her wedding day.

By the time the ceremony started about 11:00, the church was absolutely packed; Nancy and I were two of only a dozen or so non-Kenyans. The groomsmen came in, and JT appeared handsome in what looked like a Nehru jacket. Then the bridesmaids sashayed in, with a very long, very choreo-graphed jaunt down the aisle that was definitely African cool.

I know a lot of people (probably all guys) think a wedding rehearsal is unnecessary. As much as I hate to admit it, when Matthew started the pro-cessional, I saw persuasive proof that a little practice can work out most of the bugs ahead of time. He had to play it through only *eight* times before the bride found her way to the altar. At that point, I glanced over at JT and noticed he looked even whiter than usual. He had locked his knees and was ready to faint. Someone grabbed him in the nick of time and helped him sit down. But it was pretty close to getting interesting for a moment.

Then things got *really* interesting. Apparently at a Kenyan wedding, it's permissible for any family member, friend, or stranger with a camera to move to any vantage point they wish to photograph the ceremony. At least a dozen camera bugs constantly ducking, scooting, and maneuvering for just the right angle on the proceedings gave the front of the church the ambiance of a subway station at rush hour. I wondered if someone wasn't going to interrupt the minister at any moment to ask the wedding party to turn to catch a bit more natural light.

According to the wedding program, five musical groups were *scheduled* to perform. Nine different groups did. Just as one finished, another began singing from their seats and walked forward to perform. By one o'clock, I wondered if the ceremony would ever end. But after only forty-five more minutes, the service itself was over and a collection taken up to help clean the church. Then after an hour of formal picture-taking at the church, the wedding party disappeared to some other location to take more pictures. All the wedding guests lay down on the grass outside and awaited their return. Nancy decided to go home at that point, because dinner hour approached and the twins needed to be fed. I had little choice but to recline.

When the wedding party returned around four, a reception lunch was served to all who remained. And it was obvious that for many, this repast was a major reason to attend. During and after an ample meal, the celebrated couple's parents each were to give three-minute speeches. But since a minute of Kenyan time falls at the opposite end of the cultural space-time continuum from a "New York minute," each speech lasted roughly thirty minutes, by which time the festivities finally seemed to have reached full swing.

It was time to give gifts. Someone played a tape that sounded suspiciously like roller-skating music, and hundreds of people assumed their places in a gift-giving *line*. After that, there were four different cakes, and I was given the great honor of cutting the "friendship" cake. What I didn't know was that, as the cutter of a cake, I was also supposed to give a speech. I probably shouldn't have been surprised, because thus far *everyone* had given a speech. But I had not prepared, let alone practiced, what I would say in Swahili. So it was not one of my best efforts, at least in the beginning:

"I am white; you are not," at which point I saw two missionaries I had *thought* were my friends absolutely lose it, laughing so hard I thought they might become ill. I ignored them and continued, "I come from Texas. You live in Kenya. But we are united in friendship with our Lord and with Fred and Sarah." An hour later, when I saw one of those *former* friends, he immediately returned to the fetal position, with tears pouring out of his eyes. At the time, I thought the speech was not as stupid as it sounded. I think it probably lost something in the translation.

At 5:30, the celebration was still going strong, but my ride was leaving and I decided to make my exit. This was an amazing, memorable experience and, all in all, a rather grand and wonderful way to start a marriage.

One more thing: I've been a best man twice and a groomsman more than a dozen times. But I'd never had the honor I received at my friend Fred's wedding. For at the bottom of the program (which is a story in itself—how many wedding programs do you see listing a Cake Mistress or Convoy Mechanic?), the last thing on the page was a dedication: "To Steve, my first beloved computer teacher."

Who says guys don't cry at weddings?

—

I had never been able to forget my visit to that nearby national school at the end of my first year in Kenya, when the teacher had to explain that her students were lying on the dirt floor of the classroom because it was Thursday and most of the children hadn't eaten since Monday. Since my New Year's resolution on the top of Mount Longonot about not making peace with the idea of hungry children, I'd thought about those kids every day.

I knew I couldn't do anything about world hunger. *But surely,* I thought, *I can provide lunch for the kids in that one school.* Not doing *something* would be making peace with the idea of hungry children—not starving, faceless children on the far side of the world but African neighbors who now looked so much like my own Katie and Ben. So throughout the second term and the first couple of weeks of our April break, I'd done a lot of brainstorming, researching, and strategizing with people more experienced and knowledgeable than me.

Now I was finally ready to unveil my plan and the thinking behind it to all the folks on our email list:

Here are the facts:

- *The dropout rate in most Kenyan elementary schools is more than 50 percent.*
- *Most Kenyan children eat only one meal a day.*
- *When a free lunch is provided, the dropout rate is reduced dramatically.*

Here are some thoughts:

- *Most Kenyan children walk several miles to a classroom and sit all day on a bench without a back to it.*

- *It seems like they would concentrate better with some food in their stomachs.*
- *Without an education, there is little opportunity one can expect from Africa.*

The World Food Program has established the following as the minimum nutritional requirements for a lunch program: one hundred fifty grams of maize (per student), forty grams of beans (per student), a small amount of oil for cooking.

Today (the price changes constantly) it would cost me one thousand shillings or about $13.33 to purchase a ninety-pound bag of maize. It would cost me 720 shillings or about ten dollars to purchase a ninety-pound bag of beans. If I purchase oil, a little salt, and a few onions for flavoring, my cost would be up to about thirty dollars. For that I can feed six hundred schoolchildren a nutritious lunch.

This is how it would work. The school would provide a parent to cook the meal. The students would have to provide the bowl and utensils. We would provide the food and announce to the entire school and all the parents that we had enough food to last three months. That way any theft would have some accountability to it.

The problem with too many aid programs is that most of the donated food doesn't reach the people it is intended to help. We could tell you stories that we don't need to get into here. But the beauty of this plan is that all the money goes to buy local food and the schoolchildren get to eat it.

There is no middleman. I will collect the money, buy the grains, deliver the food, and make sure that the students are getting fed. I won't get paid for this, and I don't want to be. All the money goes to feed the kids.

So if you have been looking for some way to help out, we think that this can decrease the dropout rate and increase learning, and the children will know kind Americans are providing the food.

I will collect enough funds to commit to a school for one year. If we get more than we need, we will add another school. You can count on regular pictures and updates that will give you an idea of what school is like for a Kenyan child.

Obviously, I can't do this without support. How many schools we cover depends on how much support we get. My hopes may be unrealistic, but I am so tired of seeing hungry children. I would love for this to get big enough that many, many children benefit from it.

But we'll start with one school, and if you want to help, please send a check made out to Africa Inland Mission or AIM [and I gave the address]. In your note, please let them know that it goes toward the Peifer School Lunch Program. It is tax deductible, and they will send you a receipt.

The other need I have is a vehicle. The schools we want to begin with are out in the Rift Valley where there are no good roads. The job will require a four-wheel-drive van, and someday I will write an email about the adventure of trying to purchase a car in this country. If you would like to help us with that challenge, you can send a check to the same place and include a note indicating it is for the Peifer Vehicle Fund.

I always add that I know you may get a million of these requests a day. So if you can't or don't want to help, it won't hurt our feelings. Do what you are supposed to do, and don't worry about the rest.

Just know that I honestly think this is a way to go under the radar, so that all the money goes to feed kids. I think this program can really, really make a difference.

Let's change the world, shall we?

19

Daddies, Don't Let Your Babies Grow Up to Love Country

EVERY TERM BREAK WE'D BEEN AT RVA, WE PLANNED SOME SORT OF FAMily adventure. Not only for a change in scenery but also for a break from the joyful 24/7 demands of dorm-parenting, and a respite from our other campus responsibilities. We'd made an effort to expose our sons and ourselves to the amazing beauty and breadth of Africa, its diverse cultures, and some of the wonderful people God is using to do so many good things there.

However, ten-day off-road camping trips among the nomadic desert peoples of northern Kenya, hiking up dormant volcanoes, even daylong safaris through any of the national game parks no longer seemed like practical Peifer family vacations with nine-month-old babies. And the entire Peifer clan needed a vacation. With all that we'd done that term, plus the excitement and challenge of adopting, parenting, and adapting to twins, we were all on the verge of exhaustion. Even our older boys.

Spending a week resting on the beach seemed a wonderful and manageable alternative adventure for a family with two new babies. The eight-hour drive over some of the worst roads you can imagine to get to the coast was another matter. For some unexplained reason, friends who had gladly offered us rides before were hesitant about driving cross-country with two nine-month-olds in the car. (One guy even asked, "Are you taking *both* of them?") We finally decided we would rent a car, but then discovered that it would be cheaper to fly with a special deal Kenya Airways had running at the time. So instead of an eight-hour drive, we enjoyed a one-hour flight.

Beach-bumming for a week was the perfect vacation for our family that year. It was surprisingly restful and rejuvenating. Two totally unrelated highlights of that trip I will remember till I die:

Lifetime Memory 1: You don't have *any* idea how much sand you have on you if your skin is white. Ben and Katie looked like they were sugarcoated. They loved the sand and they loved the water; they just weren't wild about cleaning *off* the sand.

Lifetime Memory 2: The older boys and I went snorkeling one day. We arranged for a local fisherman to take us to the coral reef on a wooden sailboat he told me had cost him (or maybe his grandfather) two hundred dollars new. We had to wade out a fair distance to where the boat was anchored; one of the crew carried Matthew when the water got to be over his head. Just before we reached the boat, I stepped on a sea urchin—a spiky little critter that seemed perfectly and painfully designed for the sole (no pun intended) purpose of making a foot bleed.

We had already waded all the way out and boarded the boat before our cheerful Kenyan captain confessed he didn't have any snorkeling equipment on board, but he was certain he could locate some. So we sailed for ten minutes and he found friends who would lend us their masks. When we then tacked and headed out toward the middle of the Indian Ocean in a creaky wooden boat, with no life jackets, I thought, *I am surely going to be arrested for being an unfit father.*

But we eventually reached a small coral reef bordering a barely submerged sandbar where the water was shallow enough that the boys could get out and stand on it. We saw hundreds of tropical fish and all kinds of shells and starfish. *Spectacular* was the only word to describe it. After we got back on the boat and were leaving, one of the fishermen showed me the octopus he had caught in the reef. It came up to my waist, and I was glad I was seeing it on the boat rather than encountering it in the reef. But besides the bleeding, and the persistently nagging thought that if the boat went down, we were all going to die, it was a pleasant and memorable trip.

⁓

When the third term started right after we got back to Kijabe, our returning dorm boys provided some grim reminders of what life can be like in Africa. Two of the guys whose families lived in Madagascar went home during the break, but were forced to stay inside their houses the whole time because of all the riots going on there. One of them saw and heard machine gun fire on his street. Another one of the guys came back with malaria, and it wasn't the first time he had had it. Africa is always a beautiful and fascinating place, but sometimes it can be so brutal.

The relentless reminders that we lived in the third world ran the emotional gamut from I-must-be-dreaming delightful (like the pair of two-foot-tall red-beaked hornbills that took up residence on our porch) to what must be everyone's worst nightmares. Like when one of our RVA staff members walked to the mission hospital a few hundred yards down the hill from our campus complaining of a kidney stone. The local doctors sent Jeff to see a specialist at a hospital in Nairobi, who could find no problem. But since he was still in terrible pain, the mission sent him back to the States for further tests. By the time he got there, he was in critical condition and needed emergency surgery to remove one of his kidneys just to save his life. Jeff is a wonderful man (with a sweet wife and two beautiful daughters) who nearly died just a week after being given a clean bill of health at a government hospital in Africa.

—

I had yet one more reminder that we weren't in Texas anymore. The Rangers and the Cubs were playing back home. But at RVA, rugby practice had started and JT was loving it. Most of our guys in the dorm were playing that year, and let me tell you, as a dorm parent for sixteen male members of our species, I thoroughly approved of *anything* that exhausts seventh graders. Almost all our kids also came home every night with sorely bruised body parts—and huge smiles on their faces. I was fast learning to appreciate, if not understand, this alien sport, and I couldn't wait until their first game.

While seasonal sports schedules often impacted life in the boys' dorm, it was still the twins who set our daily morning ritual. By midway through that third term, the babies were finally sleeping well enough through the night that I could get up and slip away around 6:00 most mornings to exercise. I'd be back around 6:30 to get the kids up and change them while Nancy prepared their breakfast. After feeding them, we'd spread a blanket out on the floor and let them play as the rest of us rushed about getting ready for our day. But on Saturdays, I liked to get down and play on the floor with them.

And that's what I was doing one morning when it hit me: I had George Strait on the stereo. Babies are babies, and the truth is, when you have twins, you are too busy to notice their color. But suddenly I became aware that my African babies were being subjected to country music. I thought, *I can't help that I'm white, and I can't help that I'm old. But I will not train my babies to love country music; that would be too weird.*

So I jumped up, ran to the stereo, exiled the country, and restored some classic Motown to its proper place. That led to another unfortunate problem:

my uncontrollable, three-decades-old compulsion to try to dance whenever I hear Diana Ross and the Supremes. I was jammin' to "Stop in the Name of Love" and noticed the looks on the twins' faces, which struck me as a cross between morbid fascination and dread horror. I stood pondering the deeper meaning behind their expressions until JT stepped into the room and came to the rescue (whose I'm not sure). "Don't worry, Dad," he consoled me. "Matthew and I don't like *any* of your music; why would the babies?"

I stood there pondering a possible retort until long after my eldest left the room. I didn't know whether his words were depressing or reassuring. I finally decided they were both. And in an encouraging sort of way, I felt better, because for me, coming out even meant that I came out ahead.

—

I found I sometimes had to grade my effectiveness as a classroom teacher by that same high standard. As I did that third semester at RVA when the reading of *A Midsummer Night's Dream* in my eighth grade English lit class surprised me in ways I never expected. One of my best friends played Puck in our high school production, and I recall attending mostly to cheer him on. But I never read the play until college for a course on the politics of Shakespeare—a class and a professor that would have sucked all the fun out of a kiss and a bowl of ice cream.

Rereading it now at the age of forty-six was revelatory for me. This Shakespeare stuff was genuinely funny. It could speak to eighth grade students where they lived! And it celebrated language in a way that could inspire budding writers to move beyond "whatever" as an explanation for character development. As you may recall (and even if you don't, like I didn't), the character in the play named Helena is so determined to be with a boy that she tells him, "I am your spaniel; beat me and I will fawn on you more." So I asked the question, "Is this a good role model for a young woman? Is this how you would like your sister to act?" The resulting discussion was intense, and a look came into some of their eyes that I can't quite explain. But I guess I would call it the flicker of understanding.

At another point as we were reading the play out loud, one of the characters said something stupid and the whole class erupted in laughter. As they suddenly looked up and around at each other in a kind of astonishment, I experienced that rewarding (and for me very occasional) sensation of joy that real teachers experience whenever a student gets excited about something they are trying to teach.

Alas, dear Puck (I know, don't say it; *Yorick* just didn't work as well), 'twas a feeling lasting not a fortnight, when I discovered that the masterpiece of a play one of my students wrote as entertainment for the annual eighth grade formal dinner was a skit making jest of how they all had to pretend they liked Mr. Shakespeare's play just to make Mr. Peifer feel good, but how in truth they had been bored to death by it. However, I saw their eyes and heard their laughter. I know better. Though the truth doest matter but little in this sweet case. For lo, I am certain of this one thing:

Shakespeare impacted me more than them. Getting back to the profundity and humor of the original Mr. Bill was a great reminder of the many benefits to be found by stepping out of my comfort zone and trying to keep learning. Being challenged to contemplate eternal themes, beautiful language, and thought-provoking characters was a wonderful experience for me, regardless of how my eighth grade students truly felt.

—

I certainly didn't manage to make all my student interactions into such warm or meaningful personal memories. But not for lack of trying.

For one week that third term, I drew the short straw and was put in charge of the dreaded Saturday morning detention. At least *I* dreaded it, because it meant all students assigned to detention that week had to rise at 8:00 a.m. (on a weekend morning, and what's worse?) and come find me wherever I said we'd meet to do whatever I decided they would have to do. The point being that their assignment for the day—whether studying, polishing my shoes, or anything else I wanted and thought unpleasant enough—would dispel any desire they might have to continue even one more step down whatever path to perdition had brought them to me on such a fine Saturday morning.

That week I had two tough Kenyan kids. So I thought, *What would be the ultimate deterrent for these guys?* I believed my solution was ingenious. They had to follow me around for three hours, picking up any and every little tidbit of litter we might find anywhere on campus. While singing Neil Diamond songs. At the top of their lungs.

What I hadn't counted on was how into this these guys would get. In my Surreal Moments in Musical Memory Hall of Fame, the top ten will surely include teaching and then listening to two Kenyan kids singing "Song Sung Blue" at full throttle.

—

A group of Australian schoolgirls visited RVA during this same time. I volunteered to take them down to the hospital and let them distribute some of the toys our friends had donated. As I tried to prepare them for what they might see, I saw one of the girl's eyes begin to brim over.

And it turned out to be a rough week in the pediatric ward. Lots of hydrocephalus and one burn victim whose face appeared to be almost totally gone (that's the only way I could describe it). Matthew went with us, and he always tends to go to the worst-case-scenario kids. But seeing that little burn victim made him so sick to his stomach he had to walk away.

One of the biggest challenges for docs at our hospital is that whenever they treat one ailment, they find so many other things wrong. Because the water supply is foul, and most Kenyans can't eat three meals a day, the children's bodies are often full of amoebas. And malnutrition is so common, it's assumed. As a result, many of these African children have a lot more wear and tear on their little systems than most kids would.

Seeing all this for the first time, one young Australian girl came up to me and asked, "Why is it so hard for them? Why do I have so much and they have so little? Why do little kids have to suffer?"

I told her I didn't know the answers, but those were good questions.

—

I'd observed and learned a bit about what was not only a chronic problem in and around Kijabe but also perhaps the country's most pressing environmental crisis: the ongoing profligate destruction of the nation's woodlands.

Only 2 percent of the vast virgin forests that once covered much of Kenya remain standing today. That's been a major contributing factor in the growing frequency and seriousness of the deadly cycles of drought and famine that have plagued Kenya and the whole of East Africa repeatedly through recent decades.

Because our boarding school happens to be located on the edge of one of the country's last national forests, the RVA community has taken on the challenge of educating our Kenyan neighbors to understand their need to preserve and restore what historically was one of their land's greatest natural resources and is even now critically essential for Kenya's present and future generations. Our first goal was to demonstrate and help Kenyans to grasp the possibility and value of reforestation by providing the community with our own example and offering them opportunities for hands-on experience in replanting.

When you make a dollar a day, your first thought on any morning is not, *Hey, why don't I buy some trees to plant today?* But there were some dedicated RVA staff who had begun to grow seedlings. So we scheduled a huge tree-planting day with the community one third-term Saturday. For me, it was a day of deepest discouragement, which ultimately enabled me to find renewed hope in unexpected places and people.

We began that morning with a rousing welcome for the many students from nearby national schools who showed up at RVA to help. They had all been instructed by their principals and teachers to come in their school uniforms, so a lot of the boys showed up in suits. When I asked one kid if he might be uncomfortable hiking up steep hills to dig holes and plant trees dressed so nicely, he shrugged off the question and told me what he was wearing was the only set of clothing he owned.

Hundreds of us scattered throughout the town, up and down the nearby hills, and into the national forest to plant baby trees we hoped would live and become part of a big, beautiful replenished forest that could protect, enrich, and rejuvenate the land. What got discouraging on our long-planned and well-publicized community tree-planting day was how often we encountered others in the act of destroying what forest is left today. We'd be hiking up a steep trail into the forest, gently holding and protecting a twelve-inch seedling while looking for a perfect place to plant a baby tree. And then we'd meet a dozen Kenyan men staggering *down* the trail, half-carrying, half-dragging out of the forest massive pieces of the 125-year-old tree they had just chopped down.

What they were doing was illegal. But chopping down trees to make charcoal to sell for cooking and heating homes was probably the only means most of these men had of feeding their families. So it was hard to get mad enough to confront a bunch of burly men, each hauling a load twice my weight and armed with a machete. We had no way to reason with them or convince them that what they were doing to keep their children alive posed an even greater threat to the survival of their children's children in the future. People do not think about tomorrow when they don't know if they'll have enough to make it through today.

But it was hard not to scream at *someone* over the steady destruction of one of the last national forests we saw taking place right in front of us, on the day we were trying to rally the local community to help restore it. Every time I encountered a charcoal crew that day and looked down and wondered how many decades it might take for the seedling in my hand to replace the one giant tree they had taken out in less than a day, all I could think was, *We are going to lose this battle.*

Which naturally brought to mind the battle I had chosen to wage against another of Kenya's biggest challenges: its hungry children. Malnutrition was at least as big an issue as this country's deforestation and promised to be no easier to solve. That realization started a downward spiral of doubts and discouraging questions churning through my mind:

Whatever possessed me to think I should tackle such a problem? In the scope of time and history, what difference can one person hope to make by planting a scrawny little seedling or even feeding all the scrawny, malnourished children in one Kenyan school? There are too many hungry children in too many schools for me ever to feed them all, just like there are not enough seedlings or enough Saturdays even for hundreds of us to plant enough seedlings to equal the weight of just one of the trees cut down today. Replacing that tree will take more than resources; it will take time.

And by all indications, time was fast running out on Kenya's forests — and on too many of Kenya's kids. *Without the time or the resources, I'll never be able to do enough to make any real difference. Have I been the world's biggest fool to think I can do anything that truly matters? And if my efforts don't matter, what's the point? Who even cares?* Then I saw my friend Chuck Baker planting yet another seedling.

Chuck was the shop teacher at RVA. Now in his sixties, he had taught shop for forty years in the States before his wife had died the year before. They had purchased a house in southern California back in 1969 that was probably worth the better part of a million dollars by this time. Plus he had a nice pension. He could have bought and lived out the rest of his life in a nice home by the beach. Instead, he'd come to Africa to teach shop at a boarding school for missionary kids in Kijabe, Kenya.

I'd already seen him slip and fall twice that day as he maneuvered his way up steep, slippery slopes while holding and protecting young saplings in each hand. And yet I'd never heard a discouraging word nor a single complaint from him all day. Instead, Chuck talked about what a great day it was to be outside planting trees. What a privilege it was to be able to work on this project. What a great idea he thought it was. How much he appreciated all the planning and effort that had gone into organizing such an event. How blessed he'd been by the time he'd been able to be at RVA. (And more where that came from.)

As I made it a point to work alongside Chuck and listen to his words and his heart that day, my attitude of frustration and discouragement melted away. Until a brave new thought struck me: *It may look like we are losing the battle today, but in the end? We are gonna win the war. In part, because we have Chuck Baker on our side.*

I don't know if you have ever had the opportunity to know and spend time with someone you felt unworthy to be around. But that is how I felt about my friend Chuck that day as he and I and lots of other friends planted four thousand trees in and around the Kijabe community. We may have even bought the forest a little more time.

⁓

Just a week or so later, I had yet another experience that started out discouraging but ended on a surprisingly positive note with an important personal realization.

Our older sons' school back in the States sent plastic bedsheets for an orphanage we'd written home about earlier in the year. So many of the orphans tended to wet their beds so frequently that the result was not merely soiled sheets but some of the foulest, smelliest mattresses you could imagine. A logical, simple solution seemed to be rubber sheets, but you couldn't find such products for sale anywhere in all of Kenya. So it was a wonderful and generous thing for the boys' Texas school to purchase and ship a big enough supply for the entire orphanage. But because of an unfortunate miscommunication, our friends in Texas tried to send the shipment directly to the orphanage, instead of to me at RVA to deliver to the orphanage.

This is part of the email report I sent home to explain the whole frustrating fiasco that followed from that simple misunderstanding:

The orphanage's name and address on the shipment meant I would not be notified when it hit customs; neither could I sign for or receive the goods on the orphanage's behalf. And since the orphanage didn't have a phone, we had to wait and rely on Kenya's mail service to be notified when and where we could pick up the shipment. The notice, when we finally received it, informed us that customs fees and storage costs would total fifteen hundred dollars. (More than I make in a month.)

So it was that the pastor overseeing the orphanage work, a friend of his, and I all climbed onto the bench seat in the cab of the friend's 1974 Chevy pickup for the hourlong drive to Nairobi. I sat in the middle. The old truck shook so violently when it started, I didn't think we would get out of the RVA parking lot. I was wrong. But I soon wished I hadn't been.

As we began the long, slow climb up the steep grade out of Kijabe to the main highway into Nairobi, the pickup still rattling and shivering to beat the band, and a man I'd known for less than five minutes reaching between my legs at regular intervals to shift, we skidded sideways and almost plunged off the road and down into a deep ravine. When I suddenly realized there were no seat belts in the vehicle, I had, interestingly enough, the very same thought I'd had sailing out into the Indian Ocean in a creaky wooden fishing boat just a few weeks earlier: We're all going to die!

Turns out once we reached the main road, we enjoyed having a leisurely, surprisingly anxiety-free, two-hour drive into the city. During which I attempted to tell my first-ever Texas Aggie joke to a Kenyan. (In English.) I guess some things are universal. I got real laughs.

But no one laughed when I announced to the customs officials that I could not and would not pay what they were asking. I then inquired why bedding going to orphans would be charged any customs fees in the first place. I've conducted lots of business negotiations over the years back in the States and felt like I was fairly good at it. But I kept getting blank looks when I said, "It's all for orphans in your country! Why are you preventing this? Why aren't you encouraging this instead of fighting me on it?" After a very, very long discussion, they finally reduced the fee.

I then proceeded to the warehouse to pick up the shipment, and the people there wanted almost a thousand dollars for "storage." We waited an hour to talk to someone in charge before we were told no one could help us (that day). If we came back on Monday, I could be helped, but the price for the storage would go up if we waited. After another long, long discussion, they agreed to hold the price until Monday.

I spent much of the next week on the phone with the company. We spoke more than a dozen times, and after a while, my greatest gifting in life won the day: they were so sick of talking to me that they agreed to reduce the price. The pastor of the orphanage went back to town on Friday to collect the shipment. Customs informed him that they had never agreed to a lower price, and that he could be fined for being late.

We ended up paying it all, but the whole rigmarole was terribly discouraging for me. It would be so easy to throw up your hands in a situation like that and ask, "Why do I bother?" And if it was this much hassle to get a simple shipment through customs to give to a small orphanage, what kind of obstacles might I run into when I launched a daily lunch program for a few hundred schoolchildren?

But we finally had the stuff, so we went to the orphanage to distribute it on a Sunday afternoon. In addition to the plastic bedsheets, there was an individual package for each kid containing a blue floppy hat (so cool that all the seniors from RVA wanted one); a tennis ball (several kids asked me, "Why is there hair on this ball?"); a sucker; a toothbrush; and some washcloths. The children were so thrilled you could hear them exhale as they pulled out each new surprise. What turned out to be the best treasure of all was a personal card tucked into each package; I couldn't count the number of these orphans who told me, "I never had anyone write to me before."

Once the packages were all open, the Kenyan pastor asked me to say a few words. So I got to deliver my favorite line: "These were sent by people in America who love you." Then I had to explain about the sheets. It was the first time in my life I'd had a translator, and I'm sure he felt grateful to have studied English as he translated, "These are your new sheets. If you pick at them and make holes, I will come back and stand on your head. And then I will jump up and down." (As I demonstrated by jumping up and down, the sixty-year-old pastor who was translating jumped up and down also.)

It occurred to me that as discouraging as the customs charges had been, the obvious work and care that went into those packages and the joy of the children receiving them made me feel encouraged and grateful that I'm on the winning side. I'm no Chuck Baker, and I didn't spend hours putting those packages together for those orphans and raising money for the sheets, but I'd be proud to warm the bench for the people who did.

—

One day midway through the middle of that last term of the year, I spotted my oldest son walking arm-in-arm with a Kenyan and a Korean seventh grader. Since they were talking rather animatedly, I had a fleeting thought that JT and his buddies were enjoying the interchange of different cultures and, in their own small way, building a bridge of ethnic understanding that someday would enable all peoples to coexist in joy and peace. And then I heard them. They were trying to figure out how to build a whoopee cushion.

Seventh grade is its own culture.

—

Sometime in late June, I went down to the valley to celebrate a special event. One of our friends in the States raised money to replace the deteriorating dining tables at the orphanage there. I can still see the face of the young kid who came up to me and said, "Thank you. It is nice to eat sitting down."

I didn't know what to say except what I usually say: "This came from people in the United States who love you." But I couldn't quite get all the words out this time.

—

I also sent out this update on our plans to launch our hot lunch program for the fall term of the new school year:

We are grateful for all your support for the school lunch program. It looks as if we will have enough to feed two schools for a year—Kamuyu with two hundred fifty students and Nyankinyua School with three hundred fifty. Both have first through eighth grade students. Local church and community leaders told us they consider these schools the poorest in the area. So we'll start there. Both can be reached only after exciting drives over nonexistent "roads."

I first visited Kamuyu, where the biggest issue they face is that they have no running water. They started to construct a tank that would collect water from the gutters of their buildings during the rainy season, but they do not have enough funding to complete it. So they can't even offer a drink of water to their students, many of whom walk several miles to attend school where children have no water all day except what they can bring themselves.

Nyankinyua School is much like Kamuyu in structure: rock walls, no windows, and dirt floors. At Nyankinyua, they were growing seeds in the floor of one classroom. When I told the headmaster there about our lunch plan, he began to weep. He admitted it was very difficult for him to see children be so hungry; he was very grateful to have any help. I told him we will begin in September, since this term is almost over. As I drove away, I passed some of his students who were still walking home. They had already walked four miles. None of the children wore shoes.

But this is what I signed up for. I am so excited and grateful for all your help. I'll be going to the schools each month to get updates, and learn what a day is like for the children. I'll be sending you regular reports.

The adventure begins September 2nd.

20

Twins 2, Modern Dad 0

A S HARD AS IT WAS TO BELIEVE, WE WERE FAST APPROACHING THE END OF another school year at Rift Valley Academy with all the traditional end-of-school events. The administration asked the staff if we could help make one of those events a little more special and memorable by providing items to serve as prizes for those participating in the annual senior talent show. Most people made cookies, or something like that. Not me; I wanted to do something BIG—significant even.

I decided to donate, at great sacrifice from my personal collection, one of my most treasured CDs by my favorite musical artist of all time. During the show, in one of the breaks between acts, the emcee announced that they were giving away a special prize "donated by Mr. Peifer—a CD of Neil Diamond's greatest hits." This being RVA, the kids cheered mightily, although several students asked me if it was a first-place prize or a *last*-place prize. When the emcee asked who wanted the exciting prize, at least a dozen kids ran toward the stage, but quickly sat down when informed they had to *sing* a Neil Diamond song in order to win.

Sometimes I just don't understand teenagers today.

—

I was beginning to understand our twins better and better as the months passed and they continued to grow and display more and more of their distinct and different personalities.

When they turned one on July 6, we made it a festive family day. Of course, we gave the twins their first ever pieces of cake. Katie put her fingers in the frosting and licked them; Ben gobbled down his entire piece and started looking at Katie's with heightened interest.

At one, Katie was pulling up, but not quite walking; Ben was crawling, but was not as ambitiously curious as his sister. He was content to thoroughly examine one toy for a long time; she needed to see everything, constantly.

But the way they each viewed Cheerios revealed their differences in both character and world perspective. That particular American breakfast staple was difficult to obtain in Kenya, and if you did find a source, the price was often prohibitive. But they make a great snack for little fingers, as we discovered when we introduced the twins to them after a friend gave us a big box. Katie promptly displayed a new facet of her personality: she would not eat *broken* Cheerios. It probably would not be overstating reality to say that broken Cheerios *offended* her. Ben, on the other hand, considered her pickiness as manna from heaven. I was not certain that there were enough Cheerios in all of Kenya for Ben ever to get enough. The twins really did complement each other.

What Nancy and I enjoyed as much as watching the babies grow was seeing the relationships develop between them and our older boys, who each embraced big brotherhood in ways that added a unique fabric to our family life. Matthew was quite good at putting Ben down for naps. Whenever JT called Katie "Hey, pretty girl," I got choked up. As we'd said since the day we brought them home to be Peifers, it had "just seemed so natural." (With the occasional 2:00 a.m. wake-up calls still a small exception to that rule.)

Other changes were coming for all of us, as I indicated in this email I sent back to the States the middle of July:

For the last day of school, I borrowed something from author Erma Bombeck and modified it for my classes. I started alphabetically and told Ha-Sun Ahn, "You are my favorite student. I appreciate your brilliance in grammar, your witty writing, and your hilarious speeches. Please don't tell anyone in the class that you were my favorite student."

I moved on to the next student and said, "Ryan, you were my favorite student. I loved your accents when we read out loud. I appreciated how hard you worked, and your insights on Shakespeare were unique. Just don't tell anyone in the class that you were my favorite student."

By the third kid, I was pretty misty, and so were they. It was a remarkable year being back here at RVA, and I'm very grateful that I had the opportunity to teach. As glad as I am for the experience, I'm gladder that a real teacher will be teaching eighth grade English lit next year. I'm moving on to other opportunities within the school.

———

We began the official adoption process for the babies about that same time. But because we had twins and Kenya had just passed new adoption laws, no one seemed to know what those changes would mean in practice. We asked two different lawyers whether adopting twins together at the same time would count as one procedure or as two separate adoptions. Neither could tell us. So we started the paperwork without knowing the costs, or the time frame, or even all of the steps the process would entail. It was kind of scary. On the positive side, we weren't alone; no one else seemed to know any more than we did.

But we were anxious to make the adoption legal as soon as possible. We'd heard horror stories about families who'd taken Kenyan kids into their families and then faced the horrible dilemma of either not being able to go back to the States when they had to, or leaving behind children who'd already been part of their family for months or years—just because the application for legal adoption was delayed or lost somewhere in the legal labyrinth of lethargy that was Kenyan governmental bureaucracy. While our family didn't have any immediate plans for international travel, we wanted to be ready if the need arose.

———

For Nancy (none of the rest of us had planned to accompany her) the need arose to go back to the States for three weeks during our break before the new school year began. As I acknowledged in an email as her late-July departure date approached, *There are many emotions connected with her leaving. I've never been away from my bride longer than one week at a time in seventeen years of marriage, and it's difficult to imagine being separated for that long. On the other hand, we are thrilled that she will be able to celebrate her dad's eightieth birthday and see lots of family and friends. (And I realize a shorter trip would be much harder to justify in terms of the cost and time required just to make the journey back and forth.)*

Of course, I must be honest. One-year-old twins usually keep both of us really, really busy. When I think of everything that needs to be done during Nancy's absence, a deep sense of fear rises within me. Then I remind myself: I change most of the diapers; I give all the baths; I'm a modern dad who can do it.

Then I think of the time just this past week when I was on the floor with the babies when Ben bonked Katie on the head with a toy. That made her cry, so I pulled her onto my lap to comfort her. About that time, Ben threw up and seemed alarmingly intrigued by the sight of whatever it was that he'd most recently ingested. So I snatched up both babies in my arms and retreated to another room. Then the phone rang and I set them on the floor by my feet so I could answer it. I attended to whatever the caller needed in what seemed like only a minute or two. Meantime I'd forgotten the mess on the floor in the other room. But the twins hadn't; both had managed to thoroughly examine all of it.

Even so, as a modern man, I can face the next three weeks without my wife with — as the Nike ads claim — no fear. But with a great deal of panic.

At some conference back in the States, I'd been sitting and talking with a bunch of folks, including a professor from the United States Naval Academy, who excused himself from the gathering because "his ship needed to leave the harbor." I was a little puzzled until I saw him coming out of the restroom a couple of minutes later.

Until Kenya, that was probably the best such euphemism I'd ever heard. But while Nancy was gone during our break, the older boys and I took Swahili lessons together to continue to improve our cross-cultural communications skills. Our instructor confirmed what Nancy (who obviously didn't need the Swahili refresher as badly as the rest of us did) had told us already: in Kenya, when you need to excuse yourself to answer the call of nature, you say in Swahili, "I have to go tie the goat." Of course, the expression immediately caught on with the boys. I heard so many variations of goat phrases from them, you would have thought we were a family of zookeepers. I suspected this would be not a passing fad but a lasting Peifer family tradition.

Other than our Swahili lessons, there wasn't time while Nancy was gone to do much at all besides answer the call and tend to the daily needs of all four of my kids. While the daily demands were every bit as challenging as I'd expected, life without Mama never got dull. And the experience had its positive moments as well, as I reported in an email I titled "Twins 2, Modern Dad 0."

It has now been a week since Nancy left, and like most things we dread in life, the anticipation was worse than the reality. The babies have slept through the night every night this week, and other problems have been few. JT and Matthew have been wonderful helpers; they have made it fun for me and the babies. We all really miss Nancy, but I will always treasure this special time alone with my babies. This modern dad has learned three things this week:

Principle One: As long as it doesn't hurt, anything babies wear is okay. One morning I managed to wrestle Ben into an outfit that included a sweatshirt with a place to stick your hands about waist level. At noon I discovered I'd gotten the sweatshirt on completely backward. After examining him to make sure it wasn't causing any discomfort, I figured, What's the point of changing? *and let him wear it the rest of the day that way.*

Colors are another story. My wife still dresses me (not literally, you know what I mean) because I struggle with color combinations. I don't know how many times this week Grace has looked askance at me or the clothes I've put on the kids and I've had to reassure her, "Oh, that combination is cool in the United States now." She no longer seems to believe me, for some reason.

So far no one has been hurt or even seriously endangered by my clothing choices. And as far as I'm concerned, that's all that matters.

Principle Two: If you have to bet between brute force and lightning speed, it's a tough call. Katie is almost walking and can move like the Flash when she wants to. Ben is crawling, but he is pretty slow compared with her. Katie will crawl over Ben if he is in her way and slowing her down.

But she is not as successful in swiping toys from Ben as she used to be. He probably weighs three pounds more than Katie, and if he has his hand on a toy, she can no longer pry it out of his death grip. What's happening more and more is that he gets interested in something she has and will grab it away. When she used to do that to him, he would just sit there and look at where the toy was. Now that he swipes it from her, he does the same thing: he sits and plays with the toy while she rages. He isn't ignoring her in a rude way. He is just totally focused on the new toy.

Principle Three: Jealous dog equals three children. I'm on the floor playing with the babies. After a while, they crawl away. Katie comes back and wants to sit on my lap. I pick her up; she cuddles for a few minutes and wants down. Ben ambles over, wants up, says, "Da Da Da" several times and wanders off again.

Then Jessie, our dog, jumps in my lap for a turn. This has happened four times this week. The babies have a little truck book that you can squeeze and make beep. If I beep the book, all three of them come over to beep the book themselves, Jessie with her nose.

—

I had a semi funny story to end this email with, but it no longer seems funny at all:

A friend here went to get her license to drive a bus. After paying the required amount of money to the local trucking company for lessons, she spent virtually no time behind the wheel of a bus. The bus at the trucking company was decrepit, and she didn't even get out of first gear. When she completed all of her lessons, she went to the police to take her driving test. But instead of actually taking her out for a road test, they asked how long she had been driving. When she told them she'd had a regular driving license for twenty years, the police said, "That is very good," and issued her the license permitting her to drive buses and trucks. And she never had been behind the wheel of a truck. The trucking company had simply paid off the police.

I just shook my head and laughed when she told me the story. But this week, two people I know have been killed on the roads in Kenya. When you drive here, you often wonder how people ever got their licenses. I think I know now. And it's another little thing that can sometimes make this beautiful place seem so brutal.

This story sobered me up about small sins in my own life that can grow to cause such horrible problems. The guy who passes people and issues licenses without testing their skills doesn't think of it as a big thing. But I know two widows who shouldn't be widows.

—

The babies, boys, and I managed to survive until Nancy returned. We were all thrilled to have her home, but no one more so than I was. I wasn't nearly as prepared as I'd wanted to be—for the new school year at RVA the end of August or for the launch of our hot lunch program in the two national schools starting in early September.

The logistics of such a venture proved to be a fun (translated from sarcasm: "frustrating") challenge. Coordinating the purchase of supplies, delivery of food, and qualified personnel with strong enough arms and backs to handle bags weighing almost two hundred pounds each is not a simple matter when dealing with people at every stage of the process who have neither phones nor email. Even when I managed to track them down to have a face-to-face conversation, we all too often seemed to experience a failure to communicate. As in the following true and representative exchanges:

Me: Do you have beans you can sell me?

Them: Yes, many bags. *(they quote a price)*

Me: Good. I agree to your price.

Next day:

Me: I am here to get the beans we talked about yesterday.

Them: I do not have any beans.

Me: Why did you agree to sell them if you do not have any?

Them: I thought I might.

This sort of misunderstanding happened to me several times. Not because the person I was dealing with intended to deceive me and didn't care if I ended up disappointed, but because they so wanted to please me and make some money for themselves in the process. They had genuinely hoped they'd be able to get what I needed, even if they didn't have any at the time. They were truly sorry to disappoint me when they couldn't deliver. But they weren't embarrassed, much less ashamed, when this happened. They didn't feel they had been dishonest; they'd always had the best intentions. Things just hadn't worked out.

Working out transportation and personnel issues was no simpler. Because my car couldn't handle the three tons of food we were buying, I needed to hire a truck and a driver. And those negotiations, too, were different from any of my past business dealings:

Me: I will pay eleven thousand shillings.

Them: And my lunch.

Me: Okay.

Them: And my dinner.

Me: No.

Them: I will cancel.

Me: Good.

Them: Then I do not want lunch either.

During that first year we'd been in Kenya, the life-changer for me came the day I visited that nearby national school and had seen all those children lying on the ground in their classroom because they hadn't eaten since Monday.

Thankfully, we were not experiencing the same kind of famine in 2002, a little more than two years later. So the goal of our lunch program wasn't so much a desperate matter of keeping starving students alive as it was a long-term investment in encouraging kids to stay in school and keeping them healthy enough to learn. But through the hours of planning and working to get the lunch program launched, I could still see those children lying on the ground.

—

By Saturday, August 31, all the planning and all the work finally came together. We were ready to launch this program we believed would decrease the dropout rate and help children learn. The strategy was for all the maize and beans to be delivered to the orphanage we worked with down in the valley where they had a guarded, locked room. On Saturday morning at 8:00, I arrived with enough strong young muscle to load the food supplies on a truck we rented, and then we'd deliver it to two schools.

By 9:00 the truck was there, and the twenty-three bags of beans had been delivered. But the maize had not yet arrived. And the pastor who knew how to get to the schools was nowhere to be found. We seemed to be only half ready to go. But I had no idea what to do about the second half. I got in the car and drove off to see if I could locate the woman who had given me the lowest bid for providing the corn to see what had happened there. I was still looking for her when the pastor called me on my cell phone to tell me he was ready to go.

I headed back and reached the orphanage just as the maize showed up in a large truck. Seventy-five bags of maize (two hundred pounds each, more than fifteen thousand pounds in all) take up *lots* of space. I had paid the driver half the money when we'd agreed on the price, but he had not delivered it on Friday when he had promised. So I didn't have the rest of his money with me; I hadn't wanted to carry that much cash on me all day. So we had the following exchange:

Me: I will pay you on Monday.

Him: Pay me now, or I leave.

Me: Then leave half the maize; I've already paid for that.

Him: Just go get the money.

At that point, I knew it would take me an hour to get home and return with the money. And I already had the truck, manpower, and all the supplies together and ready to go now. We were, as they say, "burning daylight." Fortunately, Fred was with me. So I told the guy, "I will give Fred a note. And you can go with him to my house, where my wife will pay you the other half of the money for the corn." He agreed, so we transferred the maize, he left with Fred, and the rest of us finally headed out to deliver the food to the schools.

Except we were still on Kenyan time. So after all of about ninety seconds of driving, the pastor told me to pull over at a duka because he needed to buy some food for a conference to be held at his church. We waited twenty minutes while he purchased what food he needed. I shouldn't have worried; it was all too easy to catch up with the truck that had gone on when we stopped to shop. When we spotted it pulled off the road ahead, I thought, *What now?* As we got closer, we could see they had been pulled over by the police. I got out of the car and learned that the police had pulled the truck over because it looked to be in such poor condition. I explained the situation to the police, and they said we could go.

I had never driven a four-wheel-drive vehicle before. But we pulled off the main road, and quite soon I was driving like I had never driven before in places I'd never even imagined driving. I forded two streams, was backed up by a donkey cart, and saw several zebra and gazelle running near the first school.

Nyakinyua School had an enrollment of three hundred fifty children, all from a poor area of the valley. Beyond the school, big enough to see from miles away, was a massive telecom dish that serves all of Kenya. I thought how odd it must be for those poor children who don't have electricity in their homes or school to see every day that giant satellite dish, a technological trapping of a world and wealth beyond their imagination. Looming bigger than life. So close. And yet so far away.

We were able to deliver all the food that the school needed for three months. The headmaster was so grateful, and large numbers of children who lived nearby kept coming up to me and wanting to know, "Is that food for us to eat?" When I told them yes, they jumped up and down.

Unloading supplies for Nyakinyua, I quickly noticed a major difference between twenty-year-old Kenyans and a forty-seven-year-old, pigment-challenged American. It took me and two other smaller guys to lift and carry one bag. Each of the other guys carried a bag by himself—on his back. It would have broken mine in two.

The pastor told me there was a third school he wanted to add to the program as soon as we could. And since we were so near this third school, he asked me to drive by it on our way to our second scheduled stop. But the last hint of road ended a mile or so before we reached the poorest school I'd yet seen in Kenya. The first two schools we'd chosen for our lunch program were poor themselves—brick buildings with no glass in the windows. But Namuncha School was constructed out of wood with dirt floors and no windows at all to let light into classrooms so dark and dreary it was hard to imagine children spending a large part of the day in there, day after day after day.

Only a hundred and fifty students attended Namuncha School, all of them Masai children whose families lived in mud and dung huts, and who certainly could use a hot lunch program. We decided we had enough food already to add that small of a school to our program right away.

On our way to the second scheduled school, we passed by the pastor's church and unloaded the food he had purchased. His family invited me to share their lunch, a meal of cabbage, beans, and cooked carrots. It was good food and fun, lively conversation, although three different times in the course of the meal I yelled, "Time for an English break!" and everyone had to speak English for the next five minutes.

After our lunch, we had just started toward the second scheduled school when visibility suddenly dropped to almost nothing, like the worst fog I'd ever had to drive in. Only this wasn't fog. It was dust. I slowed down considerably, but I figured as long as I could see the edge of the road ten to fifteen feet in front of the car, I'd keep driving until we got out of this dust devil, sandstorm, or whatever it was. We'd already had enough delays. But after a few minutes of rolling across barren and rugged Rift Valley terrain at half speed and more than half blind, I heard the pastor say to me in a quiet voice from the passenger seat, "If you go farther, we will not live." I decided to stop before I asked what he was talking about. And when I did, darned if there wasn't a thirty-foot drop-off right in front of me.

I drove a *lot* slower after that, until we cleared that dust storm and could make our way much more quickly to the last school at Kamuyu to deliver the remainder of our food. What struck me there this time was seeing the conditions of the "bathroom" at a school with no water supply for its two hundred and fifty students. I don't have words to begin to describe the unsanitary conditions of the "facilities" there.

We started back home, and as I drove, I noticed I was sore in the same way you might be after riding a horse for the first time. I was sore in places I had never been sore before, from bouncing up and down all day long on the rough roads. But in life, I've noticed there are bad aches and good aches; this was a good one. Knowing that eight hundred Kenyan children, most of whom didn't eat breakfast or lunch, would have a hot, nutritious, midday meal every day at school for the next three months thanks to the generosity of so many of our friends and family back home almost made me enjoy all the aches. Almost.

I'd read there would be a big conference in South Africa the following week to address the issues of development in the third world. Colin Powell, the American secretary of state at the time and a man I greatly respected, had been quoted cautioning that, when it comes to solving many of the world's biggest and thorniest problems, "We are in a marathon, not a sprint."

I understood what he meant. But when I thought about that quote after visiting Nyakinyua, Namuncha, and Kamuyu all on that Saturday, I couldn't help but believe that if those were his children or my children attending any of those three schools, we wouldn't be thinking about the need to pace ourselves for any marathon; we would run like we were on fire.

When children have to live like that, and we know about it and allow it to continue, we're not even in the race.

21

Beyond Easy Answers
and Kidnapped Tests

As you might imagine, the beginning of a new school year at Rift
Valley Academy is always a busy and potentially stressful time of year.
Running a boarding school with an American educational curriculum in
the middle of Kenya for five hundred students from twenty-some different
countries is no small feat. In August–September 2002, we not only had all
the usual annual details to work out, but we were trying to launch the lunch
program in three Kenyan schools in our "spare time," even as I was learning
the ropes in my new role on campus as RVA's guidance counselor and college
admissions advisor.

Since I came to education from corporate America, I had not realized
how many requests for high school class changes are motivated by such serious concerns as "So-and-so is in period one biology, and I can't stand how she
flicks her hair back after she finishes a test, so I need to switch to the fourth
period class." So my new job was an eye-opening, educational challenge.

Yet the biggest source of tension in the Peifer household had nothing to
do with school starting, or even the arrival of the sixteen eighth-grade boys
who would be living in the dorm with us for the year. The problem was
Katie. Our older boys were outraged with their little sister. She'd been saying
"Da-Da" and "Mama" for some time. But her third word was neither JT nor
Matthew. It was Jessie. The dog. Which did *not* go down well with the boys.

Katie also created some tensions for Nancy. Although I was the one who
had pressed for a daughter, my wife had discovered within herself an intense
desire to have tea parties with her female child. But what we had quickly
discovered about Katie was that she is a bread fanatic. After we fixed and fed
the babies their breakfast, they would play on the floor for a half hour before

the rest of us ate breakfast. At which time, in order to "share" the meal as a family, we put the twins in their high chairs, where Cheerios kept them busy, entertained, and happy.

Until Katie saw the toast. Then she would make a series of long, deep guttural noises indicating that she wanted, needed, and *expected* more bread. And every time Katie made that sound, JT would smile sweetly at Nancy and say, "There's your tea party girl, Mom!"

~

The process of adopting the twins progressed slowly. We had another visit by a government social worker who asked JT and Matthew what they thought about having a black brother and sister. Matthew said that he loved them because they were his brother and sister. She asked what, when we went back to the States, they would think if children teased them because of the color of the twins' skin. JT said he didn't think that would happen, but it wouldn't change the way he felt about the babies.

The social worker told us she would recommend us to the courts. We then met with an attorney, who informed us that even though six months had passed since the legislature passed the new adoption laws, there was still so much confusion over how the regulations would be applied that the courts were not yet hearing new cases. We were grateful to learn that adopting twins would be considered one adoption, so we wouldn't have to pay double the usual fees. Even so, the costs would add up to more than a month's salary for us, which made me think of Kenya's one and a half million orphans, and how few Kenyans (who make an average of twenty-five dollars a month) could ever afford to provide a home and family for those children.

The most discouraging news the lawyer gave us was that our adoption case probably would not proceed until sometime the following year. Our problem was that the national elections were scheduled for the coming December, and there was considerable concern that the country might experience significant turmoil. We wanted the adoption to be finalized before then, so that if things got so bad we needed to leave the country, we could take Katie and Ben with us.

Such a scenario was hardly out of the question. Just days before we met with our lawyer, all of the missionaries working in the Congo with Africa Inland Mission (our sending agency) were evacuated because of a civil war in that country. While Kenya had a more stable history than the Congo, the Kenyan government had recently been named one of the ten most corrupt nations in the world. So there was much reason for discontent and no certainty at all about what might happen with the elections.

The one thing we were sure of was the legal names we had settled on for the twins: Katherine Izawadi Peifer and Benjamin Ikhavi Peifer. Those names reflected their African ancestry in the Luhya tribe (the second largest ethnic group in Kenya after the Kikuyu). Izawadi means "gift" and Ikhavi means "blessing." What a gift and what a blessing they already had been to our family.

—

The expression "Two steps forward, one step back" seems to apply to almost anything you hope to accomplish in Africa, whether it's adopting twin babies or providing free lunches to hundreds of children in three public schools. Less than a month after launching our lunch program, I had to write the following in an email to the supporters back home who had funded the feeding project:

All the Kenyan public school teachers are on strike, so there is no feeding going on right now. Kenya's president has threatened to hire replacement teachers; striking teachers have threatened to murder any replacement teachers who show up and teach. There have been several reported deaths around the country so far. So we are laying low until the smoke clears.

On a more encouraging note, it looks as if we will be able to add more schools to our lunch program when the next term starts in January. We're excited about that prospect and grateful for the support. I have been informed that enrollments increased in our three current lunch program schools. And one headmaster told me that was because of the lunch we provided. So thank you all for what you are doing.

—

Every fall we administer the SAT test at Rift Valley Academy. But 2002 was the first time I was personally responsible for getting it done.

The whole process of applying to colleges and deciding which one to go to is stressful for all high school kids, wherever they are. But our RVA students have missionary parents whose incomes would be considered poverty level in the United States. So standardized test scores high enough to elicit scholarships are the best and sometimes the only shot they have to afford a top-notch college education back in the States.

Only one company in Kenya was authorized to handle the SAT test. And the manager told us she would drive out to Kijabe from Nairobi to pick up the completed tests on the Monday two days after the Saturday we gave it.

When she arrived on campus as scheduled, I greeted her, handed over the tests, and watched her drive off. The problem was that she got carjacked right outside the campus. Six men, two with guns, stopped her, ordered her out of the car, and left her on the side of the road as they took off with her vehicle and everything in it, including our SAT tests. The woman was badly frightened, but not hurt. Her car eventually was recovered nearby; evidently the thieves couldn't figure out how to drive it. We were so grateful she was okay.

Fortunately, our completed tests were all there, undamaged. I say fortunately because the College Board, the outfit back in the States that oversees all SAT results for every student to every college and university anywhere, is a rather anal type of organization. I'm not sure how we ever could have adequately explained that the answer sheets for all the tests taken by our RVA students that year had been "kidnapped."

—

Another annual event takes place during the first term of each new school year: RVA's Spiritual Emphasis Week. A special, outside speaker is brought in to lead a series of meetings for the entire campus. I reported in an October email that *this year our speaker was particularly gifted and challenging. The kids responded to his message in a wonderfully positive way. One night he encouraged his listeners to make sure they didn't have any issues with one another. So for much of the evening, young people were making things right with each other.*

I got involved in this because several students came up to me and told me in so many words that they had never liked me and felt like they needed to apologize and ask my forgiveness. The reasons they gave were my insensitivity and sarcasm.

I'm sure those of you who are personally acquainted with me or have been reading these emails for a while already know I can be an insensitive clod at times. And of course many children and young people can be particularly vulnerable to teasing. Humor has been a big part of my modus operandi for as long as I can remember. But I really was convicted by the realization that I can use humor in so many wrong ways—out of habit, as a weapon, as a self-protective shield to hide behind, and as an easy way to relate to people instead of really relating to people. Humor has its place, and I don't want to become boring. But there needs to be a balance. And I'm at that wonderful place where I know I need to change, yet I don't have a clue as to how to do so. It's a painful yet exciting position to be in. I would ask for your prayers.

—

Our lunch program resumed when the four-week teacher strike came to an end and Kenyan children finally could return to school. One of them told her pastor that she was glad the strike was over because she was hungry. We were excited not only because the feeding continued but also because it already looked like we had enough new support to add two more schools to the program in January, when the second term of the school year began.

—

We held a "dorm night" one October Friday evening. The Peifer clan took all of our eighth grade guys down to RVA's lower field, where we played Capture the Flag, built a huge bonfire, and roasted hot dogs and marshmallows. You haven't really played Capture the Flag until you've played it in Africa; the pitch black night adds a different dimension. After two games in the dark, we ate. Then the guys took branches lit from the fire and ran up and down the field with them. Some of them staged a battle that had a *Star Wars* light saber look to it.

As I watched those sixteen eighth-grade boys having such a grand time with the fire, I reflected on what I thought was perhaps the greatest gift our time in Africa had provided my two older sons. It allowed them to enjoy the innocence of childhood longer than they would have in the United States. Without ready access to TV, the internet, and pop-culture celebrity, there was not quite the push in Kenya to have a girlfriend or be cool like there was in the US.

As the evening ended, one of the guys asked if we could go annoy the girls' dorm. When the other fifteen guys immediately voted down the idea, I thought, *It won't be long before all that starts, but how nice to be in junior high and still be a kid.* As I pondered those warm thoughts, one guy exclaimed, "We've got to put out the fire!" Another yelled, "Drink all the water you can!" And as I realized what they intended to do, all my warm thoughts were extinguished—if you know what I mean.

Childhood is great, but there is something to be said for growing up too.

—

I pondered a different aspect of life in Kenya a week or two later after I was invited to a harambe for a Kenyan pastor. A harambe is a celebratory event in which an entire community joins together to help someone out. It's a good thing in principle, but too often this practice seems to replace good stewardship in Africa. And when you are asked to help time after time after time, it's hard not to get numb to it all.

But this pastor was a good friend of mine; we'd had many adventures together with the orphanage and the school lunch program. If you had seen the car he drove, you would know he was not living high on the hog. He was almost sixty and had worked hard his whole life. But the harambe was to send him to England for a refreshing vacation. And he had high expectations that the missionaries would pay for a good part of it.

So the harambe, and something else that happened that same week, posed a real dilemma for me, which I tried to articulate in the next email I wrote home:

The bottom line is that I can't really understand the bone-crunching poverty of Africa, and my pastor friend doesn't understand that when I was in the States and made a six-figure income, it never occurred to me to take an international vacation, because I couldn't afford it. Now I make a tenth of that, but I am so rich compared to most Kenyans that they don't see the limit to our money, and sometimes ask things that might be inappropriate.

But is it inappropriate? This good man has worked so hard and without a break for so many years—is it truly unreasonable to have one big vacation? In the United States, we've given money to send our pastor on much-needed vacations. Why is this different?

How do you deal with that question in the context of hunger and children not being in school because their families don't have the school fees? I really don't know the answer, but I suspect that some of Kenya's problems remain unsolved because people are overreaching instead of dealing with the greatest needs. How you prioritize is a hard question for any of us; in Africa, it can often be a life-and-death question.

In the same week as the harambe, our friend Joel's wife had a baby. (Joel is the man who borrowed—and repaid—the money to buy his famous cow named Kow-Jabe.) We had offered to have a baby crib made for his child after we learned most African babies sleep on the floor because their families can't afford to have a separate bed for their little ones. So I went to Joel's house to deliver the bed.

Joel lives almost four miles away from the RVA campus. It takes him more than ninety minutes to walk to work. He and his wife live in a hut with walls of mud and canvas grain bags covering the walls to keep the rain out. Their home has a dirt floor and no windows; they cook their meals over an open fire. We put the crib in the house, and it almost didn't fit because it was so large compared with the rest of the house. The fact that most Kenyan babies don't have a bed just boggles my Western mind.

So, in the same week, I'm involved in helping someone take an international vacation and also giving a bed to a baby whose family lives in a tiny mud-walled house. When there are limited resources, you've got to make the right choice. Such choices are hard ones. And yet I think that is one of the biggest challenges in Africa today. The truth is that's an issue for all of us: How do we prioritize what is important? If someone doesn't do that carefully here in Africa, they might actually die. Sometimes I wish I could view all of my resources in that context with that mindset—recognizing that how I spend my money can make the difference between life and death.

I wish I could conclude this email with nice homilies, but Africa is way beyond easy answers for me.

—

Right after first term ended, RVA hosted another conference for all of the AIM missionaries in the region. Many of these folks lived and worked way out in the bush, and the "real missionary" stories they shared were remarkable.

One couple told how their daughter had been invited by a Masai tribe to go zebra hunting. Masai men pride themselves on their hunting skills, and Masai women never hunt. So the hunters had asked the girl as a joke, but she downed a zebra on the first try. To celebrate and honor her, the Masai hunters allowed her to wash her face in the zebra's blood.

I met another missionary at the conference, a seventy-year-old force of nature who regularly traveled in and out of the Sudan, one of the most dangerous hot spots in Africa at the time. She had been shot at more than once, survived bombings, and had to flee the violence of that country's civil war on numerous occasions. Nothing deterred her; she kept going back to help, as a teacher, because of her love for the people.

I thought about the stories I'd heard and the "real missionaries" I'd met at the conference as I stuffed envelopes in the guidance office the following week. In my new role as guidance counselor and college advisor, I had the misfortune to replace someone who not only had been the coolest person on campus but had done the job for years and knew it inside and out. I, on the other hand, had not yet had a cool day in my life. And I had to learn my job as I went.

One thing I learned quickly was that God is a great recycler who can use everything we've ever done in the past to equip us for the tasks he has for us to do. At least that was true in my case after I got to Africa. For a time earlier in my life, I had a traveling sales job that required calling on college administrators to try to sell them my company's printing and database services. I'd always considered that the worst job I'd ever had in my entire business career and the seven years I'd spent doing it a complete waste of my time. But it had afforded me the opportunity to visit almost eight hundred college campuses all over the United States.

So it was that going on twenty years later, I was able to bring a little personal perspective and firsthand knowledge to high school kids in Kijabe, Kenya, as they tried to make their college decisions, oftentimes sight unseen.

My students seemed to respond well to my talking about so many different colleges; that fall we had five times the usual number of college applications from RVA seniors, who applied to more schools than ever before.

Because all but a handful of our kids were boarding students with missionary parents living and working in so many different countries (often in remote places), it was my job and that of our guidance office to advise our students about what information they needed to include in their applications, make certain they completely and properly filled out the right forms with all the required information, and then process and double-check each application package before getting them ready to mail. It was also our job to find people returning to America who could carry the applications to mail at a US post office, because the Kenyan postal service was not safe or reliable enough to entrust with such critical and time-sensitive materials.

What this meant for me was that at the time of the missionary conference being held on the RVA campus, I was in the middle of a ten- to fourteen-day period when I was working twelve or more hours a day, digging through mountains of minutia, double-checking thousands of details, and assembling all those application packages to get them out the door before the holidays. Which I suppose was why the more moving and amazingly cool stories I heard of missionaries who were doing such remarkable things, the more I found myself wishing (usually late at night, long after my own kids were in bed, sitting at my desk in the guidance office, poring over piles of paperwork) that I could be doing more exciting, cool, and *real* missionary work instead.

During this time, something took place that hadn't happened often to me; I had what felt like a true revelation. I suspect most missionaries probably understand this before they become missionaries. What can I say? I'm a slow learner. But what suddenly became clear to me was this: in life it's not about titles or positions, or even what we do, but why and how we do what we do.

I came to terms with the fact that Guidance Counselor/College Advisor at a boarding school for missionary kids in rural East Africa wasn't the most glamorous of job titles. But I was uniquely qualified for the role. And it was what I was supposed to be doing with my life at that point.

—

Meanwhile, there were plenty of immediate, albeit intrinsic rewards to keep me going and provide all the excitement an unexciting guy like me could handle.

For example, the results of the first three months of the school lunch program seemed nothing short of miraculous. The usual dropout rate for such government elementary schools ran at least 30 to 35 percent. At the first two schools where we provided lunches (Kamuyu and Nyakinyua), not one student dropped out during the entire term. None! At the third school, Namuncha, one student dropped out. But that was because his father died of AIDS and his mother needed him at home. We had hoped to make a measurably positive impact, but these results were far greater than I ever dreamed possible.

And I was even more pumped about what I reported to our supporters in a late December email:

Most of you probably know we have been able to add two more schools to the three we already provide lunches for as of the first of the year: Karima and Rare. Karima has almost six hundred students and Rare has one hundred. We haven't seen Rare yet.

This past Thursday, when we began delivering food for the next school term, we had almost forty thousand pounds or twenty tons of beans and corn in the truck when it got stuck in the non-road. We were there for several hours until the ground dried up enough for me to pull it out with my Land Cruiser. As we were searching for and digging up rocks to chuck under the wheels to provide traction, I realized I wasn't the least bit upset. Something always goes wrong when I deliver the food supplies. It used to drive me nuts; now I understand that things just happen in Africa. I'd like to think it was a sign of maturity. (Don't bother sending me an email saying, "It's about time." I already know that. Besides, that crack is just too easy.)

I was still busy hauling rocks when a lone Kenyan man came walking along the trail and pitched in to help. That itself seemed amazing, since we were in the middle of nowhere. And he had a small radio in his pocket. As we chatted and worked, all of a sudden "This Kiss" by Faith Hill began playing on that radio. I couldn't help but laugh, and marvel at a God who would play a country and western song for me in the middle of Kenya.

Several parents heard we were coming to their kids' school and showed up to say thank you to us and to all of you. One father told me that this was the first time in his child's life that she'd eaten two meals in the same day. Another father thanked you all because you have given his children a chance. Another told me he has hope again.

A mother asked me to thank the people who saved her from "the choice." I inquired as to what she meant. She told me the choice is when you have to decide whether to feed your children or send them to school. Because of this program, she didn't have to make that choice.

Our children's school in the States gave us some money to purchase beds for a local orphanage; we'll be able to buy one hundred of them. They've been using cheap foam mattresses, and most of them are more than five years old, filthy, and in great disrepair. When I told the orphanage's pastor what we planned to do, he just sat and cried.

Being able to deliver food to hungry schoolchildren or to purchase beds for orphans this year has been a dream come true for me, a dream I didn't even know I had until I got to Africa. Thank you for helping us to be here, and for blessing the children. You have saved the parents of almost two thousand kids from the choice.

22

"Is the Momma Sick?"
Confessions of Sartorial Neglect

A
S PART OF KENYA'S NEW ADOPTION LAW, THE COURTS APPOINTED A guardian from the Kenyan Child Welfare Society to evaluate us as an adopting family and see how we were raising and would plan to raise the twins. The guardian scheduled a time to come to our home, but at the last moment, she called and asked us to come to her office in Nairobi instead.

When we arrived at the address she gave us, the building reminded me of something out of the old *Batman* television series from the 1960s—a run-down, abandoned factory that seemed a perfect hideout for criminal masterminds dreaming up nefarious plots. It was scary to go inside, and there was no signage anywhere. So we had to knock on numerous closed doors to find where we were supposed to go. The Child Welfare office, once we found it, was as dilapidated as the rest of the building, with broken windows and holes in the floor.

We were invited to take a seat in a couple of tattered chairs in what was appropriately called the *waiting* room. Two hours past our appointment time, a nice woman came out, greeted us, and ushered us to her office, where we talked with her for an hour. At the end of that interview, she promised she would come and do a home visit the following week. She did. And we had a nice visit, after which she told us the next and final step would be the official adoption hearing in court. We hoped that would be soon.

—

In mid-January I began making rounds to various schools to see how our expanded lunch program was faring in its second term. I visited Nyakinyua, planning just to observe but also to help prepare the lunches so I could get a feel for the daily operation.

The Kenyan government's recent announcement that public schools would drop their tuition requirement and provide free public education for all primary-age students was a long-overdue and politically popular decision. That welcome change in the country's educational policy was, in theory, a good thing for the children of Kenya. However, the new plan created a couple of serious problems.

First was a huge surge in student enrollment. Some schools—most of which had been overcrowded and understaffed to start with—tripled their number of students. Problem two was that Kenyan government schools had been set up to use their tuition fees to cover all educational expenses—from teacher salaries to textbooks and other resource materials and any maintenance, repairs, or improvements of facilities. And so far none of the local schools had yet received any funding from the national government to make up for the lack of tuition fees and cover their basic budget and operational costs.

The result was that public schools that had been woefully underfunded by the *old* tuition system suddenly found themselves with more children to educate and no money to do so. The nation's entire education system had gone from bad to worse. Nyakinyua, as small a school as it was, had seen an increase of almost a hundred children. It was so crowded and chaotic when I arrived there that I wasn't sure where to go or whom to see first. That led me to this conversation with the first cluster of students I saw:

Me: Where is the headmaster?

Them: Just there.

Me: Which one? That one?

Them: No, the black one. *(At this point I must point out that I was the only white person for twenty miles.)*

Me: They all look black to me.

Them: They are brown. He is the black one.

I found the headmaster. (He *was* blacker.) He and I went to help a handful of parents prepare the food. They had three huge pots filled with maize and beans on an open fire, to which the women periodically added enough broken branches and other small pieces of wood to keep the pots simmering all morning. At lunchtime, the children lined up by classroom, and we used tin cups to ladle the steaming mixture of corn and beans into empty, plastic margarine containers that served as children's bowls. There were no forks or spoons; everyone ate by hand.

You may never have seen five hundred children eat maize and beans with their hands as if they have never eaten before. But let me tell you, it was as sobering an experience as I'd ever had on this planet.

—

A few days later, I drove out to Karima, the same school I'd visited at the end of our first year in Kenya, where I'd asked the teacher why her students were lying on the floor. It now had one of our largest lunch programs, yet it remained one of our poorest schools. I found many children still sitting on the dirt floors of the classrooms there—no longer lying on the floor because they were faint from hunger, but at least in part still in school because they were *not* so hungry anymore.

Since we began providing food back in September at the beginning of the first term, Karima School had enrolled two hundred more children than they were equipped to handle. They no longer had enough desks in those overcrowded classrooms. Yet a number of those Karima students sought me out to personally thank me for their lunches. Before we started the feeding project, Nancy and I decided we wanted to make certain that Kenyan kids and their families and communities didn't think the food came from us. And that they understood the motivation behind the program. So whenever anyone expressed gratitude for what we were doing, I was always quick to say that the money to purchase the food they were eating came "from friends in the United States who love Jesus and who love you."

I had taken a list of our contributors' names and asked if any teachers might want to have their classes write some thank-you notes I would send back to the States. But when I offered that suggestion, the headmaster sadly shook his head and informed me, "I'm sorry, Mr. Peifer. We don't have any paper to do that."

I made a mental note: *Next time I come to check on the lunch program, I need to remember to bring a ream or two of notebook paper.*

—

On January 31, 2003, after reporting on the visit to Karima School, I ended my weekly email by writing about some personal news:

I'm saving the best news for last in this letter. We've had lots of extraordinary things happen to us since we've been in Africa, but this has got to go to the top of the list.

Our family has been trying to get a court date to adopt the twins for eight months.

Well, the court finally assigned us one! We were so thrilled to receive the long-awaited word that we didn't even notice the actual date until several hours later. Many of you know that we had a son who would have been five this year. Stephen lived only a few days, but his life and death changed us forever. He was born on March 4, 1998.

The day we will go to court to officially adopt the babies is March 4. When we realized what had happened, it took our breath away. These past few years the fourth day of March has been a tough day for the Peifer family. But from now on, besides sad memories, March 4 will also mark a new beginning.

I love how God can redeem the unredeemable.

—

I made another trip to Kamuyu, the school with no source of water. To prepare the hot lunches, parents must haul water for miles to cook the maize and beans. The "kitchen" itself, located half a mile from the school, had a metal roof until someone stole it. Now it was just a shell of a building. We were trying to help the people there complete a water tank at Kamuyu that would catch and store rainwater that ran off the school roof. And as I walked out with one of the parents to see the progress they'd made, he asked me what I thought of the school.

I told him I admired the way the community was trying so hard to improve things for their children. But I admitted it was hard to understand the poverty from a Western perspective. He nodded and said, "People try to hide their poverty, but there are two places they cannot hide it. Look in their eyes and look at their feet."

Back inside the school a few minutes later, I counted more than eighty kids before I found a child wearing shoes. And the look on another child's face as he waited in line for his food captured what that parent was talking about: there was a fearful longing in the eyes that chills me every time I see it. Children shouldn't have that look. So many Kenyan kids do.

—

At the end of the first week in February, I sent the following email to friends and family:

There are many interesting experiences to be had as a dorm parent at Rift Valley Academy. And one of the most highly anticipated annual events is Korean Food Day — or as it is most often referred to, Delicious Korean Food Day. Many parents of our Korean students come to campus and cook mountainous amounts of Korean cuisine.

Before I go on, let me say I think Korean food is wonderful. When Nancy went back to the States last summer and asked what I wanted brought back, the first thing

I thought of was seaweed, which my Korean dorm boys have gotten me addicted to. However, since my Korean guys get home-cooked Korean fare on campus only once a year, they feel a cultural obligation to stuff themselves beyond any reasonable limit. This results in so much methane that for a week after Korean Food Day, I live in fear that if some unwitting smoker visiting RVA happened to enter our dorm, the entire campus would be destroyed in an atomic fireball.

This term, as I go from room to room to say goodnight, the boys have gotten in the habit of asking me to rate the odor level of the room. Being eighth grade guys, it is a point of pride to be rated the smelliest. There are five rooms in our dorm, and in the wake of Korean Food Day, we have an absolute, five-way tie right now.

The greatest fear our boarding students face is that something will happen to a family member when he is away from them. That fear came true this week for one of our dorm guys. Joey is one of the nicest kids you could ever meet in your life, with a smile that could chase away the rain. We received word that Joey's sixteen-year-old brother, Justin, who was home with their parents in Zambia, passed away in his sleep.

You always feel inadequate as a dorm parent. (Truth be known, I often feel inadequate as a parent.) But never so much as when we learned this. Imagine being fourteen and having to handle such news without your parents. Nancy and I cried and cried with Joey. Then we had to tell the rest of the dorm.

Joey is pretty universally loved here. So the dorm cried and cried. Those who had suffered sibling loss took it the worst, and I was surprised how many of them there were. In eighth grade, everyone tends to take everything personally. Kids always think, What if this happens to me?

It was a very sad, very troubled night. Joey was able to go home to be with his parents in Zambia, although it was a six-hour plane flight and then an all-day car ride from there. His family lives and ministers to the people in a very remote part of Africa. Joey's older brother and sister are attending college in the States, and finances are preventing them from coming back to Africa for the funeral. There can't be too many things harder than what this family is going through; please pray for them as they come to mind.

Back in the dorm, things were pretty tentative for a few days, but eighth grade boys are resilient. By the end of the week, I heard several guys, right before lights off, asking "anyone with bad gas to please come to our room so we can win smelliest room." In most situations, this would be in bad taste. In this situation, in the unique world eighth graders live in, I considered it a sign of healing.

Believe it or not, boarding schools in rural Kenya have their own distinctive urban legends passed down through generations of students. Which is why every dorm kid believes that whenever the milk from our RVA dairy goes south (say the cows have gotten into a big crop of wild onions or something else that drastically alters the flavor), those are the days the food service folks who run the cafeteria will announce a special treat and offer students *chocolate* milk to mask the southness. I have no idea whether that's true; I've had enough funky-tasting moo-juice since we came to Kenya to doubt there is enough chocolate in the world to disguise the distinctive flavor of milk fortified with vitamin O (for onion). But true or not, the belief persists and is as prevalent in these parts as the stories I heard growing up about the legendary "man with the hook."

Since 9/11 there had been a heightened concern among RVA administrators about other kinds of threats. And after an attack on a boarding school similar to RVA in Pakistan, we were considered a "soft target" by the US embassy and had begun periodic drills in case of an armed terrorist attack. Located where we were in a rural area of Kenya, we all thought it unlikely that anything would happen. But with five hundred students on campus, the majority of whom were Americans, it only made sense to take precautions. We had a drill in the middle of February, and the entire campus went into a lockdown. That meant when a special alarm sounded, everyone immediately ran to the closest building, got down on the floor, and stayed quiet until the all-clear signal sounded. That was what the school in Pakistan had done, and no children there had been killed.

Our kids took the drill seriously, and everyone cooperated. Although I did hear this exchange in the cafeteria later that day:

Him 1: Were you afraid during the lockdown?

Him 2: I was more afraid of the chocolate milk.

—

Every year in February, the junior class holds a banquet for the seniors. It is a huge event, with many of the juniors' parents coming in to help build an elaborate set befitting that year's theme. The parents also help the juniors prepare an elegant, multicourse meal, and light the luminaries that mark the pathway where the seniors will walk, dressed in their finest clothes, as the entire RVA community—faculty, staff, and the rest of the student body—line up to cheer them on. During and after the dinner, the junior class presents an original program of entertainment. This wonderful affair and great tradition requires an enormous amount of creativity and work to pull off.

A senior this particular year captained the school soccer team, was president of his class, and had maintained a 4.0 GPA all four years of high school. On top of all these accomplishments and more, he was a genuinely nice kid whose true humility and great sense of humor made him well-liked by all. Naturally, many young ladies would have been thrilled to have him ask them to be his date for the biggest social event of their high school years. But the girl he asked to the banquet had never before in her life been asked out. She was a pretty girl, but perhaps too insecure to see herself that way. Yet Mr. Everything asked her because he really thought she was the one he should take to the banquet.

I wish you could have seen her face as they proceeded up the lighted walkway through the cheering crowd. They went just as friends, and they both knew it. But she was absolutely glowing; that's the only way I could describe her. As the couple strolled past, arm-in-arm, I glanced around at some of my colleagues in the crowd. I suspected their faces mirrored mine; it was hard not getting misty realizing what his gesture meant to her.

I also thought about how we so often look at such things as grades, athletic and musical talents, the size of our houses, and the prestige of our job titles to measure our "success" when it's often other things that really define us. This young man had already accomplished many impressive things in his first eighteen years of life. He'd applied to Harvard, and I thought he had a legitimate chance at getting accepted. I believed he was destined for greatness. But I know, as the years go by, the first thing I will remember whenever I think of him will be that look on his date's face.

―

On Sunday evening, March 2, I gave this report in my weekly email:

Nancy went to the women's retreat this weekend. So for two days JT, Matthew, and I managed the care of the Dynamic Duo. It is so interesting how twins look at life differently. When we read Lyle the Crocodile, *Ben pointed out every red car in the story; Katie showed me all the shoes the characters wore.*

Katie carries shoes around with her all the time, the result being that the shoes end up in the most interesting (and unlikely) places all over the house. Nancy always stays on top of that stuff; I tend to believe the shoe fairies will return them to their rightful places.

This morning, it was up to the three oldest Peifer males to get the youngest Peifer female ready for church. You might not think that should be a tough thing to do, but I am always challenged by female clothing. So as we all frantically rushed around with church time fast approaching, I accepted Matthew's generous offer to dress Katie (after he thoughtfully allowed me to change her diaper, of course).

Katie's favorite top has flowers on it. So logically (at least in a fifth grade boy's mind) the leggings also had to have flowers to match. Consistency of theme clearly seemed more important than the difference in kind or color of flowers. But the combined effect proved such a jarring contrast that JT's eighth grade solution was to find the brightest red socks to further coordinate his little sister's outfit. My sole contribution was the failure to find two shoes that matched, so she wore her beach sandals to church.

We have gotten used to stares that a mixed family can receive, but I'm not sure we've ever had as many people stare as we did this morning. A very nice older Kenyan woman walked up to us and asked, "Is the momma sick?"

Thankfully, no one reported us to the twins' social worker for sartorial neglect. And Nancy was home so she could dress the babies for our big date in court, which was now only two days away.

23

What Happens If You
Hit a Warthog?

Tuesday, March 4, 2003 — Adoption Day (we hoped) finally arrived.

We were instructed to show up promptly at 9:00 a.m. for court. We had heard horror stories about how long the last legal steps of this process could take. So our entire family made the two-hour drive to court with a stockpile of food, drinks, children's books, magazines — and a unsettled feeling in the pits of our stomachs.

Our first surprise was learning that our adoption had been such a long process that the paralegal assisting our original lawyer had graduated from law school and had taken over our case as our attorney. We didn't know that until we arrived at court for our hearing. We also didn't know ours was only the second case she'd ever tried. Or that she was back in court that day with her first clients, still trying to get their adoption through. (We did know many people had to go to court multiple times to get adoptions finalized.)

After a short wait, we were ushered into a surprisingly small courtroom. We sat in the back row, with our lawyer in the row ahead of us. The judge, of course, was in front, facing the entire courtroom. As the judge began his questions, Nancy noticed our lawyer had opened a booklet titled "Trying Adoptions," which she had highlighted in and was referring to during the procedure. That didn't exactly inspire confidence.

From our place in the back row, Nancy and I, along with our older sons, watched and listened intently to the proceedings, trying not to look overly anxious. The babies happily trekked from one to another of us, regularly calling out, "Mama," "Daddy," "JT," "Matthew," first to be picked up, then quickly demanding to be put down — Katie to point out and exclaim over all the shoes in the room; Ben to discover how much noise could be made by whacking an old metal filing cabinet.

The judge looked up from the file in front of him to ask why the birth father had not signed off on the adoption. We knew the birth mother had, but I thought, *Here we go! This is going to be a long process.* Our attorney consulted her book and responded that there was no certainty about who the father was. And since the twins were considered "taboo babies" in the Luhya tribe, she informed the court that the chances were the father would have nothing to do with them anyway. The judge questioned that. However, the court-appointed social worker also was Luhya, so she was able to confirm our attorney's claim.

This was the point in the proceedings, as the judge looked troubled by what he was hearing, that I began feeling nervous. But the judge finally nodded and agreed to accept only the mother's signature. Then he looked at the babies, who were making a fair amount of noise, and commented, "There are only a few people that I'm fine with making a racket in my court." He smiled at us and added, "Based on the interaction I see [and that he obviously heard] between these babies and their parents, and these babies and their older brothers, this court believes that it is in their best interests for these children to stay with you."

With that the Peifer family adoption of the twins was finally and officially approved. As Nancy said later, the babies pled their own case. Our immediate reactions are worthy of note. Nancy and I started to cry. Matthew let out a big, "Whew!" (He had been having nightmares the court would take them away from us.) JT snatched up Katie to hug her, and she graced her big brother with her million-dollar smile. Ben simply turned to me and said, "Cracker?"

Obviously *somebody* needed to stay focused on the important stuff.

—

Just a few weeks after the adoption went through, I made the following email confession:

We are missionaries, after all. So the presupposition might be that we enjoy going to church. But I can't tell you how long it has been since the new and improved Peifer family has been able to sit through an entire worship service at the local Kenyan church we attend when RVA is not in session.

African church services are long; guests will often and unexpectedly show up to sing. Last week, a group of visitors performed a song for an extended period of time that sounded to me as if the piano and the choir were having a fight. They each sounded fine separately, but together, it was a long battle. On top of the services' unpredictable length, there is no nursery at our local African church, so our twenty-one-month-old dynamic duo sit in the service with us the whole time.

Ben is our book boy. So he is usually fine "reading" until he spots something in his book that excites him. Then he begins to yell whatever that word might be—repeatedly and progressively louder: "Horsie! HOrsie! HORsie! HORSie! HORSIE!"

Katie, on the other hand, whenever required to sit beyond the narrow limits of her patience, becomes rather distressed with life in general. Suddenly there is no good way to sit, or any good books to read, or anything good about anything after a certain time in the service. At which point she does the logical thing: she screams as if we have forced her to place both hands on broken glass.

We usually handle such crises the best we can, for as long as we can. However, this week, in response to their cries, our faithful dog came running into the service to rescue the babies from whatever was troubling them. Nancy, who is as good at keeping a straight face as anyone I've ever met, lost it completely. And we were forced to leave early—again.

I'm certain that someday the Peifers will all sit through another church service together, hopefully before the twins leave for college.

—

We were experiencing an identity crisis of sorts in our home about this same time. Every Peifer male had gone through a time of being called Bubba. It's a Texas thing. But Ben really was a Bubba, just a big old sweet guy. Although most of us called him Bubba from time to time, that was how Katie always referred to him.

The problem? That was also how Ben had begun referring to *Katie.* He called his sister (the most beautiful girl in the world) Bubba all the time. I told him in no uncertain terms (and I warned the rest of the family as well) that if this continued, we might have to move from Texas to Arkansas. I hated to threaten the little guy like that, but there *are* limits. Fortunately, our social worker didn't catch wind of this affront before the official adoption went through.

—

By the time we wrapped up that second school term at the end of March, our generous supporters had provided enough funding for us to expand the school lunch program from five to twelve schools for the final term of that school year. We would feed five thousand children a day.

We spent a good chunk of our April break finding, purchasing, and delivering almost seventy tons of food. Coordinating twelve schools without phones was a nightmare. The bean truck didn't show up for five days. And we had so much maize, we had to deliver it in shifts; the trucks just couldn't support that much weight. But because we knew the headmasters were waiting for us at the schools, one of the pastors and I had to drive out to all the schools to let them know we were running behind.

I had what will probably sound like a weird objective this time out. My goal was to haul the bags of maize and beans like my Kenyan friends do. In the past, when I tried to carry the two-hundred-pound bags of corn, I'd always needed someone else to help me. I hadn't even told Nancy, but for the last three months, I'd lifted weights in the school gym every Monday, Wednesday, and Friday at 6:00 a.m., trying to increase my strength so I could do it like the other guys we hired. I didn't want to be the old white guy who took pictures; I wanted to be more of a part of it.

When the first bag was handed down off the truck and hoisted on my back, I tottered toward the door of the nearby storage room like an old drunk staggering home on Saturday night. But I managed to set the bag down without a problem. So I did it again. And again. Until I had carried ten bags. One ton, all by myself.

I wish I could explain. I don't understand why it seemed like such a big deal to me. But I was absolutely thrilled. However, the biggest thrill of all was figuring out the cost of feeding a child lunch six days a week. When we counted transportation, the cost of the maize, beans, and oil, plus the muscle we hired to help deliver the seventy tons of supplies, I calculated our total cost at $1.06 per student per month.

—

During our April break, we had an opportunity to spend a couple of days away from campus. So we took a family trip to a wild game reserve something on the order of Jurassic Park. I reported about our experience in my next email:

Instead of driving around and past animals like we'd done a number of times out in Masai Mara and some of the other national parks, at The Ark, guests are escorted out to a building in the middle of the park and locked in for the night. They have lights all around and natural salt licks, so you can watch through large observation windows as the nocturnal animals come and gather to do what wild animals do at night. We watched rhino, bushbucks, elephants, and a host of other creatures for a long time before we took the kids and retired to our room for the night. The building had an alarm system, so your room would get buzzed from time to time as different animals wandered into view.

The sleeping rooms in The Ark were very tiny. So when Katie got fussy around midnight, so as not to disturb the rest of the family, I climbed out of bed and took her downstairs to look at the animals from the ground-level windows. It was midnight or after, and no one else seemed to be awake. But as soon as we sat down in front of the window, a very large elephant came and stood directly in front of us for almost fifteen minutes. Katie kept telling me all about the massive creature ("Big ears," "Big nose"), and it was such a special moment.

I'm sitting there in the dark, holding my little Kenyan daughter, and we're watching wild elephants together when the thought goes through me: I so did not want to get out of bed when I heard Katie fussing. Now I'm here having one of the neatest experiences of my life. I wonder, how many times has God tried to bless me, and I believed it to be a curse instead?

—

The next day, we went to a nearby hotel, where part of our package included golf and horseback riding. The older boys and I went golfing in the afternoon. On one hole, we encountered three warthogs, a dozen or so baboons, and several Thompson gazelles. I wasn't too worried about baboons or gazelles, but warthogs have a reputation for being unpredictable and pretty ferocious. So I wondered how they might react to being struck by a golf ball. Which resulted in this conversation:

Me: What happens if you hit a warthog?

Caddie: It is a two-stroke penalty.

After golf, the whole family went horseback riding. I've mentioned several surreal moments from our years in Africa, but holding Ben in front of me on horseback while ambling down a trail and turning a corner to find ourselves face-to-face (or more accurately face-to-shoulder) with four giraffe was about as out there as it gets.

The wisdom of taking two twenty-one-month-olds horseback riding in Africa wasn't something we stopped to consider until afterward. (Don't tell our social worker.) But the experience was something none of us will ever forget.

—

A little later that same month, a different sort of highlight experience prompted me to write home:

RVA is almost one hundred years old and has never had a student accepted into Harvard. Not one.

Until today. The young man I wrote about several weeks ago, the one who took the radiant-faced girl to the senior banquet, was accepted at Harvard. Several months ago, when I started my new position as the college counselor, one of our seniors told me, "RVA graduates aren't good enough to get into the Ivy League." That haunted me. And I so wanted our students to know they could compete with anyone.

Which is why opening that envelope today was one of the most fulfilling moments in my life. I know I must sound like a complete wuss, but I just held that envelope and cried and cried and cried. In Africa, you don't get to see the good guys win one like this very often.

—

Another annual Rift Valley Academy tradition is the eighth grade formal. The class sponsors put together a big dinner and make it as fancy as they can. As eighth grade dorm parents, we received a twenty-page document on manners that we were to review with the boys in our dorm.

I truly loved these guys; we'd been surrogate parents to several of them for three of the past four years. But this particular assignment felt as close to mission impossible as anything we'd been asked to do since we'd come to Africa. So I asked some of my eighth grade English lit students from the previous year for tips we might share with our guys about the big night. Each ninth grade boy I asked had one suggestion: "Make sure the food is good."

That did not bode well for the evening, but we pressed on. Nancy set out a formal table and tried to explain what each utensil is for. That seemed to be an education in itself, but when we went on to explain the etiquette of fine dining, things really got interesting:

Nancy: Never leave the table unless you are ill.

Them: *(actual question)* If you have stinky gas but it isn't loud, do you have to leave?

Me: Make sure you cut your meat in small pieces.

Them: *(actual question)* If you are cutting your meat and it slides off and hits a girl in the face, can you get another piece of meat?

Nancy: Put your napkin on your lap.

Them: *(actual question)* If you spill something on a girl, are you supposed to wipe her off?

The big night came, and I got to tie ties for at least ten of the guys, and fix knots for the rest of them. Since it was raining, I shuttled the guys down to the cafeteria, which is where the gala event was to take place. When one of the guys spotted the girls (who all looked lovely), he exclaimed, "We are *so* dead," and no one laughed. That's how they felt. But when they came home, they all commented on how much they enjoyed it. Being a dorm parent can be trying, but getting to see a bunch of young men enjoy a rite of passage was rewarding.

—

It rained almost every day in May. While that certainly was preferable to the drought we'd suffered for so much of the time we'd lived in East Africa, such a prolonged period of rain is also tough for people living in mud homes, which is most of the population in our part of Kenya. So even though it was great to see everything green, too many people were cold, and too many homes were falling apart.

Kijabe's high elevation keeps it cooler than most places in Africa. Yet I didn't know anyone in our area who had a heating system; when it gets chilly, we put on more layers. Yet for many Kenyans, one set of clothes is all they have.

I had a hard time imagining being cold and never being able to get warm. We didn't have heat in our home, but it was stone, so at least we were dry.

—

In an email report on our unusual weather, I included this account of a visit to one of the schools:

This school I visited this week has eight hundred and fifty students and only fourteen staff members. At long lines of children waiting for their food, I talked to them about this and that. One little girl came up and said, "Thank you for your food." I asked her when she ate. She told me she ate lunch at school Monday through Saturday, and her parents prepared a meal for her at home on Sundays.

I asked her how she liked her lunch. She told me it tasted very good, but what she liked best was that it made her feel warm. I wasn't sure I understood, so I asked what she meant. She told me that during rainy season, she was always cold, but eating hot food made her feel warmer.

Sometimes I just need to look away.

—

In early June, Nancy and I had the opportunity to visit Empuet Nursery School, which was, to our knowledge, the first and only preschool serving the Masai tribe. This was significant because the Masai are traditional herdsmen and do not believe in educating their children. However, they do believe in free food. So because of our lunch program, many of their children were allowed to attend this school, which was especially meaningful to us.

The church where this nursery school was held had been built by one of our heroes, former RVA colleague Jim Hoeksema, the college professor from Iowa whose family finished their term and went back to the States during our first year in Kenya. Four years later, the church Jim built in his spare time was still serving this remote Masai community.

There was no good way to get to this school out in the middle of nowhere. No roads go there. But after one of the roughest rides we'd ever experienced, Nancy and I arrived at the school. Masai children have an interesting way of greeting an adult. They walk up and extend the top of their heads to you; the proper response is to place your hand on their head. The custom is endearing and sweet, unless these children of herdsmen have been amusing themselves by throwing cow manure at each other. Several of the heads seemed fairly well coated, but we just grinned and greeted.

It's easy to look at where the children live, what they wear, how little they eat, and tend to despair. But on this particular day, as we left Empuet, I felt like we were at the beginning of a revolution. Ultimately, education will be key to lifting Kenya to a different place in our world. Tradition is a hard beast to kill, but as I looked into the eager faces of those little children we met there, I sensed a hope I hadn't felt before.

—

The first week of July, I visited another one of our lunch program schools, about which I wrote:

Another tough drive to a school more remote than most, where three teachers instruct three hundred and fifty students. Against those almost impossible odds, there does seem to be education going on at Nyakinyua School. The headmaster told me that forty of those children are AIDS orphans, most of whom live with grandparents. Which explained why so many of the kids received their food and started running. They were going home to share it with their families.

As I was leaving the school, I saw a child, and I experienced a familiar punched-in-the gut feeling. Sometimes a look triggers it; other times a shape or maybe a smile. But something about one of the schoolchildren will remind me of Ben or Katie. It's at that point when this goes beyond just trying to help needy kids. I think about Ben and Katie and what their lives might have been like. And this gets so personal.

24

Headbanging Moments

OUR MIDTERM BREAK STARTED WHEN OUR STUDENTS LEFT CAMPUS AT noon on a Friday. Those who lived too far away to go home went to their in-country guardians' homes and weren't due back until Monday afternoon, which meant a long weekend for the Peifer clan.

A long weekend in Africa meant another visit to Kenya's largest and most famous game park. After all, the Masai Mara is only one hundred and twenty miles from Kijabe. We left just after 7:00 a.m. on Saturday, and with only one thirty-minute rest stop, we reached our destination about 1:30 that afternoon. The road leading to Kenya's biggest tourist attraction was one of the worst national highways in all of Africa. The park, with its eight hundred square miles of unspoiled undeveloped country, is so spectacular that words do it a disservice.

On our first visit three years before, we'd stayed with missionary friends just outside the park. This time we planned to stay at one of the camps within the park. The signage was so limited, however, that we were grateful to be with friends who had been there before. We had made reservations for our family at a tented camp. But for reasons unknown, park officials decided to put us in a cabin.

Out on a game drive after lunch, we came upon a herd of Thompson's gazelles and Grant's gazelles. When we tried to approach them, about a hundred of them spooked and ran. Watching those graceful creatures leap twenty to thirty feet in a single bound made me feel like we were in the middle of a *National Geographic* special. Later, we saw a herd of giraffes that arranged themselves in ways we hadn't seen before.

That night the entire family slept in the same room, which was a thrill for the babies. The twins got so excited, they managed to change beds every few minutes. And I had the following discussion with Katie:

Katie: Daddy up?

Me: Momma's sleepers, JT's sleepers, Matthew's sleepers, Bubba's sleepers, and Daddy's sleepers. Time for Katie to go sleepers.

Katie: *(two minutes later)* Daddy up?

This went on into the night, which was a long one. The next morning, three cheetahs walked right in front of our car. The Masai Mara is such a vast and wild place that in two days there, we never saw a ranger or an official park vehicle. In Kijabe, the local police don't have money to put gas in their vehicles; whether or not that was also the case at the park, it was obvious that if your vehicle broke down, you couldn't expect help anytime soon. And if you got out, you might be eaten.

That second night, the babies were tired and slept well. On our last morning, we were doing some serious off-roading when we drove past a small bush near grass the height of our car. When we looked carefully, we saw a large lion that moved when Katie yelled. His head was bigger than her whole body. As we were leaving the park a little later, we spotted a leopard in a tree with a fresh kill; blood was still dripping from its victim. As we watched, it sprang out of the tree, crossed in front of our car carrying its prey in its jaws, and disappeared into the bush with its breakfast to go.

In reporting on our weekend in my next email home, I told our friends and family *there is nowhere in America you could experience nature like this. It is the most magnificent place you can imagine.*

But as we drove over the atrocious roads back to Kijabe, I puzzled over why it had to be so difficult to drive to the biggest, most famous tourist attraction in Kenya. How could any country not take better care or make better use of a national treasure? There is so much about this place that makes no sense to me at all. But as I think about this, I have to wonder how much I am like Africa: what are the treasures in my life that I don't recognize, appreciate, or protect?

—

I suspect anyone who has been in Africa for any length of time has experienced that moment when the most reasonable response to all you are seeing, hearing, smelling, and/or feeling would seem to be banging your head against the nearest brick wall and screaming, "Why? Why does it have to be this way?"

Most of those moments occur for me when I'm visiting nearby government schools, whether up among the hills around Kijabe, down on the floor of the Rift Valley, or out in the Masai Mara. I'd been in Kenya long enough to know how hard parents struggle to afford the various fees for their children just to get an elementary school education. So I could never visit any of our lunch program schools without asking myself, *What do these poor parents get for their money?*

Too often my conclusion was, *They don't get much.* It isn't that the administrators or the teachers (for the most part) aren't sincere and hardworking. But without even the most rudimentary resources, and without additional staff (average class size is almost sixty), it is simply unrealistic for educators, parents, or kids themselves to have high expectations. Many of the headmasters and their teachers are either untrained or unqualified for their positions. For too many, it's their political patronage job, earned by their electoral loyalty or their tribal connections to some local official with clout. Other teachers are parents who long to provide more for their children, but never were educated themselves.

But the *shortcomings* of Kenya's "professional" educators may not be as serious a problem as the crippling *shortage* of instructional resources of any kind, at every level of the country's educational system. I shared one example with our supporters in an email:

Nancy sometimes culls out RVA library books that are old and outdated. But instead of throwing them away, we pack them up and take them out to the government schools we work with. Recently I contributed a box of a dozen or so volumes to a school which has almost a thousand students, but only thirteen teachers. The headmaster thanked me profusely for the books and then proudly informed me, "With your donation, our school library has now doubled in size."

It is always a long, steep drive back home from the valley. Some days it seems a lot steeper than on others.

—

One of my most memorable headbanging moments came near the end of the last term of the 2002–2003 school year. I'd driven only twenty to twenty-five minutes from our campus up to Kenton, one of the three pilot schools for our lunch program. What a magnificent setting! Back in the States, people would pay a million dollars an acre for the sort of views you have up there. But in a third-world country, elevation is often a curse; steep rocky roads make for tedious walking. For all its rugged beauty, Kenton obviously was a hard, rough place for its people to eke out a living.

The first time I'd been up there, Kenton School had more than five hundred students. I'd counted less than fifty pairs of shoes. As with many poorer schools, it had dirt floors throughout. Each classroom had one or two crude openings in the mud walls, just holes really. No thought of glass, or even screens, for those windows. It had been the poorest national school I'd seen up to that point.

The smiling, optimistic headmaster had informed me his goal was to someday accumulate enough textbooks to have one for every four children. To that point, he'd managed only one text for every thirteen pupils.

Things had started looking up since we'd been providing food. The dropout rate had fallen; test scores had risen. And students finally had enough energy that the school day was extended past lunch and into the afternoon. Yet despite the progress I noted, sitting in on several of the classes quickly drained me of any encouragement.

One of the biggest problems with the educational system of Kenya, as I see it, is the reliance on rote memorization, the most common instructional technique at all age levels. I certainly didn't want to belittle all rote learning, because in Kenya, it's culturally based. Oral tradition has always been a primary means for Africans to pass down their heritage from generation to generation. It is important to honor that. At the same time, students for whom rote memorization was the predominant means of classroom instruction would never be challenged to develop critical thinking and reasoning skills.

The fourth grade geography lesson I witnessed that day turned out to be a discouraging case in point. As the teacher stood in front of the class and pointed to a country on a faded, outdated map, she called on individual pupils, who stood and recited the name of the country and its capital city. Students who responded incorrectly were smacked sharply on a hand, a shoulder, or the back with the teacher's discipline stick. Answers deemed acceptable were repeated in unison by the entire class. The teacher never asked a question intended to elicit any additional details about the countries —no discussion of a nation's form of government, chief exports, history, or any distinctive characteristics of its people. Nothing but boring, bare-boned facts, drilled into young minds by deadly dull repetition, a stick, and more than a little fear. The more time I sat watching and listening in those public school classrooms, the more disturbed I became. By the time I left Kenton at the end of the day, I was beyond discouraged.

Who was I kidding? Sure, I could tell myself the lunch program was making a difference. The teachers and the headmaster said as much. And I didn't need to take their word for it. I could see the difference in the kids themselves. That dreaded, hungry look was gone from their eyes. They ran and laughed and played like kids again. But after sitting with them in the classrooms of what remained the lowest-rated (academically) and poorest (physically and demographically) school in their zone, I couldn't deny the painful truth: *Food is not enough. Kenyan kids need more; they need hope. But it's easier to find abundant food in the midst of drought than to find hope.*

Those were my thoughts, the reason for my darkened mood as the rocky rutted track of the only "road" in or out of Kenton threatened to beat me to death, or perhaps finally to put my beast of a twenty-year-old Land Cruiser out of its misery before I got home. Oh, me of little faith. So much for victorious, confident Christian living. Once again I felt incredibly sad. And I couldn't even do that right, because my *sad* came out *mad*. Which I guess explains my screaming at the merciless "road," the steep surrounding hills, the endless dust, the cloudless equatorial sky, at everything, including God, "Why? Why can't things be different?"

I coasted out of the bush and up onto the shoulder of the main national highway running across the middle of Kenya between Nairobi and Nkuru just as a long caravan of cars approached from the east. I'd never seen a presidential motorcade, but I assumed that's what was coming when a uniformed man in the lead police vehicle motioned for me to wait at the side of the road until the procession passed. I remembered someone once telling me that Kenyan law required all motorists to get out of their vehicles and respectfully stand at attention whenever the president drove past. That seemed like a cool tradition; I figured the head honcho of any country deserves to be shown a little respect. So I got out and stood stiff and tall beside my car before a brand new Mercedes bedecked with flags sped past me.

Very nice car, I thought. *Definitely presidential,* which was fine by me. But then I saw the next seven or eight vehicles in the motorcade were also brand-new, top-of-the-line Mercedes. That's when a painfully obvious insight hit me: most of the foreign aid and the other money coming into this country isn't going to improve education, relieve poverty, or in any other way help the people most in need of assistance. Any official foreign aid was not likely to trickle down past the top of the food chain, where powerful people enjoyed their perks.

As the last of the motorcade rolled west toward Nkuru, I slid back into the driver's seat of my Land Cruiser and pulled out onto the main highway, heading east toward Nairobi, and Kijabe before that. I was now madder than I'd been driving down from Kenton. I was now pounding on my steering wheel *and* yelling in frustration, "I don't know what I'm supposed to do? How do you beat political power and corruption?" And, "Okay, God, why? Why does it have to be like this?"

God suddenly inserted a thought into my head. At one time when I worked for Oracle, the second largest software company in the world, almost 40 percent of our employees were Indian. In one generation, India went from a struggling third-world country with a population deeply divided between rich and poor to an international economic powerhouse with the fastest growing middle class in the world. Technology transformed India in a single generation. Could that be the answer to African poverty as well? Maybe the same sort of thing could happen in Kenya.

What if we could build a computer center at each school that we feed? If Kenyan students could graduate with basic computer skills, they would have a reasonable hope of finding a place in the information age. With enough such technological training, there might be hope for their nation as well. Those were audacious thoughts. How would a guy like me go about even trying to start something like that? I had absolutely no idea how, or if, it could be possible, but if it was, Kenyan kids would get a shot. They would have real hope for their future.

A wild and totally impractical idea, especially considering the sagging American economy and Kenya's virtually nonexistent infrastructure. But I couldn't get it out of my mind. Despite my experience with one of the world's leading computer software companies, I didn't have the first clue how to create and build a basic computer center. But by the time I got back to the RVA campus that afternoon, I had thought of someone I could ask.

I'd met Walter in the States during our orientation training prior to our first one-year short-term assignment. He now worked in Nairobi for AIM-Tech, the support division of our sending agency, specializing in construction, repair, and maintenance of the buildings, facilities, and equipment in all of the places where our missionaries lived and worked. So I phoned Walter that evening to ask if we could get together for lunch next time I made a trip into the city. I said, "I have a wild idea I'd like to get your input on."

We met for lunch the following week. I quickly laid out the rationale behind my computer center concept and admitted I didn't know where to start or if the idea of building a computer lab for a school like the ones we worked with was even remotely possible. Walter didn't laugh at me and blow off the whole idea. But when he said, "Give me a week or so to think about this, Steve, and I'll get back to you," I tried not to get my hopes up too high.

By the time we reconnected a week later, Walter had done more than just think about the idea. He handed me detailed drawings, a comprehensive list of the required materials, and cost projections. I immediately contacted my superiors with the mission to get their permission to write a trial-balloon email asking our financial supporters if they might want to consider helping us with this new venture. Here's how I laid out Walter's plan:

Instead of constructing a building, we want to convert old metal shipping containers into classrooms. The cost is much cheaper, and the structures will be secure. Since only one of the schools has power, we will install solar panels on the roof of each lab. With a battery, inverter, and a few other items, we can get set up:

Container:	$1,200
Remodel:	$3,000
Solar Panels:	$3,000
Batteries:	$1,000
Inverter:	$650
Charge Controller:	$350
Cables:	$160
Back-up Generator:	$700
Transport:	$400
Construction Fee:	$530
Total Cost:	**$10,990**

The problem with buying laptops in this country is that they don't tend to sync the chips well, so we would probably need to buy refurbished Dell's, for about two hundred dollars each. We would begin with ten to twelve computers at each school.

Our software would all be Microsoft products: the Office Suite, Typing Tutor, Encarta, and Magic School Bus. I'm hoping to be able to talk with someone from MS next time I'm in the States to get a better idea of cost.

We'll train two Kenyans on the packages. Then they can teach all the other national teachers, who will teach the students. I think it's important that our program's not seen as one more case of wazungus (plural of mzungu, meaning "foreigners," "outsiders," "white people") coming to the rescue. A wise friend of mine once explained to me that the best solutions need to be owned by the people you are trying to help. So I just want to help provide the tools. And we will start with one school to try to work out the bugs. Then if funds come in, we will keep going.

I'm so grateful for the support you have given to the school lunch program, and I think it is so important to the children. It has enabled children to stay in school, and provided proper nutrition to five thousand kids six days a week. If you are supporting the school lunch program, please don't drop that to help with this. They are two separate programs, and both are important.

But I'm also excited about this idea for computer training labs, because if this works right, it could be the means to provide a generation of young people a chance to escape the inconceivable poverty here. I just want Kenyan kids to have a way out. I'm so tired of things being the way they are. It doesn't have to be this way.

25

Grouchy Elephants
and Usable Ants

EARLIER THAT YEAR, AN OLD FRIEND HAD WRITTEN TO ASK IF I'D BE AT our thirtieth high school reunion in August of 2003. I'd told him I would hate to miss it, but I didn't see any way I could afford to make the trip. He generously offered to pay my round-trip airfare so I could attend. But I still wasn't sure. It's such a long trip that it hardly seemed worth it for less than a three-week visit. And I hated to be gone from Nancy and the kids that long.

Although I started thinking, *I could probably do some fundraising by arranging some speaking engagements and making some appointments to talk to potential donors about our lunch and computer programs.* And Nancy reminded me that I'd managed the home front when she'd been gone three weeks the previous summer for her father's eightieth birthday. We eventually agreed for me to accept the offer and make the most of the opportunity.

The transition from Africa to America is never an easy one. When you have been surrounded by people who have so little, it's easy to feel guilty. This time it hit me on the transatlantic flight home. When the flight attendant asked if I wanted the steak or the shrimp, I started weeping. The poor guy tried to console me by saying, "It's okay; you can have both." I struggled to compose myself, but I did eat both.

—

The menu was overshadowed by something that took place at the end of that flight. For reasons I've never understood, I seem to be a magnet for odd people on airplanes. But I'd made this entire twenty-six-hour flight —Nairobi to Heathrow to Chicago—without a single awkward encounter.

Then, as I strained to wrestle my overstuffed suitcase off the luggage carousel in baggage claim, an elderly gentleman who'd been on the flight with me walked up and we had the following conversation (which is *all* true):

Old Guy: That will never happen to me.

Me: What's that?

Old Guy: I just came from three weeks in Europe and all I brought with me was *this. (points to a small piece of luggage)*

Me: That's nice.

Old Guy: Want to know the secret?

Me: *(fear rising up)* Sure.

Old Guy: I only brought three pairs of underwear.

Me: *(no response)*

Old Guy: *(undeterred by my silence)* I bought this new underwear, and you wash it in the hotel and it dries overnight. It's amazing.

Me: I'm forty-eight years old and I've never had anyone tell me about their underwear in an airport before.

Wife of Old Guy: What are you two talking about?

Me: His underwear.

Wife of Old Guy: Oh, it's great! It dries so fast.

Only in America.

In twenty-one days, I stayed in the same bed only once. Planning the trip, I'd thought, *If I spend only one night with someone, how annoying could I be?* As I reconstructed the trip, my email highlights included:

- *Traveling seven thousand miles and not winning the "person who has come the farthest to the high school reunion" (Australia won), and not being the "oldest father" either (someone had a ten-month-old).*
- *Hadn't seen my aunt in decades and falling asleep in the lovely dinner she made for me.*
- *Shouting loudly in a Walmart, "These Snickers have ALMONDS!" and frightening an old woman (possibly the one whose husband has dry underwear).*
- *Managing to lose my phone list with hundreds of names of people I was going to call in the first five days.*
- *Watching one of my flights leave without me and thus missing (1) a birthday party for a dear friend, and (2) my only opportunity to see one of my best friends in the whole world.*
- *Sitting next to two very nice Tupperware distributors on their way to a*

Tupperware convention and trying to explain why Africa might not be their next big market.

- Summoning up my courage (after forty-eight years dodging the bullet) and admitting to my younger sister that I needed her help to do clothes shopping for the children. (When it comes to shopping, she is a force of nature.)

- Seeing an old friend I hadn't seen in twenty years and being afraid to eat her peanut butter pie because it had been so wonderful twenty years earlier that I feared it couldn't possibly measure up to my memories, and having it be so good that I asked for another piece the next morning for breakfast.

- Getting in late from a delayed flight and being picked up by a kind friend who asked if I wanted a sandwich, and instead whining, "I want a pizza with American sausage."

- On the fourth day of three-breakfast-meeting-mornings, wondering if I had overbooked my trip a little bit.

- Speaking at the sixth place in one day and preparing to say, "You've got to be sick of hearing me speak," and realizing, "They haven't heard me speak; I'm sick of hearing me speak."

- Leaving a pile of my dirty clothes in a pristine hall while yelling and telling my gracious host, "I'm late for my flight; can I pick this up on Monday?"

There are so many wonderful memories of this trip. Friends driving for hours to say hi, seeing family, having someone give a huge check for the computer centers and for once in my stupid life being speechless, having the number of schools we can feed almost double, staying up late and catching up.

It was also hard. Hearing bad news, sad news, and the pain that life brings. Calling someone who is getting married and knowing you can't be there; friends out of work; friends going through tough times. I went by the cemetery to spend a little time at Stephen's grave and was surprised by how much it still hurts.

On my last day in the States, I stopped by my bank. There were three tellers that day. I waited fifteen minutes in line. My teller had been the funeral director for Stephen. I hadn't recognized her, but she remembered me. She had left the funeral home some time ago and was now working at the bank. She told me how much his life had impacted her, and how she had started making changes in her life after the funeral.

I don't know why, but when you lose a child, you have this fear that no one will remember them. It was such a gift to have that right before I headed back to Africa. As I left, I was reminded of something I had written several years ago:

He has gone to a place where babies never die, where the only tears are tears of joy, and there are no more separations and no more goodbyes.

It had been so hard to say goodbye to Nancy and the kids when I left Kenya, and then so hard to say goodbye to friends in the States. Thank you all for a special three weeks. I'm sorry for overbooking and not calling everyone I wanted to, but I'm so grateful for the chance I had to see so many. There is a place, and there will be a time, where we won't have to say goodbye anymore.

All that being said, being greeted so warmly by my family again made it all worthwhile. JT continued his holiday growth spurt and is now an inch taller than me. Matthew is doing great. The twins are growing like weeds. And Nancy is greater than ever, if such a thing is possible.

Our school administration told the staff that we needed to be in touch with today's youth. I was able to purchase a CD for seventy-five cents online called Forever in Bluegrass: The Songs of Neil Diamond Performed by a Bluegrass Band. *I think you will agree that with THAT in hand, I'm ready to take on the next group of students when school starts tomorrow.*

―

In large part because of the additional funds raised during my trip, we purchased more than one hundred tons of food, enough to feed more than sixty-five hundred children in *twenty* schools for the term starting that September. We had so much to deliver that we didn't get it out to some communities until school was in session, which meant children were there cheering when the truck drove up.

Delivery time never seems to go right. But this time we had more glitches than usual. So I went to Kijabe Town to see how things were going, only to discover that some of the maize we'd already bought and paid for hadn't been dried properly. We were going to have to dry it for a few more days before we could deliver it to the schools, which meant some lunch programs would be late getting started, and that frustrated me. I was tired and feeling downright discouraged.

Then I noticed him. A ten-year-old Kenyan kid practicing his soccer moves in a dusty, rocky, empty lot. He was barefoot. His "soccer ball" was a tightly wadded bunch of disposable plastic bags like grocery stores use, lashed together with knotted, scrap pieces of twine. Watching that boy, who was Matthew's age, kick that makeshift ball back and forth across that lot, I realized, *I may have had a rough couple of weeks, but I've got it so easy. It's a shame I have to keep being reminded.*

―

We had a new group of dorm guys for the 2003–2004 school year at RVA. After three years with our old crew, it had been hard to say goodbye. But having new eighth graders to get to know reminded me of the sacrifices many of their families make.

One of the boys was a foot shorter than his seventeen dorm-mates. He'd been homeschooled up to now, and this was his first time away from his parents. He struggled hard to keep it together that first week of the term. He and I went for a walk one day, and he told me his father was the only pilot in a remote part of Africa who flew sick people out to hospitals. If his dad were to leave, hundreds of thousands of people would have no access to emergency medical help. But there were no adequate schools around there.

He started crying. He believed his dad was doing the right thing, an important job that he felt called to do. But it was so hard to be away.

I felt so inadequate as a dorm parent. The only thing I could think to say got lost in my own tears. A week later, this same kid was running and playing and adapting well to life at Rift Valley Academy. When you are where you are supposed to be, things work out.

—

As I've said before, I always wanted a daughter. And finally having one was every bit as wonderful as I'd ever dreamed. But I admit I'd encountered a steep learning curve being the daddy of a little girl.

I don't think any of my four male children had ever shown the slightest interest in what they wore. Consequently, they were always easy to dress. Female clothing is different. Sometimes you button it from the front; sometimes from the back. There are *never* instructions.

But the hassle was worth it all whenever I'd finally get Katie's dress on correctly. She wore one on Sundays, and as we walked to church, there was no other word to describe it: she *strutted*. She looked good, and she knew it. It was so much fun to have a two-year-old daughter. And to be fair, whenever I told Katie her hair looked nice, Ben would put his hand on his head and I'd be sure to tell him, "Your hair looks really good too, Bubba."

—

On the ninth of October, I reported:

I went down to Kijabe Town School to help with lunch last week. Two parents spend much of the morning each day in the kitchen preparing the food for four hundred students.

The children wanted me to thank you for the food. Then I asked one of the teachers how the food had affected her students. (The usual response to that question is some-thing like, "They are better able to concentrate.") This teacher told me, "When the children hold their stomachs and cry because they are hungry, I lose hope and do not teach well. It is good when they eat."

I went to a remote school of eight hundred children in Kiambogo today. It took me almost an hour to get there. The moment we arrived, the children came running toward the car. The headmaster told me he has only nine teachers on staff. But that wasn't his greatest concern. He explained that his next goal was to have one textbook for every three children. And yet this headmaster was so encouraged. He told me, "It is getting so much better. Now we have food! We have more books than ever before. Soon we may have more teachers."

Perspective is a real gift, isn't it?

―

We were close to beginning construction on our first computer center for Karima School. So I drove out to check on the lunch program there and give the headmaster of the primary school an update on our time frame. The Karima community is in a remote area with no electricity, so the center definitely would need solar power. Eight hundred students attend the pri-mary grades. The nearby secondary school has another one hundred students enrolled.

We had recently added a lunch program for the Karima secondary school, so this was my first visit there. And if I had to describe those older students in a few words, I'd say they were without hope. Because they had lived longer than their younger brothers and sisters, they seemed to think they had seen all life has to offer, and it had made them afraid to hope. Chances were, any time they had ever dared to hope, Africa had dashed that hope and thrown it back in their faces. So when I told them we were going to build a computer center at their school, no one believed me.

I ran over to the primary school next door and enjoyed a much better reception. The children there hadn't given up yet. The poverty is just as bad, but they were little kids. They still believed things could get better. They cheered when I told them we would soon begin building a computer center for their school.

―

I've been accused of having too many "coincidences" for my own good, but this one is too *good* not to share.

On my return flight to Kenya from the States back in August, I'd been looking through information the organizers handed out at our thirtieth reunion and discovered that one of my classmates, someone I hadn't seen at the reunion, worked for Hope College in Michigan. It just so happened that one of RVA's Kenyan students, Josephine, had been accepted to Hope, starting as a freshman that fall. Her parents made little money per year, so extra cash was rare for them. Their daughter was going to college in Michigan, and I'd just learned she didn't have any warm clothes.

So I emailed my classmate to tell her about Josephine and explain my connection. And Molly emailed me back to say she would take Josephine shopping and make sure she got what she needed. Think about that: someone I hadn't seen in thirty years was going to clothe this young girl I helped get a college scholarship. A little thing, I suppose, just a small coincidence, unless you don't have warm clothes, which reminded me that there are no *little things*, that if we give ourselves to what we've been called to do, it's always big.

What are the odds? Molly and I went to high school together in Illinois more than three decades ago. She ended up in Michigan; I was in Kenya. One of my students ends up at Hope. I just happen to find out that Molly's at Hope because someone sends me a ticket to fly back for my thirtieth high school reunion, where I don't even see Molly, yet on my flight back to Africa, I make the connection. And when I contact her over the internet, I learn she is more than willing to help out a Kenyan kid without a warm coat.

I mean, you've just got to love these coincidences. Or the one who created them.

—

Speaking of coincidences, big things, signs, and doing what you know you're called to do:

Like a lot of all-too-human beings, I'm frequently on the lookout for "legitimate" reasons not to do what I know I ought to do. Such as exercise. A virus passed through the campus the last week of the first term, and several dozen RVA students and staff came down sick, including Nancy. After trying to take up the slack with our two-year-old twins, along with all the usual year-end responsibilities, such as preparing and sending out a gazillion college application packages for my seniors, I couldn't for the life of me remember ever feeling so tired. Yet I realized I needed a workout, so I determined to run the following morning.

Then we received a notice from campus security warning all walkers and joggers *not* to use our usual course. It seems an angry rogue elephant had been seen outside our campus and had been chasing anyone who got near him. We routinely kept an eye out for aggressive baboons whenever we were out and about. Even agitated monkeys could be a serious nuisance if you surprised them or ventured too close. But grouchy elephants were a whole new phenomenon. And a worthy reason to sleep in.

—

I was already getting into the Christmas spirit when I wrote the following email to our supporters on December 1:

The first computer lab is beginning to come together this month.

When I made the announcement to the teachers at Karima School about the lab, they couldn't believe it. One teacher told me he had prayed for a miracle, but he had not expected anything this great.

My favorite Christmas carol is "Good King Wenceslas," and my favorite part is the end: "They who now shall bless the poor shall themselves find blessings." I think of you guys when I hear it, and I pray that you have been as blessed as you have blessed us.

I am the most unlikely person in the world to be doing this stuff, but I heard two stories this week that made me realize that God uses people where they are.

Duane's journey to Africa began several years ago when his daughter broke her back and became a paraplegic. Going through that changed him forever. Last month, there was a terrible car accident here, and a young woman became a paraplegic because of it. When Duane and his wife learned what had happened, they went to see the young woman and were able to minister to her in a way that no one else could have. She was comforted and accepted the eternal hope of Christ into her heart. What Duane and his wife had gone through helped change this young woman forever.

Then when Nancy and I were babysitting today, we heard another story—about another abandoned three-pound baby. His cries were too weak for anyone to hear, so he was going to die out in the bush. But the ants descended on him. And as they began to feast on him, his cries became loud enough that someone heard him. He was found and saved. The ants, which could have been a curse, saved him.

God uses ants. He even uses me.

26

Middle of Nowhere No More

ONE BUSY DAY IN JANUARY, I DROVE DOWN TO THE VALLEY TO VISIT A school. The guy I was supposed to meet didn't show, and the school didn't have their food ready to go. So I was frustrated when I headed back to campus. The road I took out of the valley and up the escarpment was new, unpaved, steep in places, with long drop-offs, and it was more than a little intimidating in the rain. About halfway up, I stopped to offer a ride to two elderly Kenyan women who were making the long hard climb from the valley up to the mission hospital in Kijabe.

As they got in, the sky opened up and rain poured down on us. I was going uphill, my tires spinning wildly on the suddenly muddy and treacherous road, with both of my passengers regularly emitting gasps and other disconcerting sounds of terror. I was more than a little scared too.

Me: If you know how to pray, this would be a good time to start.
Them: God! Help!

He did. We reached the hospital safely. I let them out and drove back onto the campus thinking, *That's why I was supposed to go down to the school today.*

It was such a great feeling.

—

But not as great as I felt about what happened a few weeks later, when we experienced a true miracle regarding our first computer center.

The ten laptop computers we'd ordered arrived at our mission headquarters in New York on a Monday, and they were all in our home in Kenya by Friday—four days later. The people who receive, process, and ship items to

Africa from headquarters do a remarkable job in the face of many challenges. But some things sent to us through headquarters take four months to reach us in Kijabe.

Even more incredibly, I'd budgeted thousands of dollars for customs charges on ten computers. Yet this shipment cost me less duty than the two fruitcakes sent to us for Christmas. I felt truly blessed by the way the computer center plans were coming together.

―

As further evidence that my sons were experiencing a different upbringing from their father, consider this email report I sent in February:

JT is now fifteen and has gone on three dates. The first girl asked him to a Sadie Hawkins movie night. She is an absolutely beautiful white young lady. The second young lady who asked him out to a Sadie Hawkins luncheon is an absolutely beautiful young Kenyan woman. For his third date, he asked out a beautiful Korean classmate.

For more excitement, he got invited to Uganda (just a day's drive) to go whitewater rafting on the Nile River. At one point, when he wanted to get out and swim, he was informed that wasn't such a good idea, because the crocodiles would be too appreciative.

―

The following month, I marked another family milestone:

Stephen was born six years ago today. March 4 used to be such a hard day. But I look at the twins, at the more than eight thousand schoolkids we feed every day, at the amazing life we live now because of his life, and I can see him in almost everything I do, everything I am.

―

By early April, our first computer lab was finally operational. Which is a remarkable story starring my friend Walter, the same guy I'd first told about my computer lab dream the previous summer. He wasn't just what the Disney folks would call an *imagineer*—the person who took my half-baked idea, created a practical design, and even provided me a reasonable, reachable budget. Walter was also a doer who built and brought the whole thing to life.

Since our financial resources were limited, and because thievery was such an issue, Walter started with an old metal shipping container. Solar technology is like gold in Africa. So Walter figured out how to affix solar panels to the top of the container so securely that the only way to steal them would be to break them, which would defeat the purpose. When we had gotten the refurbished computers, they each had a grounded electrical plug, which wasn't compatible with Kenyan electrical sockets. I panicked. Walter just pulled the ground posts out. The guy was like a walking Nike commercial: he knew what to do, so he would *just do it.*

After we trucked the computer center to Karima, Walter lived in it for three days and nights to do the remaining work and to protect the special tools he needed to get the whole shebang up and running. While I was with him the last day, he got out a can of paint and carefully did a little touch-up work around the doors and windows. I had to walk off and cry over that. Because Walter had made this project happen. And he'd done it with excellence and a care that inspired me.

Once the center was working, the computer teacher we had hired spent the rest of her first month just instructing the school's teachers while the children were on their April break. Until then, no one on staff at this school (besides our computer teacher) had ever seen a computer in real life, so we were starting from ground zero. I instructed the headmaster to use his baby finger to type the letter A so many times that ever afterward when I visited his school, he greeted me with a wave of that little finger.

Staff members were excited beyond excited. One day during our staff training, a curious young man from the Karima community stopped by to see what was happening. He told me, "When you announced that you would build a computer center here, I did not believe you. Even when the computer center arrived, I still did not believe it."

I invited him inside the classroom and motioned for him to sit down at a computer. I showed him how to turn on the computer and type his name on the keyboard. He grinned wider and wider as his name appeared letter by letter on the lighted screen. "Now I believe," he said, with his face full of tears.

—

The Karima schools held an official opening ceremony for the computer center before the kids started their next term. Like most traditional Kenyan celebrations, the event felt confusing and exhilarating at the same time. A thousand or more people attended. The organizers had set up a tent created out of maize bags tied together. A well-used car battery powered a portable sound system operated by an announcer who maintained a continuous stream of inane patter such as "Steve Peifer is now walking toward us" throughout the afternoon, which was funnier than I can describe here.

During the "entertainment," Nancy and I, as honored guests, sat on the first row next to the region's MP (member of parliament), who proved witty and charming. Some other local officials welcomed and *decorated* us with something similar to a Hawaiian lei fashioned out of Christmas tree garland.

Then the stupid moment hit. A group of schoolchildren doing a dance invited the MP to dance with them. She obviously knew the moves, and the kids loved it. Then they asked me. You'd think my previous experience with African dance, and my lifelong history of dancing issues would have led me to gracefully decline the invitation. Instead, I got up in front of that wildly cheering crowd and began to dance. Suddenly hundreds of Kenyan kids started screaming, "Can you teach me how to dance like that?" And in that moment, Africa and America were as one.

Actually, what happened is this: for some mysterious reason, when I stood up and faced that crowd, the only dance I could think of was something I'd seen years before on *Hullabaloo*. (If you never saw that show and don't know what it is, say a prayer of thanks.) And the entire Karima community laughed at me.

Then there were lots of speeches. The MC introduced each presenter with "the hope that his [or her] *worthy* remarks will remain brief." That was not to be. But many of the speakers were quite good, with some surprisingly *worthy* things to say. Many people noted that until the computer center was built, they felt isolated and unknown. Three different people said that they couldn't understand how or why a computer lab would be built in the middle of nowhere. But now that they saw an actual computer center in Karima and all the computers for the children of their community school, they didn't feel they were in the middle of nowhere anymore.

But the most encouraging thing I heard all afternoon was when the headmaster told us that those most excited were not the community, the parents, or even the high school students. It was the younger children, because now they could believe they had a future.

—

I wrote to our supporters in my email report on that opening ceremony:

What a gift you have given to Karima and its children.

Walter and I went through the center one last time while we were there, looking for structural issues, power difficulties, or any other problems. We couldn't find any.

One reason we had wanted to make sure it was right before continuing was because we received notice of funding for the second center this week. We will have a hard decision to make as to where it goes, but another school is going to get a chance.

The world can change if we want it to change. We can be passive and allow what has occurred to continue, or we can declare, "No more hungry children and no more children without opportunity."

It's our choice, and our opportunity.

And then before concluding the email, I warned my readers that the rest of the email was going to get "weirdly personal," so they could feel free to skip through the next few paragraphs, which said:

I desperately believe in the feeding program we do, and I pray that it can continue to grow. But like much we have done in Kenya, it is reactive.

I've been in Kenya for four years, and this computer center is the first time I've felt like I have taken a stab at the beast that has robbed and raped and stolen from this country. I realize this is just one small computer center that will serve only a few hundred children. But it is a start, a real and practical way out of the poverty that consumes this land.

Besides the super important and obvious best days of my life (Accepting Jesus into my heart, Nancy's saying "Yes" and "I do," the births of our boys, the adoption of the twins), there are two other events I know will stand forever among my memories of life's greatest days.

One of those was the day after Stephen was born. He had such a cleft lip that he couldn't nurse from Nancy or take a regular bottle because he couldn't manage a sucking motion. They tried a special bottle, but none of the nurses were able to get him to take any nourishment. They informed us they would need to insert a feeding tube.

I asked if I could try, and the nurses reminded me that two of the hospital's very best, most experienced neonatal intensive care nurses had been unsuccessful. And when I asked again, they sighed the heavy sighs that I suspect only the most expert health-care professionals can sigh.

But they handed me my son, and Stephen drained the whole bottle for me. Starting that day and continuing the remaining days of his life, our son would take a bottle only from Nancy or me, as if he knew he didn't have much time, so why waste it on someone else? And that still stands as one of the greatest days of my life.

The other memorable day, which has nothing to do with the previous one, was more than thirty years ago—one early '70s summer evening cruising in a car with Tom and Charlie and Chopper when "Rocky Mountain High" came on the radio. I loved that song and I loved my friends and I knew that they loved me, and in that moment I just felt so alive and so happy.

I don't know why I thought of those two events on this occasion. But as I wept over a solar-powered computer center opening in Karima, Kenya, today, those two memories flooded my mind. And I realized what a gift it is to do what you all have allowed us to do here in Africa. So I have to say thank you for giving me another one of the greatest days of my life.

~

Somehow there always seemed to be just enough good days to get us through the other stuff. But some days there seemed to be an awful lot of that *other stuff.*

That entire April was a month to ponder the eternal. We learned some fellow missionaries we'd met three years earlier were murdered in Uganda. The Petts were former dairy farmers who sold their farm in America to come and help in Africa. They taught agriculture at a Ugandan technical school where they'd been murdered and the school burned. Murder is always a tragedy, of course. But when it involves people trying to extend kindness and the love of Christ, it seems an especially painful blow.

We also received the disturbing news that one of our dorm guys who'd gone home during the break had suffered a perforated bowel. His parents were stationed in Tanzania, and the overcrowded hospital where he was receiving treatment had two patients to a bed. Eighth grade, fighting for your life—and doing it while sharing a bed with a total stranger. The thought boggled my mind. We learned he was going to make it, but the reality of being remote hit home again.

~

On a positive note, one of my students was accepted at Princeton. When I heard that great news, I thought again about the path I traveled to become the college advisor at Rift Valley Academy.

Early in my professional business career back in the States, I worked for three companies that went belly-up in the course of sixteen months. So I'd ended up taking a job at a company selling publishing and database services to colleges and universities. It was not an especially good job; the owner was an eccentric man. But I was so gun-shy after the other companies folded that I tried to make it work.

My efforts paid off as I soon became and remained the top-performing salesman in the company for many years. But that did not make it easier for me with my boss, so I often looked for other positions. However, because I couldn't find anything that paid near what I was making, I stuck with it and endured lots of frustration and humiliation. Yet that job was the one that took me to eight hundred college campuses across North America. I learned much about those schools and the differences in quality between them and truly enjoyed the college environments I regularly worked in.

This was one reason I absolutely loved my current responsibilities at

RVA—talking to kids about colleges, helping them narrow down their best options and make their final choices, celebrating with them when they got those acceptance letters, and finding the financial resources that allowed them to pursue their dreams. Being the college counselor at Rift Valley Academy in Kijabe, Kenya, was one of the most satisfying things I'd ever done. And the value I brought to my current role was largely because of those seven tough years working a job I didn't want. Most of my life I'd considered those my wasted years. But I was now in a position where being knowledge-able about so many colleges was a big plus. And a young man from a small school with baboons on its campus was going to Princeton.

I was reminded once again: I can trust God's plan for my life.

—

Somehow the annual eighth grade formal sneaked up on me that year. From my up close and personal perspective as an eighth grade dorm parent, I found most of the emotional drama and trauma surrounding the event to be pretty funny. At the same time, I couldn't help feeling a little sad that our boys' parents didn't get to see their guys clean up so nice.

One boy was so scared that he'd forget his manners training that he wrote on his palms, "Right hand fork," "Left hand knife." Another guy got so excited about the prospect of sitting with the girl he liked that he bounced off the walls for days beforehand. But when he got back to the dorm at the end of the evening, he seemed surprisingly subdued, which led to the fol-lowing conversation:

Me: What's the matter?

Him: I was so excited when I found out I would be sitting next to her, but after two minutes, I ran out of things to say.

Me: What did you do?

Him: I looked the other way the rest of the night.

It's easy to forget how hard it has always been to be an eighth grader, and how awkward that age can be. But after two years as dorm parent for eighth grade boys, I'd reached the conclusion that some of the bravest people I'd ever known were eighth graders at RVA. To go through that stage of life away from your parents had to be so hard.

—

RVA's leadership team requested that our feeding program cease while we were to be back in the States on furlough in the upcoming year. Other veteran faculty all had their own outside projects; most everyone was stretched pretty thin. And administering the lunch program would pose a bigger challenge than any new staff member could probably handle.

I hated to have to call even a temporary halt to a program that was growing and so many people already counted on. Part of me wanted to argue that surely any number of people might do a great job. But I also realized that coordinating the details of supplying and overseeing the work at twenty schools scattered all over that part of Kenya did require a considerable investment of time and energy. So I reconciled myself to the decision and even convinced myself that it was probably for the best that the program took a rest for a year.

That decision, however, made the final food delivery drive of the school year a bittersweet endeavor. Headmasters became quite emotional as we told them we would have to curtail the program—temporarily. Again and again, I had to explain that there was simply no more money in the fund and that I needed to be there to supervise. But they had seen the fruit in this program. So as I listened to grown men with tears running down their cheeks telling me what the program had done for their schools, about children running who didn't used to run after noon because they would be too tired, I told myself, *Burn this into your heart. Feel the hurt. Let this motivate you.*

—

Driving back up to Kenton, I was struck yet again by that area's startling juxtaposition of indescribable beauty and unimaginable poverty, either one of which could take away your breath. While I didn't relish telling the headmaster about the lunch program going on hiatus next year, I was looking forward to personally delivering some exciting news to him.

When I told him, "We are going to build our second computer center here at your school," he just looked at me. Then he stared out over the hills. He looked back at me, and then he turned and stared again at the hills around us. For the longest time he said not a word. Yet I understood him perfectly. Sometimes silence can be the most eloquent thing you can say.

—

While we were there at Kenton, the school arranged some entertainment for us. They had a dance troupe and a young man who played a homemade xylophone. At closer range, I could see it was made with discarded fence posts. Yet it sounded so great. It was the most amazing thing, this kid playing this wonderful music on that junky homemade instrument. As I watched and listened, I realized that boy could well have thought, *I can't do anything on this piece of junk,* and not even have tried. But he knew what was in his hand.

I pondered his example for days. *What is really in my hand? If I looked at what I had differently, would it change the way I lived my life? If I knew what I really had, how would I change?*

—

Not long after that, Walter suggested I go out and run a routine checkup of the solar panels at our first center to make sure they were still working as expected. I needed to measure the charge left in our batteries after we booted up all ten laptops and ran them a while in the dark. Since it's never safe to be out on Kenyan roads late at night, I rolled out of bed early one morning and headed out to Karima School to do my check before dawn.

By flashlight, I used an extra key to unlock the industrial strength padlock used to secure the computer center classroom container. Inside, I flipped on the solar-powered lights, booted up the computers one at a time, and then began noting at fifteen-minute intervals—just as Walter had instructed me to do—the electrical drain indicated on our battery gauges.

Sometime along about my third or fourth reading, I heard a suspicious noise outside. Over the next few minutes, that suspicious noise grew to a full-fledged commotion, and I began to worry some mob was gathering outside with the intent to vandalize the center. All I had to protect myself and the computers was the small toolbox I'd brought with me. My choice of weapons came down to a screwdriver with interchangeable Phillips and regular heads or a semisharp panga (Swahili for machete).

I don't know what I was thinking when I picked up the panga and walked to the door. But that wasn't half as stupid as what I did next. I opened the door and stood backlighted and stock-still in that doorway, panga in hand, waiting for my eyes to adjust from the incandescent brightness inside the computer center to the fading-gray darkness outside. To my surprise and relief, I soon saw the computer center was about to be surrounded all right, but by a mini-mob of young students from the school. I recognized many familiar faces, including several I knew walked at least three miles from their homes to get there every morning. I looked at my watch to see it was just a little after 6:00 a.m.

"What is going on out here?" I asked. "School still starts at eight o'clock, doesn't it? So why are you all here so early in the morning?" One of the older and taller students stepped out of the darkness up into the light streaming out of the classroom doorway. "We come early every morning, Peifer," he explained, "because the computer teacher arrives each day at 7:00. And at 7:15 she picks ten students who will get extra time working on the computers before school starts."

Recounting that experience and the xylophone story in my next email home, I concluded by telling our supporters, *Evidently children now begin arriving at school anywhere from five to six every morning, many of them walking miles before dawn, in hopes of being first in line for an extra thirty minutes of computer time prior to the regular school day.*

So if any of you notice me taking things for granted ever again, you have permission to slap me. Hard.

Obviously the programs we've started are bearing much fruit. Please help us grow them. We're heading home on furlough soon, so may I ask you to ask your church or corporation if I could speak to them while we are back in the States? I need some larger venues in order to raise funds for expansion, and I don't know how to do it without your help. Can you help us help these kids?

Will you look and see what is in your hand?

27

America Just Wears You Down

O NE OF THE UNIQUE CHALLENGES MISSIONARY FAMILIES FACE ARE FUR-
loughs, like the one the Peifer family was about to embark upon as soon
as that 2003–2004 school year came to an end.

Most career missionaries, depending on their sending agency's policy,
serve three-to-five-year terms overseas and then return to their homeland
for a year (give or take) before they head back to the "field" for their next
term. These furlough years are not vacations or time off. Nor are they the
equivalent of academic sabbaticals. More than just R & R, the time allows
for emotional and physical recovery, spiritual rejuvenation, additional professional training, and reconnecting with family and supporters. And missionaries invest significant time and energy fundraising on behalf of their own
ministry and that of their sending agency—speaking engagements, appointments with potential donors, and so on.

The planning required for a family facing two intercontinental moves
in one year can be a logistical nightmare posing many unsettling questions.
Where in America will you live for the coming year? How do you find an
acceptable place from thousands of miles away? Where will the kids go to
school? What will you do to support your family while you're in the States?
(The monthly stipend adequate for life on RVA's campus in rural Kenya
wouldn't begin to cover the cost of living back in the States.) How big of a
financial hardship might this year be?

But one of the most significant complications is something few people
ever think about until and unless they have to do it themselves with their
own kids. Career missionaries live life in two worlds. Their original "home"
culture, where their family roots and most lifelong relationships remain. And

that second world of our adopted land, where we reside, minister, and invest our lives in people of a different culture. Maintaining equilibrium with one foot, half a mind, and a big chunk of your heart in each world, while periodically stepping back and forth from one to the other, can be a tricky balancing act, even for mature adults.

It's often tougher for the kids who are growing up, establishing their identities, trying to learn the ways of two worlds and how they as one person fit into both, either, or neither. This is why MKs often are now referred to as third-culture kids. They don't have the same cultural connection to their parents' homeland. But neither can they completely blend into the culture where they spend most of their formative years. Kids (of any age) whose lives and tangled personal roots are divided and stretched halfway around the world find it hard to feel sufficiently anchored to truly belong in either.

Three weeks before we were scheduled to head back to the States, I found myself strangely conflicted—simultaneously excited about all that it means to be going "home" to America, yet sobered and saddened by the thought of leaving Africa. This confusing combination of anticipation and melancholy was reflected in the variety of subjects covered in the last couple of emails I wrote before we headed home:

When I think about why I will miss this place, I think about Erik.

Here at RVA, Erik is a golden boy. Good looking, great basketball player, lead in the musical, some of the highest scores on the SAT in the history of the school. His dad is a surgeon who gives up millions to be a missionary doctor here in Kenya. Erik dates the prom queen, or at least she probably would be if a boarding school for missionary kids had a prom.

Anyway, Nancy and I had lunch duty last week, and for the first time in my memory, the RVA cafeteria served individual-size packages of chips. (They were probably past their sell-by date, which is when they are affordable here.)

Erik walked in, looked at the lunch, and got so elated he exclaimed for everyone to hear, "WOW! Bags of chips!" And I thought, That's one of the reasons I love this place. Where else would the coolest kid on campus act thrilled over a bag of chips?

—

The twins are not exactly sure about all this "America" business. Although we have tried hard to tell them about all the wonders of the USA, I'm not sure how much has gotten through. We have had several discussions like this:

Me: *You will have so much fun in America.*

Them: *Will Lauren be in America?*

Me: *No. But you will make LOTS of friends in America.*

Them: *Will I still be three in America?*

Me: *Yes!*

Many of you have asked what our plans are for the coming year. We hope to begin by getting some rest. The end of school is so busy and so stressful, and when you add to that trying to pack everything you have and storing it away in a different place for a year, after three straight years of 24/7 dorm duties, adopting the twins, and everything else, we could use a little down time.

So after a few weeks of rest, we are definitely going to shop for clothing. It would be in bad taste to describe for you the state of repair my underwear is in, but my friend Chris would say it's held together with baling wire and spit.

We want the older boys to get reacclimated to the States. And we'll all try to see America through the eyes of our three-year-olds, who have never been out of Kenya before.

RVA has encouraged me to get certified in college guidance, so I'll be taking a series of online classes from UCLA. And the goal the Lord has put on my heart is to come back to Kenya a year from now with enough funding to build twenty-five computer centers and expand our lunch program to one hundred schools.

In addition, our own financial support has fallen off to the point that we will not be allowed to return next year until it is at our mission-approved level. So we need to seek out new support. I hope to find some kind of work once the older boys start school in the middle of August.

I know this has been lengthy, but I wanted to end with thanks to all of you. It would be difficult to sum up all you have meant to us without getting sappy or weepy (both of which are things I like to avoid). But what comes to mind as I think of you is an old TV show called The Invaders, *about this guy who discovers that aliens have landed and are plotting to take over the world.*

And no one believes him. Worse, no one cares.

In you, we have found people who cared enough to weep with us over what we have seen and experienced here in Kenya. You have stood with us, and oftentimes it was an email from some one of you that gave us the fuel to continue the fight, and to be encouraged in it.

Which brings me back again to the last episode of The Invaders: *The main character is seated at a table with a small group of people as a stern narrator intones, "Finally, he has discovered allies. Those who also know. Those who believe." And the guy looks at the people around his table, and he weeps.*

Thank you for all you've done for us, and for the people of Kenya. You all have made a difference in so many people's lives. You've been a voice for the voiceless. You've given hope to the hopeless.

Please don't take this wrong, but when I think of you guys, sometimes I just weep.

—

Whenever you have an international trip, there always seems to be one incident that makes it memorable. Heading back to the States this time, it happened before we got out of the Nairobi airport. JT's carry-on was his saxophone. And when the security folks opened the case, an interesting conversation ensued:

Security: What is this?
JT: It's a saxophone.
Security: What is a saxophone?
JT: It is a musical instrument.
Security: You must play it in order for us to believe you.

So at ten o'clock in the evening, JT played a song for the security agents. I suspect they knew very well what the saxophone was; they were just looking for a little entertainment to liven up their late-night shift. But it was fun to see JT get into the spirit of it. He was a different kid than he had been three years earlier.

—

The only thing that seemed to connect with Katie about what we had told her about America was that there would be nice people you could call on the phone who would bring pizza right to your house.

It was a long flight; almost twenty-four hours of travel that began at 11:30 p.m. in Nairobi, so we were tired when we finally arrived in Texas. We ordered a pizza, and I wish you could have seen our daughter's face when a nice man came and left us a large sausage and anchovie pizza with extra cheese. For the next three days, whenever someone used the phone, Katie came running and yelled, "Pizza!"

After a day or so, we ventured out to a grocery store to stock our cupboards. Matthew yelled from a couple of aisles over and we all went running to see what was up.

"Look! Oreos ... Double-Stuff Oreos ... Green Oreos ... Fudge Covered Oreos ... Vanilla Oreos ..." As Matthew continued his list, JT started shoveling several packages of each into the cart. You need to understand, if we ever saw *any kind* of Oreos in Kenya, we bought them, because we knew they wouldn't be there next time we went to the store. So as I began pulling Oreo packages out of our cart and putting them back on the shelf, I explained that if a half-dozen packages weren't enough, the rest would still be there next week. And I thought, *There are definitely going to be some readjustment issues this time around.*

Or just *plain* adjustment issues. Ben and Katie were fascinated with doorbells and ceiling fans and carpet and just about everything. One day the three of us were out for a walk and a fire engine sped by, lights flashing, siren wailing. The twins started crying and wanted to be held; it took me a while to remember they had never heard a siren or seen a fire engine before. Eventually fire trucks became some of their favorite things, but it took a while.

⸺

Some of my own adjustments turned out to be quite different from what I'd anticipated. As we'd approached our furlough, I'd had a great fear that when we got back to America, someone might say something ugly to the twins. And sure enough, one day soon after our return, I took Ben and Katie with me to pick up something at a hardware store, where I noticed this big redneck guy in denim bib overalls who kept eyeing us. When he finally walked toward us looking like he wanted to say something, I casually picked up a wrench with which to hit him if he said something unkind to my babies. (In retrospect, I realized that might not have been a missionary-like response.) But fortunately, Mr. Redneck Blue Jeans stopped, looked at me, looked down at the kids, and said, "Ain't them cute?" before giving us a toothy smile nearly big as Texas, then turning and walking away.

⸺

Another day, we took the whole family by the cemetery and stood for a time at Stephen's grave. He would have been six. I couldn't help but wonder what would have happened if he'd lived. But as we wondered, Ben and Katie sat by his gravestone. It was one of the most bittersweet moments of our lives.

⸺

Within weeks of getting back to Dallas, I managed to land a job with a consulting company, working for a boss I soon decided just might be the smartest human on the planet, which was both intimidating and inspiring, in equal measures. I also enrolled in the classes I needed to get certified in college counseling. And during that first month, I got speaking engagements in Houston and Connecticut, trying to increase funding for the computer centers and the feeding program.

Perhaps one of the biggest adjustments we all had to make was to the sheer busyness of American life and culture. Evidence of which I offer here in a sampling of quick highlights, random observations, and representative summary reports from the Peifer family's eventful first six months back in the States:

• JT played football after three years of playing rugby. He had access to a great weight room and coach, so he grew even bigger and taller. Besides football, he is in a band called No Zebra, which consists of three guitars, a drummer, a saxophone, and a tuba. Both he and Matthew were blessed by the opportunity to return to Covenant Christian Academy, the prviate school they grew up in. That made their adjustment so much easier.

• Matthew loved swimming again. He continued piano lessons and started drum lessons. And he absolutely loved riding his bike on flat, smooth, *paved* roads.

• All in all, the twins were fascinated by America—by all the driving, by garbage trucks, by the wonder of McDonald's. We went to a Mexican restaurant, and Ben stood up in his seat with both hands clutching chips, seemingly overcome by the thrill of all the food.

• After swimming lessons one day, Katie was using the hand dryer. When Ben pointed out that her hands were already dry, she informed him she was "trying to get the wrinkles out."

• There was a saying among our missionary friends at RVA: "When Kenyan ice cream starts to taste good to you, it's time to go on furlough." Suffice it for me to say, my adjustment to American ice cream went exceedingly well.

• Our family went to North Carolina to spend Thanksgiving with my sister and her husband. While we were there, JT and I visited Wake Forest University. He wasn't going to be able to visit colleges as a senior the following year back in Kenya. So this was our opportunity. We had arranged to meet with two graduates from RVA who were studying at Wake. And two days before we arrived, one of them was awarded a Rhodes Scholarship, one of only thirty-seven awarded each year to American college students. As far as I know, it was the first time an RVA student had ever received the Rhodes. One thing I am sure of: it is a *good* thing to visit a college and be the guidance counselor of the high school that provided the student who won the prestigious Rhodes Scholarship. I've met with lots of colleges, but never had a meeting quite like that before.

• JT informed me he was the only person in his class who wouldn't receive a car when he turned sixteen. I asked him if that was hard on him; he assured me he would be fine with it. (Truth be known, it was harder on me.) The *next day*, I received an email from an old friend asking if JT would like her 1988 Honda with 215,000 miles on it. It had been well maintained and was far nicer than we could have hoped for.

• I woke up Katie early one morning for a holiday trip to Iowa and Minnesota to see relatives. She wrapped her arms around me and whispered, "Daddy, I was dreaming it was snowing." It did snow up north, and she was so thrilled.

• Matthew didn't make the basketball team. He was sad, but I reminded him that he hadn't held a basketball since the previous season. The coach offered to let him be the team manager and allowed him to work out with the team. He was faithful. And when a player dropped off the team, the coach told Matthew, "I need your heart," and gave him the guy's uniform. In Matthew's first game, his teammates cheered for him to get into the game, and he played the final two minutes. A father couldn't script a "sowing and reaping" lesson for a son any better than that.

• Five months of walking pneumonia had fatigued Nancy before we left Kenya. When she didn't get better the first month we were back, our doctor tested for TB. Thankfully, the results were negative. And with the help of American medicine, time, and as much rest as a mother of four can manage (which was at least more than she ever got in a dorm mothering twenty boys), Nancy began to feel more like herself again by the start of the new year.

• On what was one particularly discouraging day for me, I received this email from an RVA senior in Kijabe:

Dear Mr. Peifer: The first day I came up to talk to you about colleges, you described me as the driver of a nice Jaguar who seemed all too happy to cruise along at 40 mph without caring or realizing what I had under my hood. I believe you were right. Today, after much stress and work, I believe I've found the accelerator.

At 11:06 p.m. my time, I received an email from Stanford University which began, "Dear Greg, Congratulations."

I thought you should know because I honestly believe you set me on track; with your passion for me to succeed and your goading to press further, I've been accepted to one of the premier universities in the world. Thank you from the depths of my heart.

—

The end of February, I finally got around to sending the second email update since we had been home:

Sometimes I'm not a terribly insightful person, so it's taken me most of our furlough to learn what you may think should have been a simple and obvious lesson.

During our first week back in the States, I took Ben and Katie on a quick shopping run and introduced them to Walmart. Walking through the store, the eyes of both twins practically popped out of their sockets as their sensory-overloaded minds tried to absorb the mind-blowing realities of American retailing. Then, in the aisle next to electronics, Daddy spotted a surprise of his own, something I hadn't seen and probably couldn't have imagined three years before.

But there it was, stacked in a towering floor display. Walmart was now selling three-thousand-dollar flat-screen television sets. I stopped and stared. An alert and eager young salesperson, sensing prospective prey, sidled up beside us, smiled me a big warm Walmart welcome, and began reciting special features and spouting all sorts of specs. I tried to listen with enough attention not to seem impolite. However, she didn't seem to appreciate the question I couldn't stop myself from asking when she finally paused for breath: "Tell me, does Gilligan get off the island if you watch it on a three-thousand-dollar machine?"

I was hoping for at least a smile; I guess she didn't think it was funny.

Now, several months later, flipping through one of Dallas's daily newspapers, I happened across an advertising flyer for that same model television. When I noticed the price had been reduced to $2,396.87, I thought to myself, Wow! What a great deal!

That's when I realized: America just wears you down. They hit you with ad after ad after ad, until, after a while, you finally start to believe everything they tell you. Even about technologically overreaching TVs.

Perhaps it's time for me to go back to Africa.

28

Furlough Failure — I'm Glad It Still Hurts

OVER THE FIRST EIGHT OR NINE MONTHS WE'D BEEN BACK IN THE STATES, I'd had the privilege and opportunity of speaking to several groups and churches about the work we were doing in Kenya. Most people had been gracious, kind, and generally responsive.

One old friend, however, brought his entire family to hear me in Springfield, Illinois, and his stepson had that hostile, tortured face of a teenager who had been dragged there against his will. Because the kid looked so obviously unhappy when we met before the service, I felt it would be *helpful* to let him know how horrible it was going to be. So I warned him, "I think you ought to know, I've been arrested for boring the life out of people in three different states. And I'm already pretty tired tonight, so this could get really bad." Afterward, I asked him how I did, and he gave me the highest praise I suspect he was capable of giving: "I've heard worse." I've often thought the same thing when I finished speaking. So I didn't hold it against him.

When it comes to speakers, I find that I too have high standards and expectations, which I seldom manage to attain. Speaking gigs are never as easy as they look. And it turned out there were many challenging aspects of the speaking circuit I'd never before realized. For example, Nancy and I spoke at our own church one week for both Sunday morning services. Now, I love my wife; I love looking at my wife; I love hearing the sweet sound of my wife's voice. But after listening to Nancy give the same talk in back-to-back services, I had a new empathy for all political wives. I tried to gaze at her with an adoring look throughout the entire second talk, but it's *hard* to be Laura Bush.

In an email report about some of our speaking engagements, I admitted I was sometimes a bit bothered by the fact that just *because I went to Africa, I got pats on the back and the occasional pulpit to share. Yet I'm the same guy I always was, and I keep saying it, but there is nothing special about being a missionary.*

What is special is finding out what God has called you to, and doing it. Which means there is a special story in all of us that needs to be sought out and given a forum. I appreciate that I have one, but I long for the day when Christians see what special thing God has put in all of us.

I've been so grateful for the opportunity to speak across the country. I spoke in Ohio one morning, and then traveled several hours to speak at another church that same night. It turned out to be such a cold wintry evening, and I was curious to see who, if anyone, might turn up.

Only about fifteen people did, but they were kind beyond kind. I shared my current favorite Scripture: "'For I know the plans I have for you,' says the Lord. 'Plans for good and not for evil, to give you a future and a hope.'"

But what I will never forget about that night is a little girl who came up to me after the service with a box she had decorated. She told me she had read my emails about the hungry kids, so she had decided to go door-to-door to collect pennies for them. She told me she wanted to give them hope.

Little kids helping little kids is about as good as it gets.

That gave me hope.

Throughout the years we'd lived in Dallas, I'd made an annual tradition of watching the Final Four with some rude friends from Kansas. They would say unkind things to me all evening. I, of course, would pray for their souls —and their taste in basketball teams. We hadn't seen a Final Four together since 2001. But this year, after the game, we stayed and talked and talked. It was just hard to let it go. When I finally left, I drove maybe a block before it hit me: I won't be insulted during a Final Four in America again until 2011.

Part of my practicum for my degree in college counseling involved taking the SAT. I was thrilled to receive a perfect score on the verbal, and dismayed that my math score was so low they recommended that I refrain from driving. I felt I was learning so much from my coursework, but the clock was ticking. We'd been in a daze the first few months we got back, and already the time to return to Africa was fast approaching. I was not ready to go. But I couldn't wait to get there.

—

I told my readers in an April email, *When we return to Africa in just over three months, I think it will be easy to tell our Kenyan friends what we enjoyed the most — besides seeing family and friends — during our time in America.*

One thing has been the changing of seasons. Seeing winter become spring has been a special thrill for Ben and Katie, who have never experienced the wonders of a real spring before. That's helped the rest of us see and react to and appreciate the season like we never have before.

It has been such an unexpected gift seeing home again, for the first time, through the eyes of our four-year-old African twins. It makes for such a beautiful world.

—

My goal had been twenty-five computer centers and one hundred schools being fed. It was getting late in the game, but we had one more promising chance scheduled before we headed back overseas. Some friends had invited us to share after the morning worship services at their large Minnesota church. I had this great hope that the right people would be there to come, hear the message, and respond in such a generous way that here at the end of our furlough year we would miraculously hit our goals.

But the Sunday morning we visited, the senior pastor who had served that Minnesota church for seventeen years announced his resignation from the pulpit, saying he felt God was calling him to go to the mission field. He informed his obviously surprised congregation that there would be a meeting after the service in which he'd explain more about the decision and answer questions.

When I heard that, I leaned over to our host and whispered, "I want to go to *his* meeting." So did everyone else. Oh, a few folks showed up to meet and hear from us. And I immediately realized there was no way that church would close the gap. Yet the most wonderful thing happened to me: the remainder of that day, I felt covered in God's peace. And we ended a wonderful weekend of fellowship with dear friends, feeling both refreshed and inspired.

Even as my dream ended, the Lord birthed a new hope in me. I realized I didn't have a clue how big our computer center and lunch programs should or would grow, but I knew my hope was in him.

—

In a May email, I wrote about one big reason for hope and encouragement:

My life has had lots of surprises since 1998, but even my most optimistic friends would not have predicted this:

I won a full ride to Harvard.

You would not believe how NATURALLY this can be inserted into a conversation:

Drive-Through Window Guy: *You want a double cheeseburger and a Diet Coke?*

Me: *Did you say something about Harvard?*

DTWG: *No.*

Me: *I did get a full-ride scholarship to Harvard.*

DTWG: *Do you want fries with that?*

We live in an age when people get too much information, so I don't mention that the seminar is only for a week. Or that the scholarship was based on need, not merit. Why overload my friends with superfluous details?

My wife, for whom the term "long-suffering" was invented, has grudgingly accepted my proposal to have T-shirts made for the whole family. She has drawn the line at tattoos.

———

Fortunately, Nancy got to fly up to Boston on a frequent flier ticket to spend a couple of days with me, celebrating twenty years of marriage. Some thoughtful friends did many special things to make this anniversary spectacular for us. But just being with Nancy was pretty darn spectacular.

I missed Father's Day, which fell during the time I was at Harvard. Katie called me to complain that "a daddy should not be away from his precious girl today." I told her she was absolutely right, that I'd never been away from my kids on Father's Day before, and it was sad. But when Nancy and Katie picked me up at the airport, my daughter couldn't stop grinning. I told her that grin was the best Father's Day present ever, even if it was a bit late.

———

When I got on that plane from Kenya to America, I prayed that I would grow closer to God during our time at home in the States. I'd been able to accomplish some good things during our three years in Africa, but so much of the time, I was just busy *doing* stuff. I longed to *be* closer to God. What I had in mind included better, longer, more meaningful quiet times, in which God would serve up a big load of himself, that I might consume his spiritual nourishment somewhat in the manner of a large hot fudge sundae—with *American* ice cream.

I guess I should have been more specific in what I prayed for. Because while I did grow closer to God during our furlough year, pretty much all that growth came not from quiet times, Bible study, or great sermons but from failing at almost everything I touched.

I got turned down by more than one hundred foundations to which I applied to get funding for computers and school lunches.

I worked part-time for a wonderful company—and a boss so amazing that she could cure major diseases while flossing her teeth—that paid me generously for what work I did. But about the fifth time I was interviewing a consultant and one of the twins interrupted by pleading, "Daddy, could you please give me a wipe?" was the day I realized I wasn't meant to work from home.

I really wanted to take my kids to Disney World, so I accepted a part-time commission job, which should have been a natural for me. I didn't earn a single commission. We didn't go to Disney World.

I did start and finish a masters in college counseling. But that was harder than I'd expected and ate up much of the time I'd hoped to use to see more of our friends and family.

Yet in my failure, because of my failure, I turned to the Lord, and he met me in my despair. So I did succeed in growing closer to him—because of my failure.

And this is why I wrote a public confession of these failures at the close of another email:

I am returning to Kenya as a different man. A broken man.

I discovered my bottom line is that I like writing the checks, but it is hard to receive money. I didn't really want to depend on anyone.

So I failed. But in the midst of the failures, I confessed my failings and shortcomings to God, and he showed me how much I needed him and all my friends.

Which is Christianity 101 and should have been obvious to anyone who's been a Christian as long as I have. What can I say? Maybe the wonder of turning fifty is that wisdom will begin to thrust itself on me.

Yet despite all my failure, we still received the funding for six to eight computer centers, and enough additional money to increase the number of children we feed to almost ten thousand a day. I can't be anything but grateful for that. Even if we didn't hit the goals we set, we gave it our best shot.

—

I can't end this email on a downer. There are so many people to thank that we won't thank anyone individually in this letter; it would read like a phone book. I would say we are grateful beyond words, but those of you who know me well realize it's not quite that easy to shut me up.

So while I can't ever be able to adequately repay all that I owe you, I do have something I believe is of value to share with you:

At the equator in Kenya, the sun rises at 6:00 a.m. and sets at 6:00 p.m. There are no long summer nights.

I want to tell you: there is nothing better than an American summer. Going for walks with my children in the evening, taking the twins for their first fireworks and baseball game ("Why do they all wear HATS?"), and eating ice cream with Nancy were such wonderful gifts.

Life in America is super busy. So let this advice be my gift to you: because there is nothing sweeter than an American summer, take time to enjoy a little of it before it goes away.

—

Two days after I wrote those words, the Peifer family left our Texas home, boarded another plane, and flew back home to Africa.

—

There always seems to be that one thing that helps you know that you are back in Kenya. Last time it was driving onto the RVA campus and finding a family of baboons in our front yard. This time was a little different.

Our 1992 Land Cruiser needed some work, so I took it to the dealership in Nairobi. Since there was a supermarket next door, JT and I wandered over to kill some time. The store had its own bakery, which seemed like the perfect opportunity to get some breakfast. Behind the counter, I saw a message that let me know I was indeed home in Kenya: "Polite Notice—please do not spit in the sink."

I never saw that on a sink at Krispy Kreme.

—

All the kids acted thrilled to be home in Kenya again. The second day back, Ben asked me if he could go to the school playground. I told him yes, and he then posed an interesting question: "When do you want me back?"

That was an interesting question because (A) Ben didn't have a watch and (B) he didn't yet know how to tell time.

Oh, how our children love the freedom of Africa. (As do their parents.)

─

We were not assigned to be dorm parents again. Which was a good thing, since it had taken the entire year in America for my nose hairs to grow back after three years of junior high boy gas. So Nancy and I were going to be able to concentrate our energies on college counseling and the library this year.

The next computer center was almost ready to go, and the headmasters had asked us to begin the lunch program again in January, when Kenya's public school year started. So whatever money we collected before November 30 would determine how many schools we would be able to support for the following year. I was eager to get back to it.

But before that could happen, there were two things in Kenya that I needed to stare down again. The first was driving. The leading cause of death among missionaries in Kenya is driving accidents. And being away from it a year caused my fears to grow; I nearly panicked the first day I had to drive in Nairobi again. Of the many challenges of driving in Kenya, I particularly dreaded roundabouts, which require driving in a circle in many poorly marked or unmarked lanes with many other people, who all share different views of what is legal. I was scared to death to do it again. But I managed the first one with ease. I backed down a bus the next time. Just that suddenly, it all came back to me, and I knew I could do it. Driving in Kenya still scared me, but it was a wise, caution-producing fear, not a paralyzing one.

─

The other fear I needed to stare down was of greater concern to me, as my first email home explained:

It's so easy to become callous in Africa. There is staggering need all around and you hear so many heartwrenching stories, you can grow hard. And that can happen very quickly when you're a genetically gifted cynic like me. But I don't want to be that way here.

I remember a headmaster who came to meet me after our first computer center went live. He had traveled several hours just to ask if we could please build his school a center. I told him my first commitment was to the twenty-five schools where we had already established lunch programs. I said, "I'm very sorry. But we don't have much money. And there will have to be a long time and many more centers built before we can consider your school."

The man put his head in his hands and wept.

If you harden your heart, you don't get hurt. But you grow callous to those around you. I'm slowly learning that pain can be a valuable gift. Especially when it lets you know your heart is still vulnerable to others.

I'm glad it still hurts.

29

"Computers Make Me Think"

THE BEGINNING OF THE NEW 2005–2006 SCHOOL YEAR AT RVA WAS PAR-
ticularly tough on the Peifer family. For the first couple of months after
our return to Africa, there wasn't a single day at least one of us wasn't sick.
I guess it took that long for our bodies to build up immunity again to the
local microbes.

Good news: the second computer center had been constructed and was
ready for delivery and setup in Kenton. Bad news: the man who'd built the
center and the only one who could finish the final stages of transportation
and installation suddenly had to go back to the States for family reasons.

So the long weeks of battling through health and physical adjustments
plus all the emotional ups and downs of what seemed like a good-news/bad-
news roller coaster was exhausting. And eventually depressing.

Until a series of things happened to pick up our spirits.

First, a Harvard admissions person had contacted me to say she was coming to Africa and would like to visit RVA and meet some of our students who
might have the qualifications for, and might be interested in, an Ivy League
education. I'd written back to tell her I was still fairly new to the college
guidance game, that I'd been a "corporate pig" in my old life, but suggested
a tentative strategy for her visit if she approved. I also wanted to let her know
a little bit about what to expect, so I told her about RVA in my email:

*We had a great year last year with two kids into Stanford, one into Dartmouth,
one into Cornell, and a graduate of 2000 getting the Rhodes, but we feel like what
really began the change in our school was the first student accepted at Harvard. I will
never forget the laughter and tears when we announced it, and a little kid coming up to
me and saying, "Anything is possible!"*

To me, that is the great promise of higher education.

I have gotten to build the first solar computer center in Kenya at one of the twenty-five schools my wife and I provide lunch for, but I don't know if anything has affected me quite the way opening that envelope from Harvard did. Whether or not we ever have another student get into Harvard, one thing is sure: that acceptance changed RVA forever. It broke the ceiling, and the fear in these kids that they weren't good enough.

And my Harvard contact emailed back a warm and encouraging response that included some rather astounding news:

Well, it's the rare "corporate pig" who can make me tear up, but that you did! I hope you don't mind, but I printed out your message and stuck it in the Dean's box. Yours were good and terribly welcome words to hear; plus I appreciated the chance to remind the boss why we're spending the money to let me travel in Africa.

Well, he was obviously moved by what you wrote and took your message to this big start-of-the-academic-year retreat yesterday with the pantheon of faculty and administrative muckety-mucks, where he read your email out loud.

Encouraging experience number two came when I drove out to Karima and checked on the status of our first computer center. I admit going with a certain amount of trepidation. How would it be after a year away? Friends who had started various projects in Kenya and then left for a while often returned to see decay or destruction. But I came back to find the center in perfect condition, all machines still functioning, with tenth graders building complex databases.

Encouragement number three came the day I opened the mail to discover a personalized, autographed photo of Neil Diamond. I wasn't sure who my anonymous benefactor might be. Perhaps the friend I'd recently sent a thoughtful note saying, "Maybe this can help," to which I'd attached a news clipping advertising laser surgery as a new treatment for hemorrhoids. I immediately and proudly hung that photo on the wall over my desk and morale on campus soared. Friends and colleagues flocked to the guidance office just to see it. There quickly followed a surge of appointments made by students I suspect just wanted to see for themselves if all the rumors about this wonder of wonders were true.

I wrote about perhaps the most important and encouraging development since my return to Kenya in an October email:

Recently we attended a local church where the worst singer in all of human history leads worship. His singing could invoke laughter, but by the end of the service, you hear his heart for God, not his voice. I think heaven will be like that; we will hear nothing but the heart.

I have been visiting schools to get counts for the lunch program we will start up again at the beginning of the Kenyan school year in January. Years ago when I first went to visit schools, the poverty shocked. I eventually moved from shock to sadness to rage to resignation to cynicism.

Perhaps the greatest gift I've ever been given is that the Lord has moved me to a new stage since I've been back in Africa this time. I went to a school the other day. And I visited one class with forty-eight students in a room meant for twenty-two. There were six books in the entire class. Only three kids wore shoes.

(Those of you who know me would probably agree that I am the most unlikely "soldier" in the world. I am the kind of person Woody Allen described when he said, "In case of war, he should be taken as a hostage.")

However, now when I see children with so little, I hear a call to battle. That's the only way I can describe it. I want to strike down the enemy that has done such heinous things to children. I can see in my mind's eye all the obstacles falling away; I believe that whatever the odds, the adversary can be defeated.

The sensation doesn't last long, but it is the sweetest thing I know. I can't hear the music yet, but I think I can hear his heart.

—

We have missionary friends who are longtime "heart-hearers" with an extraordinary ministry: a series of orphanages for AIDS infants, homes that together house more than one thousand children. Their ministry is loving and giving happiness to these babies for as long as they live.

In the course of caring for these children, our friends have adopted several babies with AIDS. Their little girl Joy died several years ago. Their son Tony died that first week of November in 2005. He was about five years old. On the night of his death, Nancy called on the family to express our condolences. Mrs. Bovard told my wife that Tony had died pretty painfully, after a series of four heart attacks. But as she held him in his final moments, Tony had looked at her and then at her husband "as if to say without words that he didn't know what it was like to be an orphan."

When Nancy reported that conversation to me, I was overwhelmed with a sense of gratitude that some extraordinary people are left in the world. And we get to work with so many of them.

—

On top of everything else going on that term, car issues prompted a trip into Nairobi to get our Land Cruiser worked on—again. Kenya's roads are never safe; having your vehicle die in the wrong place can be dangerous. Fortunately everything checked out, so I made the long drive into the valley to visit one of the schools we would start working with in January.

But the car broke down when we got to the school. I am not a real missionary, so I did not handle this adversity like a holy (or "good") missionary. I hit the steering wheel and yelled a while before I calmed down enough to call a mechanic I knew and trusted. It took several hours before he could get there — of course. So I was frustrated, and more than a little angry about my predicament. The result reminded me it is best that I not be in charge, because we had a really great time playing with the kids. And in the process, I got the chance to meet a possible computer teacher for our next center.

Our paths might never have crossed if my car hadn't broken down where it did. Such a wonderful and unexpected opportunity, and I almost missed it. I sensed a lesson there somewhere: perhaps my life could be full of so many more great things like that if I didn't push fast and furiously to live it on my own schedule.

—

Representatives from the University of Pennsylvania and Harvard visited our campus as special guests, a first for RVA and a thrill for me. I wasn't sure our students knew what to make of it, but I thought they did themselves proud. And Ben discovered and informed us all that "you can't spell HaRVArd without RVA!" which impressed our visitors *greatly*. Shouldn't such a remarkable observation from a four-year-old qualify him for automatic admittance to the class of 2023? I guess we'll just have to wait and see.

—

In the same email in which I bragged on my precocious son, I also included this report:

I went to a new school today: Kinungi. They have almost one thousand students with twenty-five teachers. Because of your kindness, we will be able to add it to the schools receiving lunches in January.

When I walked into the first grade classroom, one of the students informed me, "You are white!" (I actually get told this a lot, even in America, for some mysterious reason.)

When the headmaster announced our plans to the students, there were many smiles and much cheering. But one little boy just told me, "It will be so good to eat lunch."

This is the part when I am supposed to be profound and try to sum things up. But all I can think of is a little boy in rags who seemed so happy about the novel idea of lunch.

I needed something to help my prayer life go to the next level. I had tried all sorts of plans and scenarios to make this happen, but God provided a better solution. I was assigned to teach driver's ed again starting in January with RVA's second term. The last time I'd taught driver's ed in 1999, I'd gotten closer to Jesus than I ever thought I could. So I approached this second round with very mixed feelings. Turns out this group of students was tailor-made to carry out God's plan. This is actual dialog:

> **Them:** What should I do?
>
> **Me:** To start with, don't hit that bus.
>
> **Them:** What bus?
>
> **Me:** The bus parked right in front of us that you are moving rapidly toward.
>
> **Them:** What should I do?
>
> **Me:** Oh Jesus, save me.

I would not recommend this method of improving your prayer life (at least to a friend), but I have to tell you, it worked for me.

—

In the wee hours one dark March night, I heard Ben calling, so I stumbled into his room, where we engaged in this conversation:

> **Ben:** I do not like what is under my bed very much.
>
> **Me:** What is under your bed?
>
> **Ben:** Something not very nice.
>
> **Me:** Should I lie down with you for a while?
>
> **Ben:** Yes, because it does not like daddies very much.

Evidently it didn't, because Ben was able to fall asleep right away. But this got me wondering what could be under the bed, and it took quite a while for me to doze off again.

—

The rainy season lessens some of the pain and makes everything so much greener around our part of Kenya, which was one reason the students at Kenton seemed full of energy on my visit there that March. When the school bell rang (a metal bar hung from a tree and hit by a branch), they raced to lunch with amazing gusto. After months of drought, the wonderful sight of children bursting with joyous life again made me laugh. But the best part of the visit for me was watching those children in the new computer lab.

Remember that Kenton was a school so remote and so poor that not one child there had ever seen a computer before our center opened. The computer teacher there introduced me to twelve-year-old Beth, who sat down at one of the lab's laptops and typed fifty-one words per minute right there in front of me. With only one error. After just three months on a computer.

The kids were still so poor; they still wore rags. But they acted thrilled to be eating and elated to be learning how to use the computer. I had at least thirty of them spontaneously shout at me, "I LOVE computers!"

Sometimes, it takes just a little rain to make all the difference.

—

I never expected to become friends with Margaret, but I'm grateful for it nonetheless. I met her when I first started buying maize and beans. I would go to market myself, but I could never beat her prices. She was obviously a brilliant negotiator, so I soon started buying most of my beans from her.

When the pastor I was dealing with was transferred, Margaret started going with me to the schools. Her husband is also a pastor, but because of his schedule, he asked that Margaret go with me in his stead. She has a merry laugh, doesn't suffer fools, and every time we hit a pothole, she yelled, "Oh my God, save me," which made our long trips fun and eventful.

One day when we planned to visit schools, I was delayed picking her up, and when Margaret got into the car, she told me, "You have become an African man." I thought, *Could it be the dance moves that made her think that? My innate coolness?* No. Turns out what she meant was, "Kenyan men are always late." And I was so hoping it was the dance moves.

Each time we delivered food for our lunch program was an adventure of some kind. Police pulled us over, demanding some of the grain for themselves. Or we got stuck in mud and had to move hundreds of bags off the truck, push the truck, and reload the same bags. This time it was the money. When I started purchasing food in bulk, I paid in cash. My friend Margaret, a short, stout woman, would stuff the money in a place that good missionaries can't easily describe. I finally made the rule that if you won the bid, you had to take a check.

The problem this time was that the latest bean crop had failed. So the prices were almost triple what they had been last term. Which meant it was a very big check that we gave to Margaret. The bank wouldn't cash it. They said it was too big, and told us that no Kenyan woman could have that much money. I called them and explained that there really was that much money in our account (which I assumed they knew because our account was at the same bank as Margaret's), and that we had indeed made the check out to Margaret. They still refused to take the check; we had to get another one. Eleven days later, they finally cashed the check (charging Margaret one thousand shillings for the privilege). Somehow, eventually, we got all the food distributed to the schools.

At one school, the children got so excited to see the food arrive that they danced as the bags were unloaded. Several children invited me to eat. When one of them asked me how the food made me feel, I told them that it made me feel great. Then I asked the kids how the food made them feel, and one of them, in the quietest of voices, told me, "It makes me want to try."

That sentiment made me want to try too.

—

Kenton, the site of our second computer center, held a dedication ceremony at which I was the guest of honor. Politicians spoke and children sang and recited poems. Much praise was directed to me. Here's where you need a little more background about me.

Part of the reason I became a Christian as a young man was because I had gotten what I thought I wanted. I was insecure and I wanted to be popular. So I worked hard at it. I got elected president of my high school student council. And senior year, I was elected to the homecoming court, the last goal I had set for myself to prove I had arrived, that I had made it. I remember walking home from school that day the court was announced, totally depressed. Because I realized my dreams had come true, but that they had been stupid dreams. And my stupid dreams couldn't fill the emptiness inside. That experience got me seeking, and eventually I found my identity and acceptance in Jesus.

Now thirty-some years later, I sat in front of another group of students and parents who said all these nice things to me, and all I could think was, *I so don't deserve this. I didn't contribute the money, and I didn't build the center. I am a low-rent middleman. I didn't even come to Africa to help people. I came fleeing the death of my son. All my life, I wanted this kind of attention, and now that I get it, I realize it doesn't satisfy.*

So when I got up to speak, I was able to say, with all honesty, "I don't deserve any of this praise. The praise all belongs to Jesus, who is the source of all good things. And if you will let him into your heart, his plans for you are so good and so kind."

—

One Thursday in July, I went to Kinungi School to count maize and bean bags and make an announcement. I told them we would bring a computer center to their campus in the next few weeks. I wish you could have seen the faces of those kids as they jumped and cheered and cried and laughed.

Then the headmaster asked if they could sing me a song. Almost a thousand children began singing in Swahili, and I did what I usually do when I hear any song sung in a language other than English. I smiled politely and tried to remember who played second base for the Chicago Cubs in 1969.

And then I thought, *I know this tune; I know this song.* They were singing "Days of Elijah." I was so amazed when they came to the refrain of the song and repeated:

> There's no God like Jehovah
> There's no God like Jehovah
> There's no God like Jehovah
> There's no God like Jehovah

A few years earlier, when our first RVA student had been accepted at Harvard, one of the younger girls on campus came running up to me and yelled, "Anything is possible!" At the time, I had believed it. But Africa has a way of knocking that spirit out of you, and a tough year with lots of struggles had caused me to grow weary. Then as I looked into the faces of those Kenyan students and saw their excitement about the computer center, the thought came back to me: *Anything is possible.*

I was able to pray with dozens of students after my talk. And on my drive home afterward, I kept thinking and humming, *These are the days of the harvest. There's no God like Jehovah.*

—

The 2006–2007 school year was something of a milestone multiplied in the Peifer family. We had the distinction of having a senior in high school, a freshman in high school, and two kindergartners. When school started in September, it was a sweet time for all of us to walk Ben and Katie to their first day of school.

Even as we did so, I remembered the first day of school for JT, and how in just a few short months, he would be going to the States for college. Katie had recently announced that she didn't like college. When I'd asked her why, she told me, "Because college is going to take my JT away from me."

I knew how she felt.

—

By the day I went out to Kinungi to check on our newest operational computer center, I had become discouraged again. As the headmaster and I walked from his office to a classroom in another building, he waved to some students running by and said, "That is the biggest change because of the food. Children should run. Before, they were so listless; now they run so much." And it was true; kids were running everywhere.

We entered a classroom and the headmaster asked his young students, "What do you think of getting to learn computers?" The students erupted with deafening shouts and screams. But when it got quiet again, I heard one little girl say, "I've never had a dream so big."

Every once in a while, I needed one of those "Oh, yeah! That's why" moments.

—

Later that term, I made a trip back to the States to attend a college advisor conference and participate in a college fair for counselors like me to meet college admissions officers from hundreds of colleges and universities throughout America. I carried four hundred fifty Rift Valley Academy calendars, and had hand-beaded RVA bracelets for all of the colleges.

It was impossible to talk to them all, although I gave it my best shot. I literally ran from booth to booth saying, "We are a one-hundred-year-old school in Kenya with baboons on our campus and three National Merit scholars in a class of eighty." (Say that four hundred times and see what it does to your head.) By the time the fair ended, I wondered if any of those colleges would even remember hearing of RVA, until I got an email from a man who had received one of the bracelets:

I want to tell you an amazing story about the bracelet you gave to me and my colleagues at the Oglethorpe University table during the counselors' fair. I changed my return flight home three times, and there must have been a reason.

As we were about to take off on my flight from Pittsburgh to Atlanta, I noticed the flight attendant gesturing towards me. Thinking my seat belt was unbuckled, I checked; it was okay. When I looked up at her again, she asked if I was from Kenya or Rift Valley Academy. I said no.

She explained that she'd noticed the bracelet with the Kenyan colors and the initials RVA. I told her how and where I met you. She told me she had attended RVA.

At least one college admissions officer was going to remember my school.

I was able to make individual appointments with a number of admissions people, including one from a prestigious school to talk about an RVA student who'd applied there. I was a little taken aback when he came right out and asked me, "Why should we accept this young woman?" I paused and thought what I wanted to say. *Because she is brilliant. She's seen the worst of Africa and it has made her not bitter or cynical but more determined to come back and help. She is fluent in the language of the Orma people, and I believe she is going to change the world.*

But I didn't say any of that. What I did was embarrassing. I started weeping and all I managed to get out was, "She is such a great kid." The admissions guy kindly said I was an eloquent advocate. But I walked out of that interview a few minutes later kicking myself; these RVA kids are so remarkable, but I struggled to articulate it.

—

I had to hit the ground running when I landed back in Kenya, because it was the busiest time of the year for me: college admission deadline time. With so many papers, so much information to keep straight, so many letters to write, and so much at stake, I worked day and night trying to get everything done. If Nancy hadn't come into the office and been such a huge help, I don't know how I would have survived another November. Like every year, I felt exhausted and stressed beyond my limit.

But through it all, I saw rewards. Like the senior who came to me the end of August concerned about how she would get into college. She reminded me that her older sister had not gotten much financial aid, so now she was scared she might not get enough to go to college. I pointed out that her sister had coasted through her senior year, signing up for the bare minimum load of required classes. And that she seemed to have learned from her big sister's mistake, because she had signed up for a very tough course load and obviously planned to work hard. I told her she had sown well, and I'd be praying she would reap.

Midway through November, she came up to me with a teary smile and whispered, "Mr. Peifer, I think I'm reaping." She had just received the presidential scholarship to a good college, and suddenly all the work seemed worth it. To her and to me.

—

Another Christmas and yet another rainy season had come and mostly gone by February when I wrote this email:

Now that the rains have let up a little, we have been able to go down and into the valley more often to visit schools. The good news I learned out there so filled my heart that it overflowed into a part of my soul that's felt pretty dry lately.

One of our schools, which had been rated the lowest in its zone before we started the lunch program, has just been named the best school of the year.

Those kids have been going after it so hard; the progress is amazing. I've written previously about one of the biggest problems I see with Kenya's educational system is that it emphasizes and elevates rote memorization above anything else. So it was especially heartening to visit this newly honored school and meet Gerald and Grace, the school's top computer students. When I asked Grace what her favorite part of computer class was, she gave me the most wonderful answer: "I like computers because they make me think."

30

Never Stand on
a Supermodel's Dress

BY THE END OF THE SECOND TERM, RIFT VALLEY ACADEMY HAD ANOTHER breakthrough. Our first-ever student was accepted at Columbia, which meant that in five years we had gone from having no representation in the Ivy League to every Ivy League college having accepted at least one of our students. Among the eighty graduates of that 2007 senior class, we had two students accepted at Harvard, one of those also accepted at Yale and Princeton, another student at Stanford, one at MIT, another at Penn, one student heading for the Air Force Academy, and another bound for Annapolis and the Naval Academy. RVA kids will change the world someday. And it was such a thrill and honor to be a small part of it all.

—

Kinungi held a ribbon-cutting ceremony to celebrate the official opening of their computer center, and invited Nancy and me to attend an end-of-term awards ceremony.

The head of education for that area of Kenya proudly informed Nancy that he was giving more cash awards for teachers than he ever had. The total amount could not have been more than fifteen dollars, but the teachers seemed very excited. I had the honor of handing out those envelopes. But I also gave prizes to the top three students in each class. Each of them received one pen, one colored pencil, and one regular pencil.

These kids, dressed in rags, had worked so hard. And all they got were pencils and a pen? Which, I confessed in my email report on the experience to our supporters, *goes to show just how shallow I am. Because those kids were absolutely thrilled to get the pen and pencils. One little guy ran in place when I handed him his. I went home and prayed that I would appreciate how much I have, and how much I have been given.*

We will have ten computer centers up by the time we leave in July, so I want to make sure you all know how grateful we are for you. You have fed more than ten thousand children this past term, and we are so blessed by what you have done.

But most of all, we are grateful for the God of the second chance, who gives all good gifts, even one pen and two pencils.

—

Our newest computer center was almost ready to open in Namunja, a Masai school that had nearly tripled in size from one hundred seventy to four hundred fifty students since we'd begun providing lunch there. One of their old chiefs had explained the Masai attitude to me by saying, "I do not believe in educating my children, but I do believe in free food."

Most of the Masai tribe still lived in mud-and-dung huts. The contrast between the center and the school (the poorest facility of any we'd worked with) was striking. The disparity between our computer center and how the people live must have been more mind-boggling to them than it was to me.

When I'd first told one of the teachers at the school what we were planning to do there, he just started laughing and saying, "Here? Here?" Then he laughed again. At most of the other schools we worked with, none of the children had seen a computer before we built them a center. But at least many of them knew what computers were. At this school, few students had a clue such things existed.

The day I visited, two weeks before the new term of the Kenyan school year, our computer teacher was training the other teachers how to use a computer and how they could assist her in instructing their students. Already curious and excited children came by every day to peer inside and wonder at what they were going to learn. One student who wandered by while I was there told me with a tone of awe in his voice, "I have never gone to class on a wooden floor before." All the classroom floors at Namunja were dirt.

—

Scripture talks about Jesus' offer to exchange our burdens for his. He promises that his yoke is easy and his burden is light and that when we follow him, we can trade what is heavy for what is light. I got to do lots of that in Africa.

I passed a wealth of wildlife on the road to Ewaso to tell the students their school would soon have a computer center. Here again, many students didn't seem to know what a computer is, yet the more I talked about what we planned, the bigger and bigger the grins grew as they started to understand something big and exciting would be happening for them at their school.

Sometimes, that was enough to make me happy. But as I looked at their school, made of mud, I couldn't stay upbeat. These children loved to eat, standing in long lines for food that day. So that was good. But when a shy little girl, wearing the shambles of a dress, ashamedly lowered her eyes to her dusty bare feet when I leaned down close to say hello, I knew she had no other clothes. And when I sat in another classroom next to a young boy with a cough that sounded far worse than a cold, I knew his family had no medicine for him.

Then I looked around that school where there was no power, no water, a shortage of desks, even fewer books, and not nearly enough teachers. And as I often do in situations like that, I began to rage inside for children who have to live like that. I raged for what could be and what never seems to change for many little kids in this country. I RAGED.

Scripture tells us to "be angry, and sin not." I've got one part of that down pretty well.

—

Even as we approached the end of the school year at RVA, the Kenyan government schools began a new term. So while we busily wrapped up our campus responsibilities and prepared for a six-month furlough back in the States to get JT started in college, Margaret and I had to make sure enough food for the new term's lunches got delivered. She was going to oversee the feeding program during our furlough.

—

Katie and Ben turned six and graduated from kindergarten the same month, so the Peifers enjoyed all sorts of celebrations and excitement. Truthfully, when you have six-year-old twins, there is always excitement. But this was *scheduled* excitement, which means you could fool yourself into thinking you could prepare for it. I should have known better, because I wasn't really prepared for JT's high school graduation either.

Commencement time takes on a unique emotional poignancy at RVA. Because RVA is a boarding school, the kids who've been with us for years get really close. Ten days or so before their final term ends, it starts to sink in for the seniors that when they leave campus on graduation day, many of them will never see each other again.

The night before graduation was senior night, when the kids perform skits and reminisce. I may have achieved immortality that evening; I was rapped. (I didn't know you could rhyme Mr. Peifer with red hot viper.)

Graduation itself was a sweet time. Surprisingly (or maybe not), since we're a boarding school for missionary kids in rural Kenya, one of RVA's commencement traditions is the entire senior class's rendition of the old rock song "Africa," made famous by the American band Toto. If you're old enough, you might remember the refrain: "I bless the rains down in Africa." To watch JT and his classmates stand and sing that '80s hit was to hear the song like you've never heard it before.

I summed up this Peifer family milestone in my next email:

When your oldest graduates from high school and you know he will soon be many thousands of miles away from you at college, so much goes through your head. It was American author and playwright Jean Kerr who described this stage of life by saying, "You lose not only your own youth, but the youth of your children." And there is part of you, especially the knee area, where you know this is true.

His last year of high school, JT had started to run a coffeehouse on the RVA campus. His establishment didn't have running water, so every evening when he closed up, he had to carry all the cups up to our house to wash them. So, every night, I would trek down to help him carry the cups. Part of it was that he needed the help, but a bigger part of it was to make sure I had some time with my overscheduled son. Some nights we didn't talk; some nights were profound. But mostly, it was precious, because we knew it would soon end. And part of me will mourn the end of that kind of time together; the last walk up together was a sadness beyond tears for me.

But children are life's greatest gift, and what Kerr's quote misses is the excitement you can sense in your child's future. Nancy and I know we will miss our son so much. Yet graduation felt great. It was time.

—

We will be in the US for six months, and then we will return to Kijabe for two and a half years. Nancy is going to be head of the language department here, so she will be taking some classes while we're stateside. Ben and Katie will start first grade, and Matthew will begin his sophomore year of high school. JT will get his first college semester under his belt before the rest of us return to Africa by the beginning of January.

Those of you who know me best realize there couldn't be a less likely person than me to be successful in Africa. Yet somehow God has delighted in being strong in my weakness. Thank you for all you have done. Ten thousand children fed and ten computer centers built; it's amazing.

We are so grateful for what has happened, and so eager to do more.

—

We often had baboons on our front steps in Kenya, but what made an impression on our six-year-old African twins were, I kid you not, American squirrels. Whenever and wherever they caught sight of a squirrel, they yelled as loudly as you might if you'd seen a family of baboons wandering around your neighborhood. If we spotted eight squirrels in a five-minute span, the volume didn't diminish, which made for some interesting car rides in suburban Dallas.

The other factor that made driving in America with the twins an interesting experience was McDonald's, their favorite fast-food destination. It didn't matter whether we ate inside or picked up our food at the drive-through, every time we pulled out of the parking lot, they would look up longingly at the golden arches and loudly sigh, "McDonald's." If we passed eight McDonald's during a single drive across town, they would sigh deeply over each one.

There may be an interesting correlation somewhere between the two attractions, but I never did figure out what it might be.

—

As usual, life accelerated toward warp speed from the moment we touched down again in America. Everyone but me started school within weeks of our return. The twins' first grade experience was their initial exposure to American education. Matthew loved running cross-country and started driver's ed.

JT seemed to enjoy Wake Forest, and the entire family got to visit him one weekend partway through the semester. Seeing how he already fit into the campus scene did a lot to reassure us that our son would do fine in college. When I asked Katie what her favorite part of the weekend had been, she told me, "When JT holded me."

Nancy signed up for three college classes in French, so I was able to brag to all my middle-aged friends that I was now going out with a hot coed.

I traveled almost every weekend, speaking at different churches and talking to all sorts of folks about our school lunch and computer center ministries. While I considered it a blessing to see old acquaintances and meet so many new people, I seemed to spend a lot of time *sowing* without much reaping. I worked harder than I ever had trying to make things happen, and exhausted myself in the process. That, coupled with our pastor giving his notice at our home church and an implosion at the company where I found work, led to lots of anxiety on my part.

That turned into a blessing when it brought me back to this realization:

Jesus is my provider, and I can't make anything happen on my own. Ultimately, it all comes from him. That didn't mean I made peace with hungry kids, but in the end I had to realize that only he makes the seed grow.

We didn't make Disney World this time either. But we did get to take the twins to the Texas State Fair, where eating a deep-fried Snickers and washing it down with a deep-fried latte was as gross (and wonderful) as you might imagine. The twins loved the rides, until we rode a roller coaster that went too fast for Katie. It went around three times, and to see her face, knowing there was nothing we could do but ride it out, was probably an apt analogy for a lot of parenthood.

—

Our November email report to supporters included surprising news:

We've had some amazing stuff happen lately. First, I was named a recipient of the 2007 Yale University Counseling Award honoring the high school counselor of an incoming freshman. I felt greatly honored, though I am so aware of my failings and all I still don't know about college counseling that it is hard to believe.

We also just received word that we are finalists in the CNN Heroes Awards. CNN collected nominations from viewers for people who do good work, and they have already narrowed this year's competition down to just eighteen individuals in six categories. Because we have made that cut, we will be awarded ten thousand dollars to build another computer center. If we make one more cut, we will shoot a video to explain our programs and get to go to New York for the televised awards ceremony.

We have been struggling to raise funds for the feeding program, so your prayers would be appreciated; more exposure might help bring in more money. While we realize how far we are from being heroes, and know so many people more deserving of this recognition, we are grateful nonetheless for this opportunity. We have our tickets and will leave December 27 to return to Kenya. The clock is ticking so fast. Why didn't that ever happen during math class?

—

I was on my way to a friend's funeral (twenty-nine-year-old Jared had fought leukemia bravely for several years) when the call came in: CNN wanted to fly me back to Kenya to shoot a segment for the awards show. That was Wednesday, and they said I'd need to leave on Monday. Nancy was already scheduled to attend a foreign language teachers' convention, so we had to scramble to get coverage for the kids.

I flew out of Dallas on Monday around noon and arrived in Nairobi Tuesday around 10:00 p.m. My luggage with my clothing did not make it, and we were scheduled to begin shooting the next day. We went to a hotel and I tried to sleep, but I had crossed too many time zones and sleep didn't come easily. I woke up at 6:00 a.m. and rendezvoused with the CNN crew to head to the first school. The producer/director was based in South Africa; the video, sound, and stills guys all lived in Kenya. So they were all ready to go for it. But before that could happen, we had to stop for me to buy some clothes, a first after all of my years in Kenya.

By the time we finished day one of our shoot, I'd discovered an unexpected empathy for supermodels, because the director would ask me to walk to a school, and after I did, he would ask me to do it again, "This time with more PURPOSE." Whatever that meant. At the end of the day, when the director showed me the pictures and video they'd shot, I noticed that whatever direction he had given me (turn right and look pensive; look up and be concerned), my facial expression remained the same in every shot. A pretty impressive accomplishment, when you think about it.

The second and final day of shooting began at 7:00 a.m. the next morning and didn't finish until 6:00 p.m. My flight was scheduled for 11:30 p.m., so we raced to the airport only to discover my flight had been cancelled. The airline booked me on a flight the following morning. I missed my connecting flight in Paris, and I made it back to Dallas on Saturday, only a day later than planned. A week later my luggage (which I hadn't seen since I'd left Dallas) finally caught up with me.

—

We found out we had won our category several days before the awards show in December. So Nancy and I flew to New York, where we were met by a driver, who took us immediately to the site of the broadcast for a rehearsal in a spectacular auditorium at the American Museum of National History.

I'd had to submit my acceptance speech to CNN ahead of time, which was when I discovered they'd edited out all my personal thank-yous. I asked why, and one of the CNN staffers explained, "When a famous guy, whom everyone wants to hear, starts thanking and talking about unknowns, audiences get mad. Nobody wants to hear you to start with; if you start naming individuals, people may hurt you."

After a brief rehearsal, our personal driver took us to an exceedingly elegant and expensive hotel. Upon entering our super swanky room, I came to the first of a number of unexpected but helpful conclusions I would reach over the course of our CNN experience.

Conclusion 1: I needed to turn off the part of my brain that was already trying to calculate how many kids we could feed with the money being spent on us for two days in New York, and just roll with it. So, since we had no other responsibilities and didn't have to be at the show until 6:00 p.m. the next day, Nancy and I had a blast for the next twenty-four hours playing tourists in the Big Apple on CNN's dime.

—

When our limo let us out at the red-carpet entrance at the American Museum of National History the next evening, so many photographers were waiting you'd have thought they were expecting Neil Diamond. But after stopping and posing for the third set of photographers to take our pictures, I'd reached ...

Conclusion 2: being a supermodel or a celebrity is a lot tougher than it looks. Long before the broadcast was to start, we were in our first-row seats. By the time the lights went down and the curtain opened, I wished the whole thing was over. Only a few minutes into the show, they showed the video they'd shot during my wild trip to Kenya the month before. I hadn't seen the finished piece before. But after three minutes of watching much-bigger-than-life images of me talking and walking (not very purposefully) across a number of familiar African landscapes, I came to ...

Conclusion 3: giving up my male supermodel dream had clearly been the right decision.

The clip ended, the lights came back up, and it was suddenly time for me to *just roll with it* yet again. Because who better to present an award to a fifty-two-year-old missionary working with poor, hungry children in Kenya than a *Sports Illustrated* swimsuit model? In another day in some alternative universe, it might have made perfect sense. But in the here and now of New York City in front of a worldwide television audience, it was time for me to *focus* as Tyra Banks walked to the podium to announce, "It is my honor to present the CNN Hero for Championing Children, Steve Peifer."

I have heard that some people experiencing a major life crisis or trauma have been encouraged, their resolve strengthened, by somehow hearing the prayers of the saints on their behalf. As I walked up onto the stage, I imagined all those prayers coming together as one voice imploring, *Oh God, don't let him mess this up.*

When I reached the center of that big sprawling stage, Tyra Banks handed me my award, gave me a quick, congratulatory peck on the cheek, and quickly stepped aside just far enough to allow me access to the microphone. As the applause died down (very quickly I must admit), I set the award and my notes down on the podium and began my acceptance speech: "I just got kissed by Tyra Banks! And I figured the odds of somebody like me getting kissed by her are about the same as a meteorite striking this building in fifteen minutes; so I would start ducking if I were you.

"We're so grateful to CNN for this wonderful honor, but we were given perspective on it by our six-year-old son, who said he didn't want to come to New York because he didn't want to miss the field trip to the bakery.

"My wife was the one who always wanted to go to Africa. We're in Kenya because of her; all the good things that have happened are because of her. My children are the most wonderful gift I've ever received, and I'm so blessed by their love, their support, and their fun.

"So many people have supported us, it would be another show to mention all of them. Anything that has been accomplished is because of them. *Asante sana* to you.

"We accept this on behalf of all the missionary community, who are all better people than me, and deserve the attention much more than I do. My full-time job is being the college guidance counselor at Rift Valley Academy in Kijabe, Kenya. The students are huge inspirations to me—95 percent of the time (the other 5 percent we don't need to go into right now).

"It is a privilege to be in Kenya. We came to Kenya after one of our children died. Scripture says, 'He who seeks to lose his own life, will find it.' When my son died, I felt like I lost my own life. Kenya gave it back to me.

"I'll always be blessed that we ended up in Kenya. There is such a need in Kenya, such an opportunity right now. The problems of a country are best solved by the people in that country. So in my heart of hearts, I believe if we can get a generation through high school, have the proper nutrition, and learn technology, we can break the back of poverty.

"My hope for all of us is that, in our own ways, we stop making peace with the idea of hungry children and seize the opportunity before us.

"And I am most grateful for Jesus, who loves the children of Kenya more than I ever could. Thank you, and God bless you."

I turned and walked off the set with Tyra Banks just as I'd been instructed to do. But perhaps not exactly as I was supposed to do, because the moment we got backstage, a rather large and rather imposing individual quickly approached us. "*You*," he said, looking at me. "You need to get off Ms. Banks' dress."

Of course I looked down and, to my horror, saw my feet planted on a black train I hadn't noticed but was as long as any wedding dress I had seen in my life. As I quickly stepped aside and offered my profuse apologies, I thought, *There goes my shot at hitting up one of America's top African-American fashion models for a donation to feed hungry kids in Kenya.*

That was the very same moment that I reached Conclusion 4 of my CNN experience: never stand on a supermodel's dress.

Since I would be interviewed after the show, I was escorted to the "talent room," where a lot of the other celebs had already gathered. For a long time, I stood five feet away from Norah Jones, Harry Connick Jr., and several other big-name folks. I so much wanted to ask Norah when she was planning to record an album of Neil Diamond songs, but before I could find the right moment to do so, I realized none of the other people in that room seemed very interested in speaking with me. This eventually led me to my final conclusion . . .

Conclusion 5: one of the greatest advantages of being an *actual* celebrity may be that you don't have to talk to people like me. After the show ended, and all the interviews wrapped up, CNN hosted an incredible gala bash, where we got to meet lots of nice people from the network who told us they were donating another thirty-five thousand dollars, enough to build three more computer centers.

All in all, it turned out to be a night that was surreal as any I've ever experienced. (And I went to college in the '70s.) If you need any further evidence, you can see for yourself in a short video clip that includes some of CNN's footage of our work and the presentation of my award at *www.youtube.com/watch?v=451a94jO5I4* or on our own website at *kenyakidscan.org.*

31

"I Never Gave Up Hope"

WE KNEW LEAVING TO GO TO AFRICA WOULD BE HARD THIS TIME. PACKing up a family and household to be gone for years is such a pain that the only words to adequately describe it are not in my everyday vocabulary. So I was forced to grunt often. Packing meant making choices; watching Katie try not to cry because she found one of her drawings in the trash nearly broke her daddy's heart.

Things grew worse when JT got home from Wake and we learned that he needed hernia surgery. Even though we were grateful that we could be with him through this ordeal, spending our last week with him in pain was a hard way to end our time together. To make things even harder, we were leaving Matthew behind in the States this time. When he'd first asked if he could stay and finish his sophomore year in Texas, we told him no. But after some wonderful friends offered to let Matthew be part of their family for six months, we agreed. So he planned to rejoin us in Kenya to finish his junior and senior years at Rift Valley Academy.

The holiday was different, knowing we'd be leaving the country two days after. We gave Ben and Katie approximately twelve seconds with each present before we packed them. Then we took down our Christmas tree on Christmas Day. And people we longed to see called, but we just didn't have time to get together with them.

I don't mean to complain. The truth is, besides the loss of income, this missionary thing has been fairly cost-free for me. Kenya has been a place of healing and provided opportunities for meaningful work. Finding two of our children there was incredible — and priceless. But we had all been together up to now, and I love my kids. I love to be *with* them. The thought of being thousands of miles away from our two oldest sons was hard beyond hard. Saying goodbye was wrenching.

—

So naturally we ran into ticket problems at the airport. If you'd spotted me walking away from our airline's reservations counter, I'm sure you would have exclaimed, "My goodness, that isn't the holy missionary and CNN Hero Steve Peifer saying all those interesting words, is it?" I had really cratered.

As a businessman, I learned that failure plays an important role in capitalism; as a believer, I'd learned that it's vital in Christianity. In faith, when you hit bottom, you realize you can't do anything. At that point, if you reach out to God, he meets you in a different way and touches the deepest hurts you've hidden inside where you hope no one can see them.

When I was down, I poured out all my fears to him: *Can I be a good father to my younger children at my age? How can I be away from my older children? Can we increase the feeding and computer programs? Will I ever have the money to retire when I make missionary wages during my peak earning years?*

I still didn't know the answers to those questions, but I knew I'd been able to share my heart, and I could say that I'd met him and I trusted him. This was a good thing to be able to say when — with our usual perfect Peifer timing — we landed in Nairobi just forty-eight hours before a tumultuous national election and the resulting widespread political unrest and intertribal violence that plagued the country for weeks in early 2008.

Most of us wazungus never felt personally threatened. Yet despite beefed-up, round-the-clock security measures on campus, some of RVA's long-time Kenyan staff, representing a variety of tribal groups, became terrified. Rumors swirled around and unruly mobs roamed through nearby Kijabe Town. We missionaries hurriedly helped a number of our national friends pack up their earthly possessions. And sadly watched them walk away from jobs and houses to flee back to their home regions and the supposed safety of their tribes.

We prayed for peace and justice to prevail. And things did begin to settle down once the leaders of the two major political parties reached a power-sharing compromise. By then, however, the entire country had paid a huge cost. More than a thousand died violent deaths. Hundreds of thousands had fled or been chased from their homes. And the Kenya everyone thought they knew was gone, maybe forever.

In an email report to our supporters, I summed up the challenge we now faced in a country that remained balanced on the knife-edge of political anarchy:

The tribal clashes, horrific inflation, and the falling dollar have led to a perfect storm — many displaced people have nowhere to go and no money at all. This has also led to three thousand additional students at the thirty-four schools where we now provide food.

The official government statistic for inflation is 20 percent. But this term, it will cost us six dollars plus to provide food for one child for a month. That is close to FOUR times what it was last term.

We used to get an exchange rate of eighty shillings per dollar. At this point, we are fortunate to get sixty.

So we have more kids, more expensive food, and our dollar buys much less. I have heard from a dozen schools requesting food in the past two weeks; headmasters are afraid of what is coming.

It could be a time to panic, but I seem to recall a story about a bunch of guys in a boat when a big storm came up. Lots of them were very scared, but one of them was calm and took care of everything.

In the time of a perfect storm, it is such a joy to know that guy in the boat.

—

While our goals remained the same, the period of national unrest not only added new challenges; it also served to multiply some of the old ones.

My good friend Margaret, the Kenyan woman who helped administer the school lunch program, asked me to go with her to Muchorui, one of nine new schools we had recently added to our feeding program. Although she'd proven to be adept at dodging riots and solving problems requiring diplomacy and tact, one policeman on that route insisted Margaret couldn't pass his checkpoint without paying him a bribe of nine bags of maize. I've had my share of bad experiences with police in Kenya over the years. Truth be known, I've been threatened with arrest dozens of times (though never actually arrested), usually when faced with shameless attempts to elicit bribes.

A drunken officer once stopped me at gunpoint and forced me to drive him several miles out of my way to his station. As we bounced and bumped over rugged Kenyan terrain, I asked the plastered policeman, as politely as I knew how, if he could please lower the muzzle of the automatic weapon he had resting against the back of my neck. What I'd thought was a perfectly reasonable request only ticked the man off. He launched into a profanity-laced tirade that I couldn't and didn't care to follow. The essence of his point was: how dare I, a mzungu, come to his country and challenge his authority as a policeman by telling him what to do?

Again, as respectfully as I could, I calmly explained that if the next big bump we hit happened to set off his weapon and blew off my head, there was good reason to think I might lose control of the vehicle, in which case we'd crash and he and this mzungu would very likely exit the land of the living together. He still did not lower his loaded gun. I prayed, all the way to our destination, that his trigger finger wouldn't twitch.

So, *no*, I wasn't eager to confront this policeman—or any policeman for that matter—even on behalf of my dear colleague Margaret. Over the years in Africa, however, I had learned that sometimes you need to force a showdown and face your fears. So I rode in the cab of our delivery truck with Margaret to the checkpoint where this corrupt, conniving police officer and I had the following discussion:

Policeman: You must give me nine bags before you are permitted to pass.

Me: Why?

Policeman: Because you have stolen it.

Me: Here is the bill of sale.

Policeman: I will not allow you to pass until you pay me nine bags of maize.

Me: I will do it if you do one thing for me.

Policeman: What is that?

Me: You must go with me to the school and pick out forty children who will not be fed because of what you have done. You tell me which forty do not deserve food and I will give you the bags.

Policeman: *(moving as if to climb in the vehicle with us)* I will do it. *(pauses)* I cannot make that choice.

Me: Neither can I.

Policeman: You can go. This time.

So we went. The children were happy to see us. And even happier to see the food we brought. Prices had increased so much since the elections that the families of many of these kids had nothing for them to eat other than what was provided at the school each day.

Many projects that get started in Kenya (and in other countries throughout Africa) eventually die from lack of interest, funding, or follow-through. The promised computer centers that we had under construction but had lain dormant for the six months we were back in the States had been a sign in some eyes that this was another project doomed to fail. Which was why, after Margaret and I delivered our full truckload of food—including all the bags of maize we had promised—we visited some of the classrooms to announce to the children that the computers would indeed be arriving soon. Our news was greeted with much loud cheering and celebration. And in the midst of the commotion, one little boy walked up to me and tugged on my hand. I had to lean down close to his face to hear his small voice (barely more than a whisper) as he smiled and told me, "I never gave up hope."

When I wrote our supporters to tell them that story, I ended my email by telling them, *I've been in Kenya since 1999. I've never seen it as bad as it has been since we got back. It could easily go south; we have been instructed to prepare a small bag in case we are evacuated. We don't expect that, but the huge issues in the country make anything possible right now.*

Part of me would like to go home. Every time I come back here, I have to talk myself into driving again and going into some of the areas I go to. I told this to a fellow RVA staff member who looked at me with amazement because he loves all of it. I don't.

I am really kind of a coward. So a big part of me would like to go home to America tomorrow, but that little boy's voice— "I never gave up hope"—keeps coming back to me.

~

As I added in another email, I needed all the encouragement I could get, *because these first few months back in Africa have been so crazy. Between mourning the separation from the older kids, the destruction going on in Kenya, and the guilt I felt about the CNN thing (when there are dozens of people I know who are so much more worthy), I've been more discouraged than I had realized.*

There was a point a few months ago when I wondered if it was time to pull the plug. I don't understand why we were chosen to be on CNN, but it happened, and we are going to be grateful for it. For whatever reason, I think we have a shot to impact this country. So what I want to say to you is this: I will not give up. I may go down, but I will go down fighting.

~

Evidently the Lord knew I needed a boost after a particularly discouraging day when I received an email from one of our RVA grads:

So I thought I should tell you this . . .

I was sitting on my bed watching America's Next Top Model *with two of my really good friends here at Harvard. We were talking about Tyra and how the show discriminates against "Ivy League" girls, and then we just kept going on and on about Tyra.*

And then I said, "My guidance counselor met Tyra and stepped on her dress."

They all said, "Really?"

And then as we looked for it on YouTube, we talked about how HUGE Tyra was, and then I mentioned that you got an award and that I was really proud of you.

And then they started watching the CNN Heroes clip that showed the video of your work, you, the giving of the award, and your acceptance speech. They were both really quiet and were actually teary by the end of your speech.

Then one of the girls—who is into comparative religion and pretty aggressive when it comes to my personal beliefs—came up to me later and started asking me about what the term "evangelical" meant, how important Jesus was to me, and how I would define my faith.

We talked for a pretty long time, and she actually listened instead of just crushing my opinions.

It was a pretty powerful moment. She still holds the same views, and nothing has changed. But you definitely provided a positive view of Christianity (one that is definitely not seen here very often) and encouraged a pretty important discussion.

It seems strange that this all started with Tyra Banks, but it was really appropriate that your speech touched my friends.

Could it be there were a variety of reasons we were chosen to be on CNN? If so, this one was a particularly heartening one for me.

—

The CNN exposure also offered opportunities I didn't think I should turn down, so I traveled that year more than ever before. On one trip back to the States, I landed in New York City at 7:30 a.m. after twenty-eight straight hours of travel, ran to a hotel, shaved and showered, then rushed to a meeting at noon, went back to the hotel, and hurried to another meeting that started around four and included dinner. Then back to the hotel to sleep. The next morning, I flew to Michigan for a conference. It went like that for more than three weeks. And I made an important discovery: I am too old to travel like that anymore.

I came back tired and sick, and realized the toll such a schedule takes not only on me but on my family. Thinking about the implications this experience should have on my life, I shared these insights in another email:

There is a weird dichotomy in the Christian life: We are called to excellence, and to give it our all. And yet, at the end of the day, we know that it is all in God's hands. Some Christians err on the side of not doing anything, and being presumptive of God's will. Others feel like they need to do it all, and God becomes an afterthought to their effort.

I want to give it my all, but I'm finally realizing (hopefully for the last time) that when I try to make things happen, they don't.

I had an unsolicited opportunity to speak to a foundation, which gave an enormous gift to the feeding program. I worked hard to prepare and submit a paper to one conference, was accepted to speak twice, and the first time, my voice was so shot no one could hear me. The second time, I was paired with another speaker who talked the entire time, and I didn't get to say a word.

I've said it before. Maybe I'll remember it this time: He makes the grain grow. I don't.

—

In August I visited many nearby Kenyan schools to make certain the costly food we'd purchased for that term was indeed getting where it was supposed to go. It heartened me to see our lunch programs functioning smoothly. And I found additional encouragement in the realization that despite all the country had been through and was yet going through, Kenyan kids still loved to eat and remained eager to learn. The recent turmoil hadn't much altered their daily experience at school. At least that I could see outwardly. Inwardly? I wasn't so sure.

At one school I visited, a classroom teacher enlisted me to help with an English lesson. Her elementary age students were constructing cause-and-effect sentences, and the exercise went like this: "If I ..., then I ..." One child said, "If I am tickled, then I laugh." Another said, "If I am happy, then I sing." But the one that got me was the little barefoot girl with a dirt-smudged face, wearing a well-worn, hand-me-down school uniform, who clearly spoke from experience when she stood at her desk and said, "If I am hungry, then I cry."

Driving cross-country back to Kijabe that day, a cloud of dust trailing behind me and the escarpment wall of the Rift Valley rising hundreds of feet before me, I couldn't help wondering how many more Kenyan kids might know hunger now because of the recent electoral chaos. But as that little girl's sentence kept echoing in my mind, it suddenly occurred to me, *That's it. That's the goal of our lunch program and all we're trying to do in the schools. The end of tears of hunger. That no child goes hungry and every boy and girl gets a chance to have a life with opportunity and the hope of better things for their children.*

Back in my office at RVA, I wrote an email telling about my school visits and that little girl's English class exercise. Wanting to challenge our supporters, I concluded my weekly report by telling them, *One of our most important jobs in life, if we have been fortunate enough to be born in the United States, is to protect and defend the weak. When you realize that, you understand you have been given the greatest gift and opportunity you can be given.* The end of tears of hunger. *That is still a good goal, isn't it?*

—

At another school, I noticed construction going on. When I asked about it, the headmaster told me his students' performance had improved so much that the government had decided to build water containers for the community's school, the first improvements at the school since it had been built many years earlier.

These were scary times in Kenya. Inflation, another poor crop, and near drought conditions had made living hard for so many people. We saw such a sense of relief in many communities when we brought food. And yet sometimes I couldn't help wondering if we were making any lasting difference. But as I watched the construction of those water tanks, I began to hope that just maybe we were seeing the beginning of a tipping point. The government was beginning to see improvements, and they were finally investing in the schools.

—

In October I flew to Seattle to attend a conference of colleges. The highlight for me was a college fair where we met reps from six hundred schools. We'd had some local Kenyan women make tiny baskets with the initials RVA on the side, just big enough to hold one small package of tea that said "Out of Africa." I hired Loren, a former RVA grad and a handsome young man, to go booth to booth delivering those while I focused on colleges where I knew our students would be applying that year.

In the middle of this huge convention center, at the booth of a famous college on the East Coast not known for its conservative Christian thought, I told them about one of our students who was applying there. I read one paragraph of her touching essay. The vice president of this college broke into tears and told me, "Oh my God, we need kids like that at our school."

—

Nancy had an amazing experience of her own, which I asked her to share in an email report near the end of our fall term:

One recent Saturday, I took a group of high school girls to a local orphanage. We delivered some maize and beans, and the RVA girls spent the morning playing with the kids there. I haven't been able to get those fifteen girls or Ruth, who runs the orphanage, out of my mind since, even though life here at our campus has been crazy busy. Finally, last Friday some time opened up for me, so I called Ruth and arranged another visit. I'd cleaned out the twins' closet of outgrown clothes; we'd also been given some solar flashlights I decided to take along.

I arrived and gave Ruth the clothes, then showed her one of the flashlights. (I had brought twenty to give her, but had left the rest in the car for my second load.) Ruth told me that when she told her husband I was coming, he had said, "Maybe she will bring us a torch [flashlight]." I thought that an interesting thing to specifically want when there were so many things they could use.

Even more interesting was what happened when I brought in the other nineteen solar flashlights. Ruth's whole face lit up with a smile as she told me, "You have heard God. On Monday, Kenya Power and Light came and cut our stima [electricity] because we could not pay the bill. We have been using a few candles at night, and we didn't know what to do. You are such a blessing to us."

I said, "But the real blessing is that almost six months ago — before you ever had trouble paying for the stima — the Lord put it on the heart of a man in America to send us many of these torches so that now, when you need them, they are here. Our God knows what we need before we even know we will have the need. That is what is so wonderful about this."

⁓

I shared my thoughts on yet another example of God's provision in the end of that same email:

One of my best friends in Kijabe is Dr. Rich, the dentist at our local mission hospital. He may be the nicest human on the planet, beloved by all. There was a baby abandoned at the hospital, and his wife began going down every day to hold her because newborns need to be held. The hospital was overcrowded, so the nursery staff asked if the Riches could take the baby home until some room opened up.

What happened next surprised them all. Dr. Rich is in his early fifties, with a son in dental school, a daughter at the University of North Carolina at Chapel Hill, plus a senior, a sophomore, and a sixth grader still at RVA. They weren't looking for any more children, but the entire family fell in love with this baby, and suddenly began thinking about adoption.

That startled me. Right now, one of my favorite Scripture passages is in Matthew 17, where Jesus is expected to pay a temple tax, so he tells his disciples to go fishing and look in the mouth of the first fish they catch, where they will find a coin that will more than pay the required tax. I've puzzled over that for years; why would he tell them to do that? I think part of it was that Jesus was fun and that was a cool way to give them money. The other reason is this: Jesus wanted them to know that he was in charge, and his ways are not our ways.

These are perilous times, but I believe in the God who puts coins in the fish's mouth. And I bet the baby does too. Her name indicates she might understand a lot. Her name is Hope.

—

I like the word yako. In Swahili, it means "yours," but being the creative sort, I have found myriad uses. Unlike my wife, who had managed to become fairly fluent in Swahili, I had found my breathtaking mastery of one new word of Swahili a year was not equipping me to interact in the community. So I quit worrying about all the words I didn't know and began utilizing the words I had learned, in whatever circumstances I found myself in.

For example, I could greet almost every Kenyan by saying, "You have no yako." And while I could never be certain how they might interpret that, it almost always resulted in improved communication by making sure they switched to English when conversing with me. But my strategy had further uses. My friend Margaret often asked me to pray for rain, so I would tell her, "You love yako so much." She knew that I meant rain.

We were paying for Peris, a young Kenyan woman, to take a computer class. So I often reminded her, "You must work hard on your yako." In no time at all, she knew exactly what I meant. What's more, it almost always brought a smile to her face, no matter how yako the day was, or how yako she felt, which in my book qualified as doubly effective communication.

I kept telling Nancy this technique could be adapted for use in any language. She wasn't easily convinced.

—

That verse the apostle Paul wrote about God's strength being "made perfect" (or "best illustrated") in and through *our* weakness had always been (and sometimes still is) a tough truth for me to swallow. But our year back in Kenya had been an instructive case in point, a year of great weakness and much failing, and having God be strong in me in spite of it all. I'd always hated looking like a failure, even when it was painfully obvious to everyone else. But this had been a breakthrough year for me not only in that I had been reminded just how weak I was, but in that I'd started not to care who knew it.

As someone who had always had an answer for everything, even when I didn't have a clue, this had been the year of "I don't know." In so many issues in Kenya this year, I didn't have a clue what to do. It felt humbling to start conversations with, "I don't know." But I also found it freeing. And it taught me to seek the Lord's wisdom and strength in a new way.

One day in December, I went with my wife to the local orphanage for little girls that Nancy's new friend Ruth and her husband, Edwin, ran. They and twenty girls ages five to sixteen lived in the simplest way you could imagine. The government was supposed to help them, but hadn't quite gotten around to it yet. No doubt because, as Edwin told me, "There are so many orphans." Ordinarily, such a sobering and matter-of-fact statement would be my cue to lament the current state of affairs in Africa and Kenya in particular; to despairingly recall all the headmasters who'd called me that week to ask if we could add their schools to our lunch program; to think about how I'd been forced to tell them no because I hadn't raised enough money to add *any* schools this year; and to remember how listening to grown men cry is horrible.

But before my mind could flash through all of that, Edwin added, "With what little we have, we are satisfied." His words hit me with conviction. For the first time, I realized it could be, and truly *needed* to be, possible for me to feel grateful for what we had been able to do, without always bemoaning my failures. Rather than feeling guilty about what we weren't able to do and focusing on the disheartening mountain of need, I could keep my eyes on the one who can move mountains and calm storms.

After all, we ended the year with 18,300 children being fed lunch every school day. Virtually every one of those schools had risen to or near to the top of the school ratings for their zones. And the 30 to 50 percent dropout rate that had plagued public education in Kenya for years had plummeted to near zero in our lunch program schools. And we had fifteen computer centers operational now. To focus on all the good things that had happened was not surrendering or giving up the fight, or making peace with the idea of hungry children. Rather it provided more encouragement and determination to continue the battle.

We'd returned to Kenya and begun the year with disturbing riots and unrest. We ended 2008 with hope and many needed reminders of who was in charge. And looking forward to a Yako New Year.

32

Dead or Alive?
Answer in Five Minutes

W E DELIVERED MOST OF THE LUNCH PROGRAM FOOD FOR THE NEW TERM in January. But the last two crops had failed because of near-drought conditions, so prices went up, people became desperate, and tensions were getting pretty close to the edge. We'd never intended our lunch program to be emergency food, but for too many terms for too many families, it had become just that.

The son of a friend attended Texas A&M University, where he came up with a simple but effective fundraising idea. Every Tuesday at lunchtime, he sat in front of the cafeteria and offered to make peanut butter and jelly sandwiches for fellow students. He explained our lunch program and requested donations from what his fellow students would have spent in the cafeteria. So far he'd brought in enough money to feed all of the students at one of our schools for an entire year.

In the harsh economic climate in America, as well as in Kenya at the time, I loved that a young man in Texas could make a difference in the lives of so many kids half a world away with a little creative effort. That was the kind of news I was determined to focus on in 2009.

~

I never had been good at the romance thing; I once took my wife to see *Schindler's List* on Valentine's Day. But with age and experience (also trial and error) comes wisdom. And after adding a big dollop of that holy missionary stuff, I thought I finally had the goods. And I was going to prove it.

At the annual banquet that RVA's junior class organizes each February to honor the seniors, the juniors write a play, build an elaborate set (with a lot of help from their parents), perform the play for the seniors' entertainment, and even provide (again with parental assistance) the multicourse meal. The only people allowed to attend are the seniors, the juniors, and the sponsors of each class. But for some reason, this year Nancy and I were invited.

A related annual ritual that has become every bit as important as the banquet itself is *how* you ask someone to go with you to the senior banquet. "The ask" has become such a big deal at RVA that the administration sets specific rules to limit *when* you can ask, as well as what can and cannot be done as part of your ask. Yet each year there seems to be no limit to what creative students will do to become legend in the annals of Rift Valley Academy's senior banquet tradition.

Well, Nancy made it quite clear she expected to be *asked*, that I shouldn't presume anything, which made me a little nervous, although Katie let me know that if Momma said no, she would go with me. That took some of the pressure off, but I was determined to make an impression.

I needed to take someone into town that week, and the one thing you can always find at a bargain in Kenya is flowers. So I bought one hundred roses in Nairobi and spent less than twelve dollars. The plan was to bring them home, and when Nancy came back to the house that evening, wow, would she get a surprise.

She *did* get a surprise, but ...

The school encourages us to hire local people to work in our homes, and so I had asked our house-helper Teresa to arrange the flowers. I clearly should have asked her to yako the flowers, because when Nancy and I walked in a little later that evening, we were *both* surprised to find that Teresa had carefully and conscientiously taken the flowers and *stacked* all ten bundles of them, ever so neatly, on the table. So my underwhelmed wife and I had the fun of trimming the bottom off the stems of one hundred roses.

It may be a guy thing to buy his wife one hundred roses. It is *not* a guy thing to ask, Where will we *put* one hundred roses? It turned out there wasn't a good answer to that question, and the final answer wasn't romantic. I did, however, get down on one knee and ask my bride to accompany me to the banquet. She said yes! (Though she had to help me back up off the floor.) Maybe I didn't have the goods just yet.

—

The week before the banquet, it occurred to me that I owned only one suit, and I had not worn it since the CNN thing. When I tried it on, I realized I needed to lose twenty pounds in five days, and that was my *best* option. The day came, and only by huffing and puffing like the Big Bad Wolf did I manage to pull on the pants.

Later, Lamaze breathing techniques became the key to surviving the five-hour event. The only adequate analogy that comes to mind is the rural Texas expression, "Like putting twenty pounds of manure in a fifteen pound bag."

Romance: I've got it *covered*.

—

I knew I'd vowed to focus on the positives. But conditions in Kenya made that difficult, as I reported in a March email:

Five men attacked the guard at one of our computer centers. They hit him in the head with a machete, broke down the door, and stole all the computers. When I first heard the news, I didn't know what to do—it was so discouraging.

But one of my favorite Scriptures is Genesis 50:20: "You intended to harm me, but God intended it for good to accomplish what is now being done, the saving of many lives." There is a handout mentality prevalent here, and part of what we are trying to do is help children acquire the tools to make a living rather than expect a handout.

During one of my calls to the school about the robbery, I could hear children in the background loudly weeping. Their parents called an emergency meeting and voted to hire three guards. They didn't ask for any money from me; they just did it. That community has seen the value of these centers, and they are going to fight for them.

The situation in the valley is grim. Three crop failures in a row have forced us to go all the way to Uganda to find maize. Prices have skyrocketed, and there are an additional one thousand students enrolled in the thirty-four schools we work with. Bottom line: we have enough money to buy food for only half a term. Again, I don't know what to do. Please pray for wisdom for us.

—

RVA offers special interim activities for juniors and seniors during the second trimester; so Nancy and I were asked to lead a group of RVA teenage girls on a trip to Tanzania during our April break. Meeting with our kids ahead of time, we asked, "Why Tanzania?" When every one of the girls admitted it was her second choice, I didn't consider that an auspicious beginning. But their honesty proved a great start to an astonishing week.

We spent that time among the Datooga tribe, a group that still lives in mud-hut villages in an amazingly beautiful national park. Someone we had never met from Canada donated and sent us solar flashlights, and we purchased Swahili Bibles to take with us as well. So we were able to present those both as gifts to our Datooga hosts. Wandering the village the next day, seeing many people reading the first book they had ever owned was thrilling beyond thrilling.

Our group consisted of Nancy and me plus a bunch of girls, so the rest of the team held several meetings with the women in the tribe, meetings in which, for obvious reasons, I didn't participate.

Which was why, one day, I was sitting by myself under a tree, reading a book, when a snake dropped in my lap. I learned two interesting things:

1. My instinctive response when a snake falls in my lap is to scream like a seven-year-old girl.
2. Snakes *hate* it when an old guy screams like a seven-year-old girl.

While screaming, I leaped to my feet and flung the snake as far away as possible. A Datooga gentleman came running to find out what was wrong.

Me: A snake just dropped in my lap.

Gentleman: Was it bright green?

Me: Yes.

Gentleman: *(serious concern on his face)* We must get you to the hospital immediately.

Me: It didn't bite me.

Gentleman: Are you certain?

Me: Well ... uh ... I don't think it bit me.

Gentleman: Well, the hospital is two hours away. If that snake *did* bite you, you will be dead in five minutes.

It's amazing how many details you have never noticed about your wristwatch until you have to wait and wonder whether you will be dead or alive in five minutes. Fortunately, nothing happened during my countdown—besides personal and spiritual growth.

Nancy and our RVA girls had their own interesting time with the women of the tribe. My wife did an educational presentation about AIDS, which was notable in itself, because eleven years earlier, Nancy would have fainted dead away before she would have spoken in front of any group. Let alone talk about such a sensitive subject. By all accounts, she did a great job. Then the really interesting time began. The question and answer session that followed did not focus on *how* AIDS could be transmitted. They said, "In our culture, a wife cannot refuse her husband if he wishes to be intimate. We know our husbands are being intimate with other women. What would you tell us to do?"

For years, the rap against missionaries was that they could be cultural imperialists, and historically, that has sometimes been a fair criticism. Our goal should be not to make people more like us but to help them to be more like Jesus. So in a situation like this, do we tell women to deny their culture? Or do we tell them to do what their husbands want when the infection rate is tremendously high?

Sometimes I longed for the days when answers seemed so easy.

—

Following our week in Tanzania, we flew back to the US for the remainder of the school break. Our mission allowed us to take one trip with each of our children to look at colleges, so Matthew and I toured thirty campuses while Nancy and the younger kids visited family. All in all, it was a special time for me to spend with my second son.

While we spent most of our time in America traveling, I had a day to meet with my Kenya Kids Can advisory board. I reported that as a result of the economic crisis in America and deteriorating conditions in Kenya, we were able to provide only about 70 percent of the usual amount of food we give to the schools. I said we were grateful for what we could do, and prayed the Lord would make the 70 percent last longer than it should.

I also reported that we'd just received excellent new curriculum that should take our centers to the next level. A friend who has a PhD in computer training had come to Kenya to observe our centers and produced some outstanding educational materials targeted specifically for the teachers and kids in our program. Finally I asked the board to please pray for protection and wisdom, "Because some of the centers are being attacked by thieves, and the police have informed me it isn't their problem."

I always feel the need to keep my board informed. But I also expect them to challenge me and hold me accountable. One of my oldest friends in the world cut right to the chase in that board meeting. He reminded me of the exciting vision I had when we'd launched the feeding program, and how I'd used that vision to persuade him to join my board. But he then expressed his disappointment that I'd not referenced that vision at all during our board meeting. So he came right out and asked, "What is your purpose? Are you still planning to change the country?"

My immediate response was an easy and certain yes. But in my next email communication, I elaborated on that answer:

My friend's blunt question made me realize how easy it is to get so bogged down with daily details and difficulties that you focus on your problems instead of your purpose.

So . . . this is our purpose:

1. *To get a generation of Kenyans through high school with good nutrition;*
2. *to provide them with hope and an opportunity to learn technology; and*
3. *to let them know the reason this happened is Jesus' love for them.*

If we can do that, we will change the lives of so many kids who have never had a chance, which will indeed change the whole country.
And that is what I signed up for.

—

Most of our lunch program schools ran out of food weeks before their term ended in July. I got frantic calls from several headmasters, but we just didn't have any money left to buy additional food. Hearing that many students had started leaving school around 11:00 a.m. each day to search and beg for food painfully reminded me that we were in a war, and there was no easy ground to take anymore. Everything was a fight; nothing was easy.

—

Sitting in a computer center and feeling as discouraged as I could remember, I had a little girl tell me her dream was to own a pair of shoes. Then another class came in, and suddenly I was watching kids without shoes learn how to query a database. The progress they were making felt exhilarating. It struck me that I'd spent a lot of time in this battle feeling as if I was getting the crud kicked out of me. But watching those kids master a difficult lesson was like standing up after a year of being beaten to a pulp and slugging the bully right in the mouth.

If we remember we are in a war, every once in a while we get to hit back.

—

Shortly after that I drove out to check on Njira Primary School, the most remote school we provided food for. They were out of food, even though we'd given them enough to make it through the term. I suspected theft, but then I discovered that there were two schools nearby that did not receive food. And Njira had shared their food with the children of these other communities.

Somehow, in this war we're fighting, that had to hurt the other side.

—

During our August break, we received word that a pilot and his mechanic with our mission had been killed in a plane crash. Perhaps it's not unexpected that people who willingly put their own lives at risk to help the poor some-times pay the ultimate price. But when that happens, you're still surprised by how much it hurts. Each man left behind his wife and four children. It was just such a great loss.

The Psalms tell us we should look to the hills and the heavens when things get rough. But during this sad time, the Lord directed me to look a little lower. To a driver.

Joshua's father runs a driving service RVA often uses. Since it wasn't safe for me to drive at night because of my poor night vision, their dependable professional service was a blessing for late night trips to and from the Nairobi airport. I had a flight out one evening that summer, so I scheduled a ride. Joshua picked me up, and when we reached the city ahead of schedule, I asked if he wanted to stop for dinner. As we ate, he told me a heartening story.

When he was in high school, Joshua and four of his closest friends started meeting together to pray for Kenya. During one of their prayer meetings, the five of them each felt led to make a vow: they would all go to law school, they would all enter politics, and they would all work to bring justice to their land.

Joshua, who had already earned a college degree in accounting, told me all five friends were now in law school, and they still met regularly to pray for each other and for Kenya. The odds of those young men remaining true to that vow, and for all of them to be accepted to law school and to be able to pay for it, were beyond what I could imagine. I felt as if I was hearing about something holy and historic that someday could bring justice to an entire country.

—

They say humor is universal. But some days you couldn't prove it by me, as evidenced by the incident with which I began a November email:

One windy afternoon, I warned a bunch of students walking across campus that if they weren't careful, they might take flight like the Flying Nun. When that elicited nothing but puzzled looks, I made an urgent note to self: MUST UPDATE POP CULTURE REFERENCES. The blank stares continued as one of them asked, "Nuns can fly?"

—

Two weeks ago, I visited one of the schools we work with. The kids know me so well there that whenever I drive up, they all yell, "Peifer!" and come running to the car to greet me. But I'd never grasped the extent of my fame, nor just how isolated they really were, until this last visit. Another vehicle pulled up while I was there and a swarm of students ran toward it yelling, "Not-Peifer!"

Those kids are thriving. Our computer teacher there is excellent. And the day I visited, they took a final in Excel that I don't think I would have passed. They did great on it. They were so happy and full of life that as I left there, I realized one thing I never adequately communicate is just how fun this can be. The kids love to laugh, and I walked away thinking, This is working. I get to be part of something that helps little kids.

Despite the frustrations and the challenges of this work, it fills holes deep inside of me. Which reminds me of the Scripture where Jesus says, "My food is to do the will of him who sent me." I always figured that verse was for holy people, but it's true even for people like me.

—

And then there are the weeks when everything is stripped bare, and stuff you have seen a million times hits you as if you've never seen it before.

I took a video camera out to one of the schools, thinking that since it was almost Thanksgiving in America, it would be fun to film Kenyan students talking about what they are thankful for. Some of it was funny; some of it was touching. Then a little boy dressed in rags told me, "I am thankful for my clothes."

Usually I can hold it together until I drive off; I couldn't that day. A flood of tears ran down my face as I realized how much I have and how much he didn't. I ran off like a fool full of crazy sorrow over how much need there was, and how little we could do. Sometimes it just gets you sad.

—

On the last day of school each term, Kenya's government schools give out prizes to their top students. I was invited to the awards ceremony for the remote Masai school at Ewaso. The first time I had visited that community eight years before, a little girl screamed when she saw me because her parents had always told her that if she was bad, the white man would come and *eat* her. They all know me there now and greet me without fear. But that was only one example of how cultures can change.

Because of our lunch program, the population of the school had doubled, with virtually no dropouts. Students who lived in mud huts were learning how to use computers, and they delighted in the fact that I scored the lowest of all of them on their computer exam. One of them asked if I did poorly to encourage them, and I had to confess that while I wished that was what had happened, they were all smarter than me.

We don't want to be cultural imperialists, and there are many things to appreciate about Masai traditions. The Masai aren't ruled by their possessions. A lock on a door would be a shock; they are a people who share whatever they have. They love and respect nature. They live out the true meaning of *community*. But there are toxic parts of their culture as well. It isn't uncommon for fifty-year-old men to marry ten-year-old girls. Drunken beatings are common. Women have no legal rights and often are treated horribly. After her husband dies, the most common cause of a Masai widow's death is starvation.

But this community was starting to address these issues. As part of the awards ceremony, students performed a skit about an old Masai man wanting to marry a ten-year-old girl, and they mocked him during the skit. Then a young woman recited a poem she had written that went like this:

> I want to be a pilot.
> I want to be a doctor.
> I don't want to fetch water.
> I have dreams.

This was happening not as a result of external forces but because any people, as they become educated, begin to see and understand what they need to cast off. The Masai have clung to their ways longer than other tribes, but even they are changing.

—

The encouragement I found in that (and so many other things I'd begun to notice) was reflected in the year-end Christmas email greeting, when we thanked and assured our supporters:

We know your secret identity. You go around disguised as doctors and teachers and salespersons and stay-at-home moms, but we know who you really are. You are the people who feed almost twenty thousand students a lunch every school day. You are the people who built seventeen solar computer centers, with another three scheduled for completion in 2010. You are the people who hear the cry of the children of Africa, and you have not made peace with it. We are so grateful for you, and your secret is safe with us. This has been a challenging year in so many ways, but we can look anyone in the eye and say, "We are hard pressed on every side, but not crushed; perplexed, but not in despair; persecuted, but not abandoned; struck down, but not destroyed."

33

I Don't Like Living by Faith

YOU MAY HAVE HEARD THE OLD BLESSING/CURSE (IT COULD BE EITHER OR both), "May you live in *interesting* times." That's what we've been doing for almost a decade and a half now, in what has to be one of the world's most interesting places, as we were reminded by multiple unusual developments on RVA's campus early in the new year.

One day a boomslang (a deadly venomous snake) was found coiled atop a kid's backpack, which had been left on the ground outside the cafeteria door. That same month, one of our seniors received a concussion when he crashed his motorcycle into a *gazelle*. During that same period, there was more illness, and more lingering illness, than any time in all our years at RVA. A particularly virulent stomach bug struck so many people on campus that in a staff meeting one afternoon, the principal had to ask who might be willing to fill in for our sick home economics teacher. Nancy volunteered me.

I refused to take offense when laughter swept through the roomful of colleagues. In a campus-wide email appeal later that evening, titled "Save the Children," the principal implied many possible serious and even horrifying consequences to which innocent youth would be exposed if *no one else* stepped into the breach. It turned out that what too many had already been exposed to was the H1N1 virus (aka swine flu). So many people were out that the principal had no choice but to call upon my unique skills. I hasten to assure that there were *no* serious injuries, except to my pride, when he sent out an email that night after my first class asking would *someone else please volunteer* to teach home ec.

It just happened to be my turn to do chapel that week. So before I gave my previously scheduled talk, I seized the bully pulpit (so to speak) to explain the whole thing from my perspective. Then I asked every student to stop by the principal's office and ask him this question: "Do you think you are being sensitive to Mr. Peifer's feelings?" The killing blow was next: they were to wave their finger and say, "I don't think you have been." (And he thought I was just going to take it.)

Before the wave of illness receded, we had a hundred cases of swine flu reported out of a campus population of some five hundred people. No one had to be hospitalized, but many were pretty sick for a few days. We tried to stay on campus for the duration of our mini-epidemic, because what would make many Westerners sick might kill an African with a weak immune system. By the time the worst passed, everyone was tired beyond tired.

So when another RVA student got accepted to MIT, many folks who were so sick of bad news and so ready to rejoice erupted in sudden celebration that included much jumping and yelling and weeping for joy. It's hard to explain how much something like that means at an isolated school surrounded by baboons. Campus-wide morale soared.

—

Great news is always a wonder, and the Peifer family received some of the greatest when JT became engaged to the lovely Janelle; they told us they planned to be married after he graduated in May of 2011. We felt fortunate to have gotten to spend time with our future daughter-in-law the previous summer, when she visited Kenya with JT and the entire family had gotten to know and fall in love with her.

Right away Katie had told us she knew why her brother JT had fallen for Janelle. When we asked why, she said, "Because she reminds him so much of me." And now that they were engaged, Janelle invited Katie to be in the wedding. You should have seen my daughter's face when she got her first look at the bridesmaid dress she would wear.

—

Three more computer centers had been completed, and I went to visit the one at Karia. The children were hard at work when I arrived, and I didn't want to interrupt. So I stood outside the lab chatting with the headmaster when Paul, the computer teacher, came out and indicated he wanted to speak to me.

Paul started by saying he needed to tell me about a major problem he was having. I don't know what you do when you've hit the limit of major problems you want to deal with, but my immediate response that day was to let out a deep sigh. With a twinkle in his eye, Paul went on to tell me his *problem* was that after every class, he practically had to chase the children away from the center because they loved it so much they wanted to stay and keep learning.

—

When I finally had the chance to go to one of the other schools with a new computer center, the computer teacher there reported an even more extraordinary "problem." Students had begun skipping lunch to have more time on the computers. And since lunch was the only sure meal of the day for many of those kids, the teachers had begun closing and locking the center at lunchtime to make sure the kids all ate.

I was surprised to find a new headmaster at one of the schools we worked with. The previous one I'd dealt with had never finished high school; he'd gotten the position only because of political connections. And because pretty much everyone considered the school a write-off, no one had ever expected much. But student test scores improved so much after we started providing lunches, that the local government authorities decided to get serious about education in that community. The new headmaster had a college degree and told me he wants to take the school to a new level.

We created our programs to try to address some of Kenya's most discouraging problems. Now the "problems" our programs were creating provided encouraging signs of progress. How cool is that?

—

In an email that spring, I wrote about another wonderful and personally encouraging surprise:

Longtime readers might remember that when we first came to Africa in 1999, a young Kenyan named Fred did some work for us in our yard. I taught computer for first through sixth graders at the time, and during a drought when we didn't have much yard work, I invited him to come to the computer lab with me. Fred was afraid even to touch a computer at first, but he had soon mastered replication and ghosting, and before long the school hired him to work full-time with kids in the lab.

A couple of years after, he got married; he asked if we would loan him a significant sum of money to get some college training in computer skills. We lent it to him, but after years of making regular payments on the loan, he stopped paying and we stopped seeing him. We've lent money a number of times knowing that sometimes it might not be paid back. We just assumed this was another case in point.

But Fred came by today and paid off the rest of the note, a large sum of money. He told us he had finished his computer training and was now the database manager for a hospital. He and his wife had three kids now, and recently they had been using the remainder of the money we'd loaned him to purchase rental property. He now owns his own home and the three rental properties free and clear. He is a deacon in his church, and he is obviously doing very well.

It was such a reminder to me that when God directs you to invest in people, sometimes you get to witness the wonder of his working in ways you might otherwise never get to see.

—

We were in the process of building three more computer centers with plans to have a total of twenty centers up and running and twenty thousand children eating lunch each day by the time we left for furlough in July. This time we had the national personnel and sufficient infrastructure in place to keep both programs operating with no problems while we were gone—as long as the funding was there. Of course, that was still an issue.

For months I'd been wondering where the money would come from to provide food for next term, but we had seen so many miracles already that we had hope. JT and Janelle raised more than eight thousand dollars at an event they sponsored at Wake Forest. Covenant Christian Academy, our kids' school in Texas, raised more than thirty-eight thousand dollars at their annual auction. And God made it rain. Kenya had its biggest crop in years; suddenly there was so much maize, the prices plummeted. We weren't there yet with necessary funds, but I could see possibilities that weren't there before.

As a missionary, I am ashamed to admit I don't like living by faith; I'd much rather have the money in hand than to know I'm going to have to trust God for it. But when I see him move, and know it could only be him, that is perhaps the sweetest experience on earth.

—

As evidenced by my email account of this memorable case in point:

On our anniversary, Nancy and I went to Nairobi to celebrate and spend the night. On our way back to RVA the next day, we stopped to shop and eat lunch. As I walked past an Indian family, they asked me if I was "Stephen." Since I had just been to an ATM to withdraw some cash, that unsettled me a bit. I told them the only person who had ever called me Stephen was my mother, and that was only when she was upset with me.

They explained they had seen me on CNN, and wondered if I might join them for lunch. After agreeing to do so, I hurried off to help Nancy finish her shopping, and then we joined them. They asked us questions about our lunch and computer programs. We learned they were part of an influential family in Kenya that had already made a contribution to those projects. But at the end of our lunch, they practically floored me when they told us they would like to give one hundred thousand shillings (roughly thirteen hundred US dollars) a month to our work.

For some time, I've been wondering how we would manage to pay our computer teachers and complete our last three centers. This contribution by itself will cover half of all our teachers' salaries per month.

Jesus made a way. He always makes a way for us to do what he asks us to do. Every screwup in this work is from me; every good thing is from him.

⸺

If you've read this far in the book, you probably won't be surprised to hear me say that being in Kenya has taught me new ways to pray. And new things to pray about.

Every day working at Rift Valley Academy, I am surrounded by remarkable, uniquely experienced young people of character and intelligence I've always believed had the potential to change the world someday. I knew that a lot of people—parents, relatives, friends back home, and the RVA staff—regularly prayed for their safety, from things like deadly snakes on backpacks, motorcycle meetings with random wildlife, swine flu, and other health issues in a land with limited medical resources. A lot of those same people are praying for our students' emotional growth and adjustment living at a boarding school, for the effectiveness of their education, and about these kids' futures. I've done a lot of praying about those things myself—during our years as a dorm parent, at exam time, and especially every year during college application season.

With all those prayers, and all I've experienced and learned of God's grace since we came to Kenya, I figure most of the major concerns of our students are pretty well covered. So I've felt led to sometimes set my prayer sights a little lower, to focus a little less on lofty concerns and aim for more here-and-now, practical prayers.

Which is why, when encountering students as I walk across the RVA campus, I regularly pray, out loud, that God will give me a water balloon to throw at their heads. I've found that nothing brings people together like hearing an old guy beseeching heaven, "Lord Jesus, please give me a full water balloon that I can throw at Josh's head." *Many* students have asked why I do it. I remind them that Scripture says to ask him for *all* things. They usually don't know what to say to that. Most of them simply walk away shaking their heads and pondering my deep spiritual insight.

I once had a student tell me she didn't think my prayer was appropriate or very nice. I responded by saying, "Lord Jesus, please make the water balloon I throw at her extra cold."

And some people used to say I can't relate to young people.

—

In July of 2010, Matthew experienced all the wonderful graduation traditions of RVA, a school our second son had attended since second grade. This schooling had been a great experience for him, which had culminated in a really great senior year.

Matthew and I had established a tradition of our own over our years in Kenya; he and I played racquetball every Sunday afternoon. We started when he was in second grade, with the long-term goal that he would beat me in the final month of his senior year. He'd started beating me when he was a sophomore. So he was a little ahead of schedule, or maybe I was behind. But it had been a good way of regularly connecting with my seriously overscheduled son.

So the day after graduation, we walked down to the outdoor courts beside the gym at the lower end of the hillside campus to play our final game. When we finished the game, I probably surprised and no doubt embarrassed him by suddenly bursting into tears. I confessed to my son, "I never wanted it to end."

But games do end, and children grow and move on. And that part of life is hard, especially when you live overseas and expect to see your college-age and adult children only once a year at best. I couldn't quite make peace with that part of our lives. But Nancy and I were both excited for Matthew. And we were grateful that all of us would be back in the States on furlough for a year as he started at the University of Richmond in the fall and to see our oldest graduate and get married the following spring. We anticipated an exciting Peifer-family-milestone year.

—

We had many of the usual readjustment issues coming back to America, plus others I touched on in an October email:

You would think a wife who is aging well would be a GOOD thing for the husband, and mostly it is, except when she is standing next to you and you are seeing friends you haven't seen in three years.

> *Old Friend:*   *Nancy, you look so great!*
>
> *Same Old Friend:* *Steve, how* are *you?*

Comparisons can be CRUEL.

—

We have gotten to see JT and dropped off Matthew at the University of Richmond, and I have had eye surgery that resulted in my left eye going from 20-800 to 20-40, which will take some time getting used to. I'm still shocked to see the dark-ringed, wrinkly-eyed guy who shaves my face every morning. Thank you for not telling me what was really going on with my face.

—

Nancy went to Chicago to visit her father, and I decided to do something special with Ben and Katie. We were going to see their first 3-D movie. They just loved the experience.

    The movie we saw was Despicable Me. *If you haven't seen it, it is about a bad guy whose life turns around when he adopts some children. Ben and Katie couldn't understand why that movie made me cry.*

—

The National Association for College Admission Counseling (NACAC), a professional organization to which I belong, honored me with their Excellence in Education Award at their annual national conference in September, perhaps the highest recognition a guidance counselor can receive. But like so many things in my life, it did not occur quite the way I wish it had.

    NACAC had been good enough to tell me I would be getting the award, but our computer had crashed and I'd lost the email telling me the details. So when I arrived at the convention midday on Thursday, I went straight to the official NACAC booth to ask when I would receive the award. The nice lady told me, "Saturday," which sounded perfect, because it would allow me time to think deep thoughts and prepare a great speech to give while wearing the first new dress shirt I'd purchased in a decade.

    So I walked on into the opening session of the conference dressed for success, wearing a yellow T-shirt and jeans. One of the authors of the mega-blockbuster book *Freakonomics* spoke, and I distinctly remember thinking, *I am so lucky I don't have to follow that guy.*

    Then they presented an award — to a professionally dressed woman who walked up on stage carrying pages and pages of a prepared speech. I suddenly had a sinking feeling, and having forgotten to bring the reading glasses I needed since my recent surgery, I leaned over and asked the woman next to me, "You have young eyes. What does the program say about awards today?" She assured me that they were giving only two awards. *Whew!* After thanking her, I listened to the presenter of the next award begin. And then I saw my picture flashed on the big screens on either side of the stage.

Since I was sitting in the back of a large auditorium, I had to literally run to make it to the front as the speaker finished saying whatever nice things she told the audience about me, RVA, and our work in Kenya. I am never nervous before I speak. Perhaps I should be, because I'm not much of a speaker. Fear might eliminate the meandering I tend to do when making a speech. But that day as I climbed the steps of that stage, I was nervous as I asked Jesus if he would somehow help me salvage this situation. And he gave me a word to share with the nine thousand of my professional colleagues in this mostly secular organization. I don't remember what I said word-for-word, but I closed by saying something like this:

After my son died, I had the same dream for months. I could see him in trouble, and I knew if I could get to him in time, he would be okay. I would run as fast as I could, but I would always wake up before I could reach him.

I haven't had that dream for years now. But today I can see another nightmare in my mind: a huge ocean wave is racing toward Africa. Fortunately, we have time and opportunity to get the children of Kenya to safety. In fact, you and I can save all the kids we decide we want to save.

How many children do we want to save?

In spite of everything, my brief impromptu speech seemed well received, and I heard many positive responses, including two I will always cherish. The first was from a young woman who said, "When I get *old*, I want to do something noble like you." The second was from a guy at the door of a college reception I tried to sneak into:

Guy at Door: Your speech was awesome, dude. I actually cried.

Me: *(walking past him through the door)* Thanks so much.

Guy at Door: Hey! Just a minute. Where *is* your ticket?

When I informed my superintendent at RVA that it truly was a big honor to be given the NACAC Excellence in Education Award, he emailed me back to say, "They must never have observed your driver's ed class."

—

Other Peifer family highlights from our furlough year back in Texas:

• We used our hotel and airline points to finally take Ben and Katie to Disney World.

• Because of the issues with the famous book *Three Cups of Tea*, I was asked to replace the author as a keynote speaker at a big educational convention, which for the attendees must have seemed like winning lunch with Angelina Jolie and having me show up instead.

• JT graduated from Wake Forest and two weeks later married the lovely Janelle, a young woman he had met his first month of college. They set up housekeeping in Charlottesville, Virginia, where she was already working on her PhD in clinical psychology. (When Matthew applied to Richmond, we had no idea that both the older boys would end up forty-five minutes from each other.)

• Nancy presented a well-received paper on integrating biblical truth into curriculum, which made me even more impressed with my impressive wife of twenty-six years.

• My bride and I used part of the advance for this book to take an anniversary cruise to Alaska, which was a miracle that we didn't expect to be able to enjoy once we entered the mission field.

• And somehow, even with donations way down during tough economic times in America and Africa, we managed to feed twenty thousand students a day for the year.

—

In an email detailing some of these highlights and more at the end of the year, I wrote:

All that sounds so nice.

But this has also been a year with beginning to deal with the hard issues that adoption can bring. One of our young ones will have a fun day and then in the evening begin to cry, and when we ask why, they can only answer that they are sad.

When your children are hurting and you can't fix it, it will break you like nothing else will. With the help of a counselor who deals with the special issues adopted children face, we've seen wonderful progress being made. And we think we understand better how to avoid burnout and protect ourselves and our family.

We are all broken, but we have the Hope that came to earth for all of us two thousand years ago. So we end this year of furlough with that Hope and gratitude to all of you for your continued love and support.

More than anything, we realize what a privilege it is to serve the poor of Kenya, and we are ready to get back.

34

No Fear in Kamuyu

S OON AFTER WE GOT BACK TO KIJABE, THE KENYAN GOVERNMENT informed us we had to officially register our computer program if we wanted to continue operating the centers at their public schools. Back before we'd ever set up the first computer lab, we had talked to a number of government officials and they had advised us *not* to register.

Now we had to, which meant jumping through regulatory hoops and paying taxes on the salaries of our computer teachers. I wanted our computer program officially recognized and registered under the name of our website *KenyaKidsCan.org*. But some Kenyan bureaucrats rejected our name and assigned us what they evidently thought was a better, more appropriate name: Organization for Children in Computer Technology.

Catchy, don't you think? Oh, well.

After years of stumbling and struggling, we realized that having strong Kenyans in principal positions makes all the difference. Somehow, the Lord led Margaret to us to administer the school lunch program and Lucy to train our teachers and oversee the computer centers, two people who are trustworthy and have a true vision for excellence and honoring the Lord. This is how both programs continued while we were gone for a year during our most recent furlough.

Yet funding continued to be our biggest challenge. We didn't have the money to start any more centers. And since the gifted guy who'd built the previous centers for us had recently left the mission field, we felt the Lord was leading us to concentrate on maintaining and improving what we had in place, before expanding to any more schools. Truth was, we were struggling just to cover our teacher payroll, about twenty-eight hundred dollars a month. So our goal for the coming year was to do better with what we had and wait until the economy (or something else) changed and it became possible to grow again.

We were far enough behind on food donations that we considered offering lunches on Mondays, Wednesdays, and Fridays that term. We had decided we had no choice but to make that cutback, until the money came in at the last minute. Even then we thought that we'd be late purchasing and delivering the food. But with another teachers' strike, I was told, "Do not come. It will be very much dangerous." By the time the strike ended, we had everything we needed to begin delivering enough food to the schools for the full term, five days a week.

The costs increased again—up to $2.05 to feed a child for a month. That's a small amount to impact, maybe even save, a child's life. But when you multiply that amount by twenty thousand students for a three-month term, it adds up to an imposing figure for missionary educators who already raise their own support. There was little we could do beyond trusting God: to help us know what to do, to guide us in doing it, and to provide the resources to take the next step.

—

We had spent a year in the States feeling healthy. But Nancy and I and Katie and Ben each had health issues at one time or another our first few weeks back at RVA. Having lived in the developing world for twelve years, we understood that was just part of the readjustment process. Of course, knowing that didn't make us feel any less sick or frustrated, though it did give us reason to believe things would get better and a realistic hope it could happen sooner rather than later.

—

Three items from our first emails of the year, once we got to feeling better several weeks into the term:

From student announcements: "Mr. Peifer is delighted to announce that the broken glass on his historic, personally signed picture of Neil Diamond has been repaired and is available for viewing in his office with an appointment."

—

Nancy and I got to go to Kamuyu Primary School last week, the first such visit we'd been able to make since we've returned. Being back at a school reminded me of the Scripture where Jesus says, "My food is to do the will of him who sent me." Let me tell you, watching little kids who have absolutely nothing fully engaged on computers during an Excel class, and getting it, may just be the most nourishing, not to mention exhilarating, thing I can think of.

The headmaster reminded me that when I first came to his school, the students feared me. When we brought the computers to the school, they feared the computers.

There was no fear at Kamuyu last week.

—

I also recently went down to the school in Munyu, a community that has been devastated by AIDS. Because of the food that you have provided, they have added more than two hundred students to their ranks. The computer classes were lively, with our only Masai teacher adding something special to the lessons.

Before we started out work there, Munyu school had always ranked lowest on the national tests in their zone. They have topped the list for several years in a row now.

Everything seemed to be going well the day I observed class there. But with a raging inflation rate, I knew money had to be getting terribly tight for many families. So as I was making conversation with the kids, I asked a young boy how he was doing. He told me his father was dead, his mother had AIDS, and he lived in his older brother's back yard. There was no food for him except for what he ate at school for lunch. During the weekends, he went out and begged for food.

He later told me that he felt lucky because he had a brother. Since he could live in his brother's back yard, he didn't have to sleep on the streets. He also made it a point to tell me how grateful he was to be learning computers and that he was so happy for the food at lunch.

I drove home and prayed. I wish I had a wise homily to end this with, but I just prayed.

—

Throughout much of Africa, ugali is a staple dish that consists of boiled cornmeal. If that sounds appetizing, you need to read that last sentence again.

We sponsored an end-of-the-school-year luncheon for all of the computer teachers, and a number of them remarked that I didn't eat any ugali. When I asked why they ate it, three different people gave me slightly different answers to the effect that if you ate ugali at night, you would not wake up with hunger pains, which is a real issue for most Kenyans. I found an excuse to turn and look away. I thought it would embarrass them to see me cry.

Perhaps the greatest gift Africa has given me is the gift of tears. I'd been afflicted with cynicism most of my life. But Kenya has managed to pierce my hard heart again and again.

—

Since the wide world of photography went digital, Peifer family members have taken thousands more pictures than ever before. We've attached hundreds of them to our email reports for graphic illustration of the people, places, events, and stories written about in those reports, upon which so much of this book has been based. But as I suspect is true of most American families, we have printed out relatively few photographs over the last ten or fifteen years.

Which is why, not long ago, I decided to go back through years' worth of pictures we've taken since we first came to Africa and print out a large pile of highlights. There's just something different about shuffling, one after another, through a big stack of photographs you can hold in your hands, setting a pair of pictures down side by side to notice the differences, the similarities, and the changes wrought by time. Or spreading the whole batch out across a tabletop and noticing patterns and themes you just don't see when you're examining thumbnails on Photoshop or scrolling through a collection, one picture at a time, on your screen.

Of course, we have countless photographs of schoolkids eating lunch. Shot after shot showing hundreds of hungry kids scattered around barren, dusty schoolyards laughing, talking, and enjoying what is, for most of them, their only meal of that day. Close-ups of individual faces waiting eagerly for food, hands holding tightly to dented tin plates, old coffee cups, disposable plastic margarine bowls, even opened-up, half-pint milk cartons—anything that could be used to hold food and eat from—contented faces being efficiently filled by fingers full of hot beans and maize. Lay the photos out together and what you notice first is happiness, clearly conveyed by smiling faces and hopeful eyes.

Comparing lunch program pictures taken over the years, I was surprised to see that the kids looked so much better in the more recent shots. Years of improved nutrition had a noticeable effect; the children at our lunch program schools look younger and more alive today. Being hungry ages you prematurely; eating regular nutritious meals helps kids look like kids should look.

Even bigger smiles (if that's possible) can be seen on countless more faces of children pictured attentively focused on laptop keyboards and screens in our computer center classrooms. The expressions captured in those photos suggest more than happiness, contentment, or hope. I see excitement, intensity, and wonder.

I look at those photos and realize we will never have a way to measure the impact our comparatively few computer centers might someday have on the country of Kenya. I already know dozens of former students who have landed good jobs and begun to establish careers using the basic technological skills they learned in our centers. But it's impossible to estimate how many more thousands of Kenyan students have first dared to believe and hope they might someday escape the poverty that surrounds them, in a computer class where they also discovered a thrill and thirst for learning that could enable those hopes and dreams to come true.

When I look at our photos of the schools themselves, I see as much deterioration as I do improvement. Many classroom structures are shabbier, more overcrowded, and at least as understaffed as when we started working with the schools. Yet looks can be deceiving.

Of the thirty-four schools we work with, *every one* is ranked academically first or second in its zone. When we started, every school was ranked last, except for one that was second to last. Something as simple as a nutritious lunch plus a little bit of hope can add up to remarkable academic achievement.

In our photos, I see the familiar faces of many committed Kenyan educators. Teachers who keep showing up at their schools each day to face unimaginable working conditions and a student-teacher ratio so high it boggles the mind. And I can't look at the photos from computer center dedication ceremonies and see the encouragement on the faces of proud principals without remembering also the tears of administrators I've had to tell that we wouldn't be able to add their school to our lunch program. Or that we would not be able to provide a computer center for their community anytime soon.

We are truly gratified and humbled by what progress and results we've seen. We remain realistic, however, about how painfully tough life is for so many people in Kenya, and how much more still needs to be done. Our long-term goal is to continue growing our work with Kenyan government schools, and to raise additional support for more computer centers and more children getting good food. My dream, my prayer, is that one day soon, we will reach the tipping point where enough of a generation of Kenyan people will become sufficiently healthy and educated to believe in themselves, and that they then will elect a Kenyan government that will begin to serve, care for, and believe in its people, so that the world may learn and be amazed to see what a great country Kenya is and what Kenyans can do.

So our ambitious, ultimate aim is still the same today as it was in the beginning. But it's not so much thinking *we* can change a country as it is that we now know that if a couple of simple, proven ideas catch on and reach a tipping point, our lunch programs and computer centers could help equip a generation of Kenyans to change their country themselves.

—

Each picture I recently printed out captures a moment in time. Together they tell a fourteen-year story in which so much has happened. The photos I see of myself quite vividly show just how much has changed for me through those years. And pictures can't tell the half of that story.

I need no visual prompts to remind me of what I can never forget: that I came to Africa a broken man. When you bury one of your children, a part of you dies. Such a big part of me had died with Stephen, so much of me had been shattered by that loss, that I would not have risked investing in someone like me. But so many wonderful people did; they believed in and supported me and our family, which allowed us to be a part of something that has been life changing, as much for me — for all of us Peifers, in fact — as for any Kenyan kid with whom we've ever worked.

I look at the pictures from our earliest Africa years and know I'm a different man today. Africa has given me so much more than the gift of tears. Every year in Kenya has broken me in ways I'd never been broken before. And that brokenness has changed me — is still changing me — in ways and in areas of my life that so desperately need changing. I'm a better husband, a better father, a better man than I was before.

Just recently I've begun to change the way I deal with my RVA students. Early on, my style and aim as a college counselor were often results oriented — *how many* students can we get accepted *where* with *what* amount of financial aid. Recently I've shifted to more of a relationship-oriented approach. I've tried harder to listen to and know students so I can better help them hear the Lord as to where they should go to school.

As this book goes to press, our first Rift Valley Academy student in 105 years to attend Duke just completed his first freshman semester. His parents, who have sacrificed so much to serve the poor in Africa, cried when they learned their son would be able to graduate from such a school without taking on much debt.

Another of our sharpest recent RVA grads applied for and received a full-ride scholarship to Harvard. After she got the wonderful word about the scholarship, her father tearfully confessed to me that he'd taken on a burden of guilt when his obviously gifted daughter had begun thinking and talking about colleges. Because he and his wife had been unable to make any financial provision at all for her education, they felt like inadequate parents. They didn't even know how the family could afford for her to go anywhere to college. Now to think she was going on a full scholarship—to Harvard, no less—felt like a miracle; he was overwhelmed by the grace and provision of God.

Another RVA grad was accepted to Harvard and placed on a waiting list for a full scholarship. A long and anxious wait ended with great news and another celebration. But a day or two into her first semester, with a fall chill in the air, our Harvard coed got a note summoning her to the financial aid office. After her wait-list experience, she feared they were going to tell her there'd been some mistake and her full scholarship, or some part of it, was being rescinded. But no, the financial aid counselor smiled and told her that as a student from Africa, she qualified for another five hundred dollar stipend to cover the extra expenses entailed in adjusting to a new climate, culture, or whatever. She promptly went out and bought the warmest winter coat she could find at a nearby Goodwill Store and had enough cash left over that her parents didn't even have to provide her any pocket money for her first semester.

When I hear stories like that, I feel overwhelmed by God's grace in allowing me to play a small role in his miracles. And for the privilege my college-advisor job grants me to have a ringside seat to watch and learn how often he provides in such wonderful ways in the lives of so many of our RVA students and their families.

—

Naturally, a great many of the photos I recently printed are of family. Candid photos of everyday moments mixed in with milestone events. I see how deeply life in Kenya has impacted our entire family.

Nancy was the one who had always wanted to come to Africa. Not me. But the choice we made to take a year (of escape for me) to serve as dorm parents at a little school for missionary kids in rural Kenya turned out to be the single most monumental decision of our married lives. I've watched my already wonderful spouse flourish and blossom—as a wife, mother, and woman. She loves teaching high school French, has chaired our school's world language department, and now is in charge of Rift Valley Academy's professional teacher development programs. It's been a thrill for me to see her embrace this latest role and instill a vision for all of us on staff at RVA to pursue the professional training needed to get better at what we do. She has been innovative and passionate, and it has already made a difference.

My amazing wife completes me today more than she ever has before. The decision to fulfill Nancy's dreams in Africa led me to dreams of my own I never knew I had. Dreams so big.

I look at the photos of our oldest boys and note how they've grown since they came to Kenya with us as fifth and second graders. And I think of how many people have wondered (some have come right out and asked) about the "sacrifices" we've made and the "price" we've paid to do the work we do. They have no idea how much the rewards outweigh any costs.

Living most of their formative years in Africa has endowed JT and Matthew with a perspective on life that the greatest fortune on earth could never buy. Growing up where and how they did infused in them a realistic and wonderful worldview that allows them to look past all the superficial markers —nationality, race, economic status, social standing, academic prowess— that often divide us as human beings. JT and Matthew see the people they encounter in life not as groups or categories but as individuals with uniquely human attributes and needs. Kenya matured our boys into young men of character, conviction, and compassion like no other life, no other place, could have done. My sons make their dad incredibly proud.

And I can't look at photos of Katie and Ben over the years without a sense of wonder and gratitude to God for how they have completed the Peifer family. None of us can, or ever want to, imagine how different all our lives would have been without them. Every day they fill our lives to overflowing with excitement, joy, and love, while somehow keeping us young and reminding us just how old we really are, all at the same time.

And every year when we celebrate their birthday, every year on the anniversary of their adoption into the Peifer family, and countless days in between, I look at our daughter, Katie, and our youngest son, Ben, and I think of the brother they've not yet met. On whose gravestone we inscribed, "Having fulfilled the purpose the Father had for him, he returned to the Father March 12, 1998."

That was our testimony then. And it's still our testimony now that we understand so much more of "the purpose the Father had for him," because this whole story started with Stephen.

—

But as we spread out all the photos and sort through the memories, we realize everything that's happened since and everything we pray will happen in the future as a result of our story is really all about Jesus. He is our beginning, our middle, and our end. And he can use anything and anyone for his purpose.

I think again of the story we heard about that premature baby boy abandoned to die in the Kenyan bush. How his cries grew too weak for anyone to hear, until the ants came to feast on his nearly lifeless body, and how he cried louder then to be heard, found, and saved.

I remember how God used ants in that story, and how he used a baby who lived only eight days to start this story. I look at all the pictures, and I flash through thirteen years of memories recorded on the DVR of my mind, and I'm reminded again how he's used even me.

If he can use me, he can use anyone for his purposes. He can use even you. Wherever you are. Wherever you go. You don't need special talents, special training, or even a special calling to get your own story started. It's not that hard if you have eyes and ears. See the needs all around you. Hear the cries. Accept the gift of tears. And do whatever little thing he asks you to do, if only to feed a child lunch or to teach kids basic computer skills.

I promise. Once you find his purpose for you, you too will discover a dream so big.

Epilogue

JANUARY 30, 2012 — EVEN AS I READ BACK OVER THE FINAL PAGES OF THE manuscript for this book, the dream goes on. As does real life and the lessons to be learned from it.

The chicken breasts I'm grilling smell terrific and look almost done. Time to empty the pan of chicken juice and guts. So I head for the outside trash container around the side of the smaller house we live in now that we have only two kids with us in Kijabe. When I dump the contents of the pan into the barrel, a rather large monkey leaps straight up out of the garbage can screaming in protest. Or maybe that's me screaming in surprise. I'm not sure which. But I do know the monkey gives me an indignant look like, "Do you MIND?"

I'm pretty sure that it is raining, and that that is the reason my pants are damp.

—

My second case of bronchitis in two months has me back down to the mission hospital. Although Dr. Taylor, my American doctor in Texas, is the greatest doctor in the world, the care at the hospital doesn't suffer much by comparison. One of the most humbling things you can do is to be in the presence of a missionary doctor; they have sacrificed so much to be on the mission field. Although they are caring and fun, I always leave in awe.

The issue at the hospital isn't the care; it really is first rate. The challenge comes when you go to pay your bill and pick up your meds at the hospital pharmacy. The idea of an orderly line just hasn't made it to Kenya yet, and there are times when it has taken two hours to settle my account. It is only thirty minutes this time, and then I sit on a bench with dozens of others waiting for my prescription to be filled.

I am sitting next to a Kenyan woman I would guess is near my age. She shows evidence of the hard life most Kenyans have lived: her shoes are in tatters, her dress is neat, but very worn, and her back curves from a lifetime of carrying firewood and water. We begin to talk, and I try out a joke. She tells me "Your jokes are not so funny" with such a merry laugh, that I can't help but laugh along.

She tells me her story. Her son and his wife died of AIDS, and she is raising her three grandchildren alone. Her husband died years ago. It is sad that I've heard this story so many times; I can take you to villages where there is nobody alive ages twenty to forty; AIDS wiped them all out.

I look at her: she is a short woman who is as stout as she is tall, and she has the odor of someone who walked six miles in the African sun to come to the hospital. What strikes me is that when I look at her, my first thought is, *She is so beautiful.* She has endured what most of us couldn't possibly imagine, and she still has joy. A few years ago, I would have seen that she was black and not looked much beyond that. I walk home rejoicing in her beauty and think, *How God has changed me because of Africa.*

—

I go to one of the schools we work with and I see a young boy bleeding from his cheek. I ask what happened and learn a teacher has beaten him with a stick. Although Kenyan teachers are taught not to hit students on top of the head because it can damage hearing, there are many other places that are fair game. The boy is filthy, wearing a torn sweater and no shoes, and shows no evidence he has been near water for a long time.

I go to talk to him and discover that Timothy is an orphan, that he sleeps on the front porch of his cousin's house. His crime is that he sneaked into the classroom, but he has not paid his school fees. For that, he has been beaten by two teachers in two different classes. Yet he stays on campus for the lunch and for his afternoon computer class. I talk to the headmaster and he agrees to let Timothy stay on, although the man tells me there are dozens of students in the same situation, and he cannot do it for all of them.

I see Timothy and I realize that a few years ago, I could not have looked beyond his hygiene; now I look at him with awe because he is so brave and he hasn't given up. God has taken my judgmental, critical heart and allowed me to go deeper. I'm reminded of Jesus' words when he said, "If you've done it unto the least of these, you've done it unto me." I say goodbye to Timothy and walk away thinking, *I am not worthy to wash his feet.*

———

I wasn't at RVA last year, and there are several students who had their first year as juniors, and I don't know them at all. The problem is that now that they are seniors, I need to write letters of recommendation for them, and I don't have a clue. I ask Karol (not her real name) to come in so I can interview her and compose a recommendation.

Karol looks like you might think a missionary kid would look. She is beautiful, with blonde hair and a sweet smile. I've listened to her lead worship, and as she plays the guitar and sings, I think, *This is the poster child of a missionary kid.*

It takes Karol a while to warm up to me and to know whether she can trust me. She begins to tell her story; she has attended seven schools in the past nine years. Because of family health issues and unrest in the area where her parents work, she has gone from one school to the next. She feels like she never fits in, and as she begins to make friends, she has had to leave again.

I labor over my recommendation, and I fearfully send it to colleges. I've tried to be honest. There are educational gaps, and because she is relatively new, she hasn't been involved with much. I say in my recommendation letter that college can be a time of healing for her; four years in one place will do wonders for her. I tell them that she is a treasure, and that the wise college that will nourish her will reap a wonderful young woman.

The college responds, and I open the email with a sense of dread. Instead, I am blessed and humbled by the news: the vice president has read my recommendation to the entire admissions staff. They have cried and pledged to be a safe place for her. She is accepted to her first choice school.

She comes in to talk, and I tell her that college is going to be a place of rest and refreshment for her. That if she will seek counseling while she is there, the wounds from her past can be healed. She begins to weep. She tells me that she is so proud of her parents and the amazing work they do. She knows that it wasn't their fault, and she sits and cries and cries.

I don't know what to do for the longest time, so I pray and God gives me a word for her: "Karol, it isn't disloyal to honestly deal with legitimate hurts." She cries harder, but this time there is hope in her tears. In the next few weeks, I see a more confident person beginning to peek her head out. It strikes me that I have usually settled for the surface, but Karol's real beauty is below the surface, and I'm so grateful that God has let me see deeper.

—

Jun (not his real name) is another senior, a Korean, who comes in to talk. We have an awkward conversation; his English isn't very good, and he defers to me so much it is hard to have anything but a surface conversation. I pray and I probe, and it comes out that when he came to our American school, he didn't know a word of English. Staffing is always problematic at RVA, and we rarely have a teacher who is trained in ESL (teaching English as a second language). Jun tells me that he was always outgoing until he came to RVA; now he retreats into himself.

I sit there, listening, and I am convicted. I tell him that I have been at RVA for thirteen years, that Koreans make up 15 percent of our student body, and I haven't bothered to learn even how to say hello in his language. I tell him I have disrespected his culture, and I have dishonored him because I was oblivious to his struggles. He looks up and sees my shame and my tears.

I tell Jun how courageous he is, and that having endured something so hard has given him the tools to overcome many hard things. I tell him that he has inspired me; I know I could not have done what he has done. He is silent, and his eyes glisten. I tell him that if he gives himself to ESL in college, there will be no stopping him. He leaves grateful. I marvel that in all of my weakness, God has somehow been strong.

I pray over my recommendation letter and try to portray someone who, against all odds, has somehow managed to succeed. I get a call from a college; they tell me they would be honored if he came to their school. I put my head in my hands and weep. I have seen God overcome all of my errors, and in the process provide a good college for a student *and* teach me about becoming more culturally sensitive.

I walk home so grateful for the evidence of continuing change. With no good reason except his love for me, the Lord hasn't given up on me yet.

Thank you for buying this book. If you found this story compelling, please share it with friends and family.

The children of Kenya featured in *A Dream So Big* continue to need our help. There are several ways you can do more to give them a brighter future:

- Visit the *www.kenyakidscan.org* website, which provides instructions on contributing financially to the school feeding program and the computer center program. You can also keep up with Steve's latest blog posts from Africa.

- Review this book and link to it on Amazon.com, Barnes and Noble, and other ecommerce websites. Your comments will help build "buzz" for the book and reach other potential buyers.

- Link to the book on Facebook, mention it on Twitter, and feature it on Instagram or your social platform of choice; use your social network to spread the word.

- Make *A Dream So Big* the featured text at your next book club meeting, or feature it at your men's or women's group, place of worship, or civic club.

- Suggest your teacher add the book to your university or high school reading list, or do a report about the book for a literature or social studies course.

- Add Kenya Kids Can to the charity list at your place of worship or workplace; some employers provide matching funds to listed charities.

- Make a tax-deductible contribution to the Kenya Kids Can programs. Send a check to African Inland Mission Int'l, PO Box 3611, Peachtree City, GA 30269-7611. Or phone toll-free, +1 (800) 254-0010. Reference the program ("Peifer School Feeding Program" or "Peifer Computer Centers") to which you would like the funds applied. It costs pennies to feed a child each day.

Share Your Thoughts

With the Author: Your comments will be forwarded to the author when you send them to *zauthor@zondervan.com*.

With Zondervan: Submit your review of this book by writing to *zreview@zondervan.com*.

Free Online Resources at

www.zondervan.com

Zondervan AuthorTracker: Be notified whenever your favorite authors publish new books, go on tour, or post an update about what's happening in their lives at www.zondervan.com/authortracker.

Daily Bible Verses and Devotions: Enrich your life with daily Bible verses or devotions that help you start every morning focused on God. Visit www.zondervan.com/newsletters.

Free Email Publications: Sign up for newsletters on Christian living, academic resources, church ministry, fiction, children's resources, and more. Visit www.zondervan.com/newsletters.

Zondervan Bible Search: Find and compare Bible passages in a variety of translations at www.zondervanbiblesearch.com.

Other Benefits: Register to receive online benefits like coupons and special offers, or to participate in research.

ZONDERVAN.com/
AUTHORTRACKER
follow your favorite authors